# Line Drawings

# Line Drawings

## Defining Women through Feminist Practice

## CRESSIDA J. HEYES

*Cornell University Press*

ITHACA AND LONDON

First published 2000 by Cornell University Press
First printing, Cornell Paperbacks, 2000

Printed in the United States of America

**Library of Congress Cataloging-in-Publication Data**

Heyes, Cressida J.
    Line drawings : defining women through feminist practice / Cressida J. Heyes.
        p.   cm.
    Includes bibliographical references and index.
    ISBN 0-8014-3684-2 (cloth). — ISBN 0-8014-8669-6 (pbk.)
    1. Feminist theory.   2. Feminist criticism.   I. Title.
HQ1190 .H49   2000
305.42'01—dc21                                                    99-059252

Cornell University Press strives to use environmentally responsible suppliers
and materials to the fullest extent possible in the publishing of its books. Such
materials include vegetable-based, low-VOC inks and acid-free papers that are
recycled, totally chlorine-free, or partly composed of nonwood fibers. Books that
bear the logo of the FSC (Forest Stewardship Council) use paper taken from forests
that have been inspected and certified as meeting the highest standards for environ-
mental and social responsibility. For further information, visit our website at
www.cornellpress.cornell.edu.

Cloth printing        10  9  8  7  6  5  4  3  2  1
Paperback printing    10  9  8  7  6  5  4  3  2  1

FSC   FSC Trademark © 1996 Forest Stewardship Council A.C.
      SW-COC-098

**For Vivien, David, and Rod**

# Contents

# Acknowledgments

I never imagined I would actually write a book, first because I thought I might have better things to do, and second because it seemed too daunting a task. It is a mark of the extraordinary support I've received from colleagues and friends over the last seven years that both prognoses have been proved wrong.

My first debt is to my mentors, Marguerite Deslauriers and James Tully. Marguerite coupled her demand for careful, analytical philosophical writing with a political commitment to my slightly unorthodox approach. Jim first introduced me to the study of Wittgenstein as a political philosopher and kept faith in his potential for feminist appropriation. I continue to be deeply grateful to them both, and for the ongoing support of the Department of Philosophy at McGill University. I was also fortunate to spend five graduate years with a wonderful cohort of proto-philosophers (special mention to Dale Turner) who, without a doubt, also contributed to any virtues this book has.

A number of friends and colleagues have generously commented on part or all of the manuscript, shepherding it through various stages of development. For their intellectual generosity and kind criticism, I am indebted to Karin Cope, Sue Dwyer, Linda Nicholson, Naomi Scheman, and Vicky Spelman.

For their critical engagement with the ideas I have developed here, I thank the participants in the following conferences and colloquium series: Canadian Society for Women in Philosophy 1998, Departments of Philosophy and of Women's Studies at the University of Alberta, Departments of Philosophy and of Women's Studies at Michigan State University, History of the Human Sciences Research Group at Durham University, SOFPHIA 1996, Department of Philosophy and Centre for Research and Teaching on Women at McGill University, and the members of Midwest Society for Women in Philosophy. Thank you to the anonymous reviewers for *Hypatia*, where an earlier version of Chapter 4 first appeared as "Anti-Essentialism in Practice: Carol Gilligan and Feminist Philosophy," *Hypatia* 12 : 3 (1997), and to three anonymous reviewers for Cornell University Press.

During a brief tenure at Michigan State University, I benefited from conversation with a small but dedicated feminist intellectual community. I am grateful to Maxine Baca Zinn, Marilyn Frye, Mary Gebhart, Kim Hall, April

Herndon, and Peter Hovmand for supporting my work and being ready interlocutors. Thanks are also due to all my feminist students at MSU, especially the students in my "Philosophical Aspects of Feminism" course, for their enthusiasm and willingness to learn and teach.

This book could not have hoped to address the mutual implication of feminist theory and practice without drawing on my own experience of activism. I learned an enormous amount from my former co-workers at the Sexual Assault Centre at McGill—especially my colleagues on the co-ordinating committee, and those women who participated in our crisis intervention training program and volunteered at the center between 1994 and 1996. Thanks most of all to Natalie Blitt.

Alison Shonkwiler at Cornell University Press guided this book astutely and humanely through the first phases of its journey, and I owe much to her and to Catherine Rice, her successor at the helm. Thanks also to Judy Davidson for stepping in at the end of the trip to compile an excellent index.

David Kahane has been my most stalwart supporter, undertaking endless commentary, copy-editing, and emotional and nutritional sustenance. His belief in the value of the project has kept me going through some tough times.

This book is dedicated with love to my mother, father, and brother, who first taught me how to be a happy political underdog, and who have supported my education and career unreservedly, even when it took me far away from them.

Finally, thanks to P. for her affection and ever-constant company.

C.J.H.

# Line Drawings

# Introduction

## Philosophy and Purity

This book stands at the confluence of several trends in feminist theory and my own experience of political organizing and feminist practice. It also reflects an ambivalent relationship with the activity of philosophizing, an activity that is now my profession. For several years I have been thinking and writing about what it means and might mean to be a feminist in the context of doing philosophy and politics. Like many other radical scholars, I hope to see social justice enacted in the most tangible ways; however, I find that I am constantly pulled back against my will (I think!) to philosophical questions that immediately abstract (and dissociate) from the concrete. At first I thought this was because philosophy and activism had nothing in common, that I was naively looking in quite the wrong place if I wanted to find pragmatism in this most abstruse of academic disciplines. Like many women graduate students, I considered quitting to go out into the "real world." But somehow my questions would not go away, and imperfect though the university proved to be, it seemed the only venue in which to explore them. Then I thought that perhaps I was not very good at formulating the *right* philosophical questions, and that with practice my academic theorizing would fall into place (this turned out to be partially true, but not for the reasons I anticipated). Finally, however, I realized that there is a way of philosophizing (call it "doing Philosophy"—a culturally and historically specific, parochial, contested, and troubled activity) that caused my questions to crystallize into a form I never intended them to have. Armed with this realization, and taking a perverse satisfaction in my new knowledge that some "canonical" philosophers had analyzed the same phenomenon, I tried to rework my questions, and even to answer some of them, in a voice that was not distorted by the tradition I had inherited. This is a project with little closure (indeed, the demand for closure is perhaps antithetical to the project); at every moment when I have thought that the picture holding me captive had finally been dispelled, it has resurfaced in another guise.

In what follows I attempt to outline some of the details of this picture and to show why it exerts such compelling control not only over those working most contentedly within its frame but also over those who have challenged its limits. In particular, I look at a series of debates in feminist philosophy that are by now firmly established; debates that perhaps feminists ought to have moved beyond, but have not. These debates address the methodological questions commonly lumped together under the rubric of "essentialism." In the context of contemporary political philosophy, questions of essentialism are questions about how to theorize, how to relate to different others in the context of political organizing, how to connect practice and theory, and how to understand the mechanisms of power that construct our understandings of ourselves and one another. These are topical concerns that I suggest can be answered neither by dismissing feminist preoccupation with essentialism as passé nor by acceding to the terms of a philosophical picture that dissociates itself from these questions.

Perhaps the most obvious way in which my own feminist questions have been shaped by Philosophy is in their demand for abstraction and purity and its insistence that only purity can make sense. Philosophy requires both that its questions be removed from practice and experience (or at least from the experiences of those who are not its implicit archetypal subjects) and that its adherents conform to what María Lugones labels a "logic of purity." This logic understands the social world as "both unified and fragmented, homogenous, hierarchically ordered."[1] My impurities—as a woman, an immigrant, a female philosopher, a radical teacher, a socialist, and a young person in a position of authority—make me both the target of those who want to maintain their dominance by destroying, denying, or marginalizing these ambiguities and someone whose questions are not reflected in much mainstream social philosophy. In Lugones's words:

> If women, the poor, the colored, the queer, the ones with cultures (whose cultures are denied and rendered invisible as they are seen as our mark) are deemed unfit for the public, it is because we are tainted by need, emotion, the body. This tainting is relative to the modern subject's urge for control through unity and the production and maintenance of himself as unified. To the extent that he is fictional, the tainting is fictional: seeing us as tainted depends on a need for purity that requires that we become "parts," "addenda" of the bodies of modern subjects—Christian white bourgeois men—and make their purity possible.[2]

I want to understand the mechanisms that make these appeals to purity compelling even for those, like myself, who think we have rejected them. How does a desire for purity creep back even into philosophizing that is avowedly and self-consciously impure? How do words and deeds intended to be radical slip into the logic that Lugones criticizes, with its oppressive consequences? How does privilege, too, feature in this story, and why might my experience as a subject with privileged aspects make my questions about purity, politics, and exclusion take a particular shape?

These questions have an unexpected resonance with Wittgenstein's *Philosophical Investigations*. On my first reading I was struck, on the one hand, by how I had inadvertently been "held captive" by my philosophical education, and, on the other, by the ways I had never been trapped in the fly bottle at all. First, I could identify with Wittgenstein's depiction of philosophy as "the bewitchment of our intelligence by means of language," and saw, particularly in his critique of essentialism, the rejection of a kind of seductive quest for purity of understanding that Philosophy encourages and had encouraged in me. Wittgenstein contrasts his image of the crystalline purity of logic (a requirement rather than a result of investigation) with the rough ground of actual language and action. This image captures not just a philosophical critique of logic but also a fantasy of escape common among philosophers—an escape from the troubles of the mundane, from the human interactions that in fact constitute the texture of our daily lives. As Terry Eagleton envisages, in the script for Derek Jarman's film *Wittgenstein*: "A young man . . . dreamed of reducing the world to pure logic. And because he was a very clever young man, he actually managed to do it. And when he had finished, he stood back and admired his handiwork. It was beautiful: a world purged of imperfection and indeterminacy, like countless acres of gleaming ice stretching silently to the horizon. Each object in this world sparkled in the purity of its being, each thing cleanly demarcated from its neighbours."[3]

On the other hand, the "seductive" face of philosophy has, I think, always been a more attractive prospect for men than for women philosophers. Purity is more obviously within reach for those men who participate in what has become an institutionalized profession. They are less often reminded of their earthly, imperfect, and fallible minds and bodies, and are less likely to have political complaints about the status quo that this philosophy supports. Somehow it seems that "reducing the world to pure logic" is a fantasy peculiar to white, bourgeois, western, Christian male philosophers. As Lugones says: "The logic of transparency shines in the constructed lover of purity himself, the modern subject, the impartial reasoner. He is the measure of all things. He is transparent relative to his position in the hetero-relational patriarchy, to his culture, his race, his class, his gender. His sense is the only sense."[4]

The fantasy is also an impossibility: the perfect world of ice is uninhabitable, for it contains no friction. Eagleton's Wittgenstein struggles with the knowledge that perfection and action cannot co-exist: "He grew up into a wise old man who came to understand that roughness and ambiguity and indeterminacy aren't imperfections—they're what make things work. . . . He had to dig up all those gleaming acres of ice until he discovered the rough ground beneath them. And the words and things scattered up on this ground were all battered and tarnished and ambiguous; and the wise old man saw that this was the way things were. But something in him was still homesick for the ice, where everything was radiant and absolute and relentless. And so, though he liked the *idea* of the rough ground, he couldn't bring himself to live there. So now he was marooned between earth and ice, at home in neither."[5] My first response to this recognition is merely to affirm that that is what I have always known. Those for whom the ice is made an unattainable ideal—no matter how vainly we aspire to reach it—are more likely to feel at home on the rough ground, and to make the most of it.

This search for "the crystalline purity of logic"—for the ice—seems to me to be attractive to male philosophers because it is in part a disavowal of the messiness of the social worlds we move in and inhabit, and in part a form of psychological (and perhaps—foreshadowing Gilligan—pathological) dissociation from the ethical and political complexities of these worlds. It's tempting to characterize this dissociation as the exclusive preserve of men. But not only does this claim conveniently ignore the struggles of some male philosophers—Wittgenstein among them—to get off the ice and back to the rough ground (and the possibility that some kinds of men never aspired to it), it also elides the ways feminist philosophy itself has often continued to use its inherited philosophical strategies to escape friction. Just as Wittgenstein is exasperated by his earlier attempts to disengage from the complexities of language, to find "super-concepts" that require no giving of examples, so I was simultaneously attracted to and repelled by the phenomenon in feminist theory that I now call "methodological essentialism." On reading Elizabeth V. Spelman's book *Inessential Woman*, I realized that Spelman was talking about some of the same things as Wittgenstein, albeit in more political and accessible terms. Much feminist philosophy seemed to me to be struggling with the desire for easier, less messy ways to capture the essence of "women" while trying to remain true to its roots in feminist movements. We have sometimes tried to reduce complex phenomena to their simplest forms, eradicating their concreteness in favor of abstraction and purifying them of specificity. "Monophilia and purity are cut from the same cloth."[6] Essentialism, then, for feminist theory, seemed to have something to do with the same "craving for generality" that erased the "particular case" that Wittgenstein identifies.

My approach to Wittgenstein's work has always entailed spinning out the fragmentary ideas that he advances in the *Philosophical Investigations* rather than attempting to remain loyal to his philosophy. Indeed, Wittgenstein himself explicitly encouraged this attitude during his life, and I take him at his word. Not even the most willful reader can interpret the *Investigations* as a comprehensive philosophical program with clearly defined parameters; it is a partial, hesitant, elliptical text that tacks from theme to theme in unpredictable fashion. Of course, this is in part the allure of Wittgenstein's work: it invites the free association of ideas, eccentric connections, and multiple interpretations and thus can speak to a wide array of philosophers. Recent work in social and political theory takes up the *Investigations* in ways Wittgenstein would never have countenanced (certainly a feminist interpretation would have horrified him) only to move beyond the text to offer analyses that are inspired by Wittgenstein but far from derivative of his work. This book is thus situated in this emerging genre of work that calls itself "Wittgensteinian" but rapidly overtakes the content of his ideas.

Wittgenstein's critique of essentialism is actually one of the more identifiable and discrete sections of the *Investigations*, albeit complexly connected with his larger picture of "philosophy." My initial goal when I started on this piece of theory was thus to bring together Wittgenstein's critique of essentialism with those of Lugones and Spelman. This was to be one original contribution of the book: to construct an anti-essentialist Wittgensteinian feminism. But I wanted this work to be more than critique, to offer more than another soul-searching account by a white woman of exclusion in feminist theory. In particular, I wanted it to speak not only to my concerns as a "private" feminist philosopher but also to my struggles as a "public" feminist activist. I wanted it to be action-guiding, pragmatic, and constructive. These desiderata were motivated by several sets of experiences. For example, I was surprised by the ways that concerns about essentialism have filtered through to general discourse in and about feminism in the academy. As I discuss later, "essentialist" is usually a disapprobative adjective, intended to imply racism, ethnocentrism, or some form of exclusion. Often feminists accuse other feminists of being "essentialist," and I analyze the content of these claims at some length in this book. But essentialism is not only an issue debated by feminist philosophers. Sometimes these accusations are made by antifeminists, those ambivalent toward more radical feminist claims, or those who see in feminism an unwelcome challenge to their own political projects.

In the terms of the debates about identity that have characterized recent political philosophy, two kinds of knee-jerk response to essentialist critique have emerged. The first is the response that avoiding "essentialism" demands that we give up on social groups altogether. On several occasions when I responded to a straightforward example of sexism by making a claim featuring the term "women," a sly look in my opponent's eye preceded the trumping riposte, "Ah! But by talking about 'women' aren't you being an 'essentialist'?" And the general move of pointing to differences among women as a way of dismissing feminist claims rather than nuancing them has also become a relatively familiar phenomenon. For example, an increasingly common rhetorical move on the part of antifeminist interlocutors, in my experience, has been to attempt to cut the ground from under my feet by pointing to racial difference as a decisive argument against the salience of gender in any given feminist analysis. Rather than understanding the criticism as an entrée to a better kind of radical analysis, exponents of this rhetorical move most often lapse into a liberal individualist position that denies the centrality of social groups per se by appropriating the language of the essentialism debates.

Second is the reverse phenomenon: that offering any critique from exclusion implies that we must "talk about everything," leading to an endless proliferation of categories that merely attenuates any social theory. The notion that to criticize a particular social theoretical account for what it excludes necessarily implies that every conceivable social group should be included merely sidesteps anti-essentialist critique. The evasion "Well, what about class? age? race? sexuality? Where will it all end?" is the flip side of disavowal of the reality of social groups. The latter position rejects the group in favor, usually, of the individual, while the former admits the existence of groups but casts them as too numerous to theorize (thus inconsistently evading the need further to justify any particular analysis, while nevertheless defending a specific—usually monolithic—view). Both responses—supposedly to essentialism and anti-essentialism, respectively—are stubborn refusals to engage critically with particular political objections to a given theory. Specifically, they are refusals to ground the reality of social group membership in anything other than theoretical parleying. My initial response to both these attacks is not only that they do not address the substance of their opponents' claims but that they treat social groups as immaterial units to be divided and proliferated by philosophical fiat. Which groups are relevant in a particular context, what we can justifiably say about them, and what our claims might exclude are enormously complex methodological issues in political philosophy, but they are nonetheless vital to continuing conversations about the contours of oppressions. Claims about what we can and cannot say about "women," or any other social group, are claims about social realities. Which axes of oppression, power, difference and identity will be relevant in a particular political problem-space is (minimally) a question that cannot be resolved by a priori appeal either to the irrelevance of group membership or its hopeless multiplicity. Social ontologies therefore need to be constructed and negotiated in dialogue with the social phenomena a theory purports to explain. The arguments I make in this book about how we should analyze tacit exclusion, about the empirical and material bases of generalizations in social theory, and about the relations of power at work in theory building, all aim to provide alternatives to these two related dismissals.

The sense of hopelessness implicit in these criticisms does not imply that feminists should give up their worries about essentialism and exclusion. It seems to me an inevitable feature of oppositional discourses that our own self-criticism will be appropriated, distorted, and used against us by our political challengers. When my own position within the feminist milieus I know best has been a powerful one (as, for example, a white woman, as the sometime beneficiary of heterosexual privilege, or as a highly educated woman), it has doubtless contributed to a relative inattention to how my own experience of gender oppression has shaped my perception of the oppression of women in general. And concomitantly, the ways in which I am marginalized (as a young woman in an aging male profession, as a feminist philosopher, as a woman with a different cultural background from most of my colleagues, or as a woman with strong political commitments that are at odds with the dominant belief systems in North America, for example) have given me added insight into how systems of oppression operate. The concerns about false generalizations about women that I discuss here under the rubric of essentialism are, I believe, very real political problems for feminists, reflecting both the inadequacies of white, heterosexual, middle-class women in responding to racism, heteronormativity, and class oppression within feminist movements, and a failure to recognize and respond to these omissions in our processes of theory building. But nonetheless, I am disquieted by the shorthand deployment of "essentialist" as a strategy for dismissing controversial feminist claims both within and outside feminist contexts rather than as a genuine precursor to discussion of how to improve feminist methods.

Finally, I wrote this book concurrently with my involvement in feminism in more pragmatic domains, most notably as a counselor and advocate for survivors of sexual violence, and a co-ordinator for volunteer recruitment and training in a sexual assault center. Although I had always been very public about my feminism and was used to fighting the feminist corner against sexist opposition, when I took up this work I was soon shocked and dismayed by the extent of sexualized violence against women and the ways that violence is condoned by and contiguous with gender socialization in general. I had understood feminist analyses of sexual violence in simple theoretical terms for a long time (knowing that a woman is more likely to be raped by someone she knows than by a stranger, for example). But this activism brought a different kind of knowledge, of aspects of this problem that are too often hidden—of the ways people in positions of power try to evade responsibility for violence, and the ways people close to survivors of violence are too often complicitous in retraumatizing them, for example. Most notably, I came to see gender as a horribly real and often absolutely overwhelming axis of difference in the context of sexual violence. I sometimes felt as if all men stood on one side of the line, and all women on the other, and that nothing more remained to be said.

At the same time, the organization in which I worked was struggling to improve its services; part of this effort focused on dynamics internal to the organization around racism, ethnocentrism, heteronormativity, and the sometimes troubled relationships between volunteers who identified as survivors of childhood sexual abuse and those who did not. Our struggles to improve our organizational strategies, not only in our contact with our clientele but also in our contact with one another, provided me with much more concrete understanding of the limitations of invoking "sisterhood" as the solution to our common oppression. They also convinced me that differences between women are the motor of feminist organizing not a barrier to its success, no matter how difficult they may be to negotiate. As Marilyn Frye has written:

> All . . . formations of women (including those initially conceived as unified by specific differences such as sexuality or race), if persisted in for any

length of time, have profoundly involved their participants in articulating, elaborating, appreciating, defining, exploring, recognizing, negotiating, consolidating, and traveling differences among women. This has been practically, politically, historically inevitable. If women were going to be together in women-focused, women-defined, and women-defining spaces and enterprises, women were going to engage in many varieties of what might be called "the practice of differences."[7]

My experience of many feminist—especially lesbian feminist—spaces has been that they are more racially and class diverse than other kinds of political enclaves. Although some feminist contexts are undoubtedly exclusive, it is in part the diversity of many others that has prompted some of the feminist theorizing of "differences among women."

But the necessity of working with difference and our conflictual—albeit in many ways productive—internal struggles over differences stand next to a frequent need to resist in unequivocal terms our opponents' oppressive characterizations of women. Feminists working in coalition often struggle to accommodate a nuanced political strategy and need to construct interim notions of "women" that perhaps do not capture every important case. We need to do so because we grapple with the pervasiveness of rhetorical spaces that favor unified and universal constructions of gender, which endorse a "modernist political idiom."[8] As Wendy Brown asks, in an analysis of Catherine MacKinnon that connects with my own: "Can a radical postfoundationalist feminist political discourse . . .—with its necessarily partial logics and provisional truths, situated knowledges, fluid subjects, and decentered sovereignty—work to claim power, or to contest hegemonic power?"[9] This discourse not only is a product of feminist philosophizing but also emerges from the complexity of our political practice: as we try to offer more sophisticated accounts of gender identities and oppressions, of relations of difference and power among women and within feminism, we face the challenge of an antifeminist world that can only make discursive space for the simplest, least nuanced kinds of feminist claims. This situation presents us with a set of contradictions, and not enough of the feminist philosophy I know seems adequate to the task of providing signposts for a feminist practice that has to confront this paradox.

I provide this personal account of how I came to write this book as a way of explaining—if not justifying—the somewhat controversial direction of my work from theory to practice to theory. Many feminist philosophers, myself included, aspire to make our work "relevant" and to locate our more abstract musings on the rough ground of "activism." As I discuss toward the end of this book, that distinction itself is problematic, as is the privileging of either "theory" or "practice" within any feminist discourse. Thus my goal is not to use examples from practice to adjust my theory but rather to abandon a certain kind of theory altogether in favor of a discussion of "theoretical" issues that are deeply enmeshed with, and worked through with reference to, particular concrete examples. This has been a frustrating process, and I have often wished that the messy "rough ground" of practice were more susceptible to theorizing of the neater, smoother kind. To paraphrase Lugones, I have sometimes worried more passionately about the harm my practice was doing to my theorizing than vice versa.[10] Too often my thoughts about feminist theory have taken off in one direction while my practice required a different kind of intellectual framework. This book is an attempt, then, to reconcile my own theory and practice without giving up either the circumspection and imagination of philosophy or the immediacy and pragmatism of political engagement.

How do these various questions fit with established debates in contemporary political philosophy? The essentialism controversies in feminist philosophy not only are central to contemporary feminist studies but also speak to broader concerns about political identity. To use identity as the basis of political mobilization—as in some sense all feminist, antiracist, and queer activists do—raises quite different political questions from those raised by appeals to political beliefs simpliciter as the basis of shared goals. Some of these questions are by now very familiar. Does invoking a shared identity necessarily conceal or destroy differences?[11] Is this a bad thing? Must we choose between "essentializing" our identities and disowning them? Is any subaltern political identity merely an artifact of oppression, and how should this concern shape our politics? How does one mobilize around an identity that one ultimately wants to change, undercut, or even destroy altogether? Do "pluralist" political theories—or the strategies they might imply—damage our ability effectively to resist structures of oppression? How can such theories be rhetorically successful in hostile political environments? All of these questions have been widely debated by feminist, queer, and critical race theorists. I have been especially interested in the answers to these questions in the context of feminist concerns about essentialism, but they play out in other discourses too. Essentialism is by no means a problem (if it is a problem) only for feminists.

I return to some of these broader questions, but here I want to describe three specific lacunae in the existing feminist philosophical literature that motivate this work. The first is the evident confusion in contemporary feminist theory surrounding the use of the term "essentialism." If Wittgenstein is correct that the meaning of a word lies in its use, then feminists will find it hard to know what "essentialism" means. The term and its cognates are used indiscriminately to express disapproval of many kinds. Some feminist theorists have already presented analyses of the state of the discipline of feminist philosophy which crucially identify both the conceptual vagueness and the regulatory effects of charges of essentialism, but which also ultimately sidestep the substantive issues at stake. These articles tend to be limited in scope—opinion pieces that express regret at the lack of critical analysis of essentialism but do not pretend to provide such analysis.[12] Thus I hope here to complement this literature and provide an etiology of the feminist preoccupation with essentialism, as well as distinguishing different uses of the term and different pejorative imputations.

Many feminists have pointed to the putative tension between generalizing claims about women and demands for attention to "difference."[13] This dichotomy has been described, reiterated, and criticized in numerous ways. The tension itself seems to lie in different places. Is it a problem in language? Is it an ontological difficulty stemming from the ways we categorize different objects? Is it an empirical problem concerning what women have in common? Is it a political difficulty emerging from our organizing strategies? However we characterize the tension, the dichotomy of overly general essentialism and hopeless particularity must be false. In keeping with Wittgenstein, I found that work in the discipline of philosophy in particular tended to reiterate this dichotomy, repeatedly presenting feminists with a specious choice between difference-denying generalizations and a hopeless fragmentation of gender categories. Thus my second motivation for this project was a sense of frustration with the way this false dichotomy was persistently offered up without either a philosophical escape route or any recognition of the concrete feminist praxis that seemed successfully to evade it. Preoccupation with the theoretical trope of "difference" seemed to me to reduce concretely based power struggles within feminism to philosophical fetishes to be toyed with in increasingly obscure ways.

Thus, finally, I was motivated by a desire to see the essentialism debates relate more explicitly to political practice. Several feminists have gestured toward potential routes for avoiding essentialism by stressing the material nature of feminist problems as well as the fact that feminist practice seems to have been able to negotiate difference in ways not adequately captured by feminist philosophy.[14] While I found such approaches potentially useful, they always appeared at the end of an argument, as conclusions rather than as premises to be elaborated. I want to be specific about how particular identity claims actually are constitutive of feminist practice, to make a new contribution to understanding how essentialism matters for feminist methods. The two areas I chose to explore—research methods and organizing against sexual violence—reflect my own preoccupations and interests, and there are other contexts in which the same kinds of analyses might usefully be applied. But I noticed that these were two fields where generalizations about women played a particularly important resistive role.

"Research" is one set of methods by which feminists have attempted to uncover the contours of women's lives hidden by patriarchy, and they have pointed both to the exclusion of all women from many research projects and to the sexism implicit in much empirical investigation that does purport to address or include women's concerns. The development of feminist methodologies has therefore been a project central to much work in feminist sociology and theory of knowledge. But until recently, feminist research has too rarely addressed philosophical questions of identity and essentialism by working toward methods that epistemologically and pragmatically address the complexities of differences among women. Put simply, I saw a gap between the kinds of things I, as a feminist researcher, had to do or assume in order to conduct empirical investigations and ground claims about women and the anti-essentialist philosophy that challenged aspects of this enterprise.

As an activist working against sexual violence in a small feminist organization, I found a similar discontinuity. For example, the feminist discourse I argued for and within on most days made unequivocal claims about the significance of gender in shaping our clients' experiences of so-called domestic violence. When I argued about issues such as "date rape" with university administrators, male students, or hostile journalists, however, I found that my struggle of necessity focused on introducing gender (often unmodified) as relevant in discussions overtly (and, to my mind, naively) dismissive of its significance. At the same time, I knew that my practice had changed and continued to change in the light of, for example, my increased awareness of racial difference and racism in the context of sexual violence. But these changes did not seem to imply that gender was any less significant than I had first thought, only that it was differently significant. Thus there did not seem to be an irreducible conflict between the theoretical lessons of feminist anti-essentialism and the particular forms of feminist practice with which I was most familiar.

These factors, then, provided the motivation for this book. In Chapters 1 and 2 I construct an etiology of the use of the term "essentialism" and its cognates in feminist theory. I identify four distinct uses of the term, with metaphysical, biological, linguistic, and methodological connotations. I argue that neither metaphysical nor biological essentialisms in their pre-social constructionist incarnations are at stake in most contemporary feminist debates (although questions of social ontology and of the materiality of women's bodies are). I bring together different substantive uses of "essentialist" to pinpoint a methodological problem within social constructionist discourses, outlining the putative tensions between feminist generalizations about women that risk underestimating politically significant differences between us, and anti-essentialist approaches that seem to undermine feminist political analyses and goals. In Chapter 2 I look at the political implications of methodological essentialism, defending Elizabeth Spelman's critique of essentialism against the replies of Natalie Stoljar and Susan Moller Okin. Like Stoljar and Okin, I have been disturbed by the ways feminist critiques of overly general claims about "women" have permitted gender to be treated as an illegitimate category of analysis. One of the themes of the book is my own skepticism about gender skepticism, or my "anti-anti-essentialism." Analyses that depict anti-essentialism only as a kind of relativism about gender, however, fail to see the importance of contextual theorizing or the more general potential for constructive strategies following on from anti-essentialist critique. Although I am sympathetic to the fears evoked by other anti-anti-essentialists, I argue that they miss the point. Spelman's analysis does not preclude the possibility of legitimate generalizations about women. It does, however, make critical commentary on essentialist feminist theory its main focus and stops short of offering an alternative "anti-essentialist" method.

So what are the implications of feminist critiques of methodological essentialism for feminist philosophical method? In Chapter 3 I turn to Wittgenstein's critique of essentialism and his proposed alternative, to outline a feminist method that understands similarities between women as "family resemblances" and uses purposive line drawing to ensure the political efficacy of feminist categories. Wittgenstein's therapy for philosophers, I maintain, can also be useful for feminists: it encourages a healthy distrust of the discipline of "philosophy" while reconstituting feminists' endeavors through the injunction "look and see." These two aphorisms—"look and see" and "back to the rough ground!"—together motivate my own philosophical attention to feminist praxis. For those feminists who are "bewitched" by essentialism, a Wittgensteinian approach offers a methodological path between two extremes: on the one hand, asserting women's sameness in ways that minimize important power-laden differences and, on the other, insisting on an a priori shattering of gender categories that undercuts important feminist political theories and objectives.

The essentialism debates have for too long remained at the level of metaphysical and epistemological questions about generality and "difference," sidestepping analyses of power that might show how homogeneity comes to be imposed, and when "strategic essentialism" might be most useful. We—especially the "we" who find our lives and concerns reflected in existing feminist approaches—are too willing to be excited by the idea of diversity rather than by the political struggles required to ensure genuine social justice. Justified generalizations must capture the social realities of gender oppression while remaining aware of the shape of the social ontologies they deploy. Put simply, the oppression of women is real, as made manifest by the familiar phenomena of violence, economic stratification and inequity, cultural imagery, sexual exploitation, stereotyping, (self)disciplining of bodies and so on through a motley of examples. But theorizing these social realities in all their complexity requires both a keen sense of the epistemological and ontological exigencies of a plural social theory, and an attentiveness to the precise design of the phenomena under scrutiny. My arguments in Chapters 4 and 5 are constructed to reclaim the importance of women's lived experience for feminist practice in a more subtle way than "anti-essentialism" has previously been able to do. One consequence of a Wittgensteinian analysis of the kind I recommend is the need to give specific and concrete examples of the contexts in which feminists have to arbitrate between different claims about what women have in common. Without this specificity, it is not clear that there is very much at stake for feminist practitioners in the essentialism debates. It seems to me that to develop accounts of the implications of anti-essentialism for feminist practice is a significant but as yet untapped interdisciplinary project in feminist studies. We have failed to move on from the tropes of anti-essentialist critique to more carefully discriminating and praxis-oriented encounters with feminist political projects.

Therefore, in Chapter 4 I ask what the injunction "look and see" actually implies, examining one practical context feminists might rethink in light of the tension between essentialism and anti-essentialism. "Look and see" cannot be the conclusion of an argument, a wave of the philosopher's hand toward forms of inquiry that lie outside our ambit. Nor can we uncritically assume that women's lives are transparently accessible to feminists, when our own analyses have long revealed the epistemological and political complexities of methods of empirical inquiry, and the ways they have been shaped by the inquirer's particularity and partiality. No undertheorized appeal to materiality or lived experience can be presented as the simple "truth" about women, but theoretical engagement with these categories nonetheless is grounded in the social reality of gender oppression. I attempt to redress, on the one hand, the lack of feminist philosophical examination of specific attempts to justify empirically based generalizations about women. By contrast, I show how philosophical critiques of essentialism might relate to ongoing projects in feminist social research that aim to refine existing methods.

To develop this approach I present an extended case study of Carol Gilligan's recent work on girls' experiences of relationship at adolescence, in which she attempts to reconcile a feminist theoretical framework that emphasizes relatively generic features of gendered psychology with more explicit recognition of the diverse race and class contexts in which gender is shaped. Feminist theorists have long treated Gilligan as an arch-essentialist. I argue, however, that she has been unjustly criticized for her tendency to make overly general claims about women and girls, men and boys. I interpret her most recent book—*Between Voice and Silence, Women and Girls, Race and Relationship*—as an attempt to respond to charges of methodological essentialism. I maintain that Gilligan successfully evades the kinds of essentialism with which she had previously been charged but that she continues to struggle with the essentialism of her research method. She fails fully to recognize how relations of power in her methods of inquiry and processes of theory building shape the similarities and differences she is able to acknowledge. In articulating a way Gilligan might rectify this problem, I point toward forms of anti-essentialism that interrogate the relations of power among women and how those relations shape political theories of identity. I argue for a particular research method that is sensitive to the influence of researchers' identities in producing their research findings and that diffuses researchers' power to construct the identities of their participants.

In the final chapter I turn to another locus of feminist practice, examining the same debates in connection with feminist discourses around sexual violence—the quintessentially essentialist feminist issue. I take another alleged essentialist—Catharine MacKinnon—and review her response to critics who suggest that her feminist theory creates a monolithic account of womanhood that fails to understand the particular location of women of color. MacKinnon claims that her theory is based in women's experience and the feminist practice that emerges from that experience; thus, she maintains, her theory is both materially grounded and politically well-judged. I argue that merely to assert the transparent reality of women's experiences and the primacy of practice begs the question of how those experiences have been represented and how political practice has itself been constructed from particular locations. MacKinnon overgeneralizes diverse women's experiences in ways that my Wittgensteinian analysis precludes, and argues that feminist practice can be straightforwardly theorized merely if we "look and see" without recognizing the complexity of this claim. Thus MacKinnon's arguments underdetermine the nature of anti-essentialist feminist organizing against sexual violence.

In the second half of Chapter 5, I look at the challenges facing feminist organizations that do reshape their practice in the light of politically significant and power-laden differences among women, at the same time as they persist in understanding gender as a political category that is absolutely central to their work. These case studies again illustrate the overwhelming importance of feminist attention to how relations of power construct generalizations about women. But these relations cannot be cast as always pernicious: feminists need criteria for deciding whom to include and exclude from political identity categories and coalition formation—and when. Working through these conflicts redirects feminist attention to mechanisms of power, suggesting that renouncing the very idea of a political theory with general ambitions—a position often associated with anti-essentialism in feminist philosophy—in fact precludes anti-essentialist feminist praxis.

In my conclusion, I point to some of the many other contexts in which these debates might usefully be applied to rethinking political practice, including controversies about race and racism, the politics of sexuality, and challenges to the structures of feminist organizations. These particular concerns seem a long way from the discussion of Wittgenstein with which I begin. Nevertheless, they are Wittgensteinian in spirit, moving my own discussion out into the world to "look and see" with a critical eye. They also reflect an ongoing dialectic between the hugely diverse philosophical tools we have inherited from western philosophy and the political exigencies of concrete feminist engagement, with its compromises, struggles, and rough ground. Like Wittgenstein, I am willing neither to renounce philosophy in favor of some kind of extraphilosophical pragmatism—even if I could make sense of this imperative—nor to accede to the allure of the frictionless ice and remove myself entirely from political engagement. But the resulting dialectic raises its own questions and contradictions; they are the substance of this book.

# Chapter 1

## Essentialism and Anti-Essentialism in Feminist Theory

Sometimes an expression has to be withdrawn from language and sent for cleaning,—then it can be put back into circulation.

—Ludwig Wittgenstein, *Culture and Value*

The word "essentialism" and its cognates regularly appear in contemporary social and political theory, particularly in theory addressing the politics of racial, sexual, or gendered identities. Their meanings are generally taken for granted, and their force is generally disapprobative. Essentialism is presumed to be a negative aspect of feminism. Consider the following examples:

One use of a theory of discourse for feminist politics, then, is in understanding social identities in their full socio-cultural complexity, thus in demystifying static, single variable, essentialist views of gender identity.[1]

To maintain that femininity predisposes women to certain (nurturing) jobs or (collaborative) styles of work is to naturalize complex economic and social processes and, once again, to obscure the differences that have characterized women's occupational histories. An insistence on differences undercuts the tendency to absolutist, and in the case of sexual difference, essentialist categories.[2]

The critique of essentialism encouraged by postmodernist thought is useful for African-Americans concerned with reformulating outmoded notions of identity. We have too long had imposed upon us from both the outside and the inside a narrow, constricting notion of blackness. Postmodern critiques of essentialism which challenge notions of universality and static overdetermined identity within mass culture and mass consciousness can open up new possibilities for the construction of self and the assertion of agency.[3]

Some theorists who have ceased looking for *the* causes of sexism still rely on essentialist categories such as gender identity. This is especially true of those scholars who have sought to develop gynocentric alternatives to mainstream androcentric perspectives but who have not fully abandoned the universalist pretensions of the latter.[4]

All of these examples, taken from articles with otherwise disparate theses, presume that "essentialism" is a way of conceiving of political identities and that it renders these identities "static," "absolutist," "overdetermined," and "universalist." This chapter and the next identify versions of "essentialism" in four feminist contexts—metaphysics, biology, language, and method—and argue that the specific problem I label "methodological essentialism" generates a serious political challenge for contemporary western feminist theory. Metaphysics, biology, and language are all implicated in this isolation of a particular methodological conversation within feminist theory, but nonetheless the reduction of the charge of essentialism to either a priorism or biological determinism does not capture the most important political issue at stake. The questions I am posing by way of this typology are first, is a given form of essentialism manifested in the work of any contemporary feminist theorist, and second, is this form typically the object of feminist anti-essentialist critique? I argue that essence-talk in recent feminist thought is rarely concerned with realist forms of metaphysical or biological essence, although "essentialism" has a philosophical history that is deeply embedded in strong claims about the true nature of things in the world, including women and men. These pre-social constructionist claims do not capture the complexity of the feminist debates: no feminist author uses these claims, and they are not the targets of feminist critics of essentialism.

However, forms of essentialism occurring *within* social constructionist discourses have come to occupy an important problem-space in recent feminist theory. Biology is still relevant here: the tendency of many feminists to hive off the sexed body as a pre-social site upon which constructions of gender are imposed has been challenged by thinkers whom Elizabeth Grosz labels "sexual difference" feminists.[5] Recognizing that the materiality of bodies still needs to be rendered intelligible to feminists within the terms of social constructionist discourses, "instead of seeing sex as an essentialist and gender as a constructionist category, these thinkers are concerned to undermine the dichotomy."[6] Thus feminists have struggled to reconcile the essentializing moments perceived to adhere to any discourse about bodies (with the histories of determinism and reductionism familiar from feminist critique of the history of ideas) with the need to theorize rather than dismiss women's bodies and lived experience. This book situates, rather than engages, this particular aspect of the essentialism debates. Nonetheless, my later discussion of feminist practice is intended explicitly to draw attention to the importance of materiality—including sexed bodies—in constructing claims about women.

In this chapter I describe linguistic essentialism and outline a feminist anti-essentialist critique. This critique offers a challenge both to realist claims about linguistic reference, and to the assumption that classes of objects are individuated in terms of necessary and sufficient conditions of membership; that is, that members of a class each exhibit common properties, possession of which makes them such members. The problem of linguistic categorization, for essentialists, is constructed around sorting potential members of categories into those that fall inside the boundary and those that do not. As Chapter 3 argues, the focus of feminist attention on this understanding of the reference of category terms contributes to an impasse, obstructing the construction of a politically viable anti-essentialist feminist method. Any alternative understandings of language within feminist theory, however, also need to recognize the strategic importance of drawing boundaries and to provide political analyses of better and worse examples of this activity.

In situating all these questions for the essentialism debates, I identify the specific problem of methodological essentialism, which pertains to the use of generalizations in feminist political-theoretical work. I take seriously the claim that feminism's need to use gender as a basic category of analysis, when set against the deep extant differences and divisions among women, represents an epistemological and political tension that frequently remains unresolved both in feminist theory and feminist practice. On the one hand, some feminist theories and forms of feminist political organizing have made overly general assumptions about "women," or used the term in exclusionary ways that presuppose a set of necessary and sufficient conditions of membership defined in relation to the identities of the powerful. On the other hand, some feminists have argued that essentialism is inherent in the very use of general terms, and that, to be faithful to one emancipatory vision, feminists should retain a deep and persistent skepticism about gender, aiming to fragment and proliferate gender categories. Both of these polar positions, and many in between, are represented in contemporary feminist theory, if not by the entire oeuvre of any author, then at least by certain moments in her work. These first two chapters describe the tension between overly general assumptions about "women" and challenges to the category itself, before offering a Wittgensteinian solution in Chapter 3.

## Essentialism in Feminism

Feminist theorists have presented "essentialism," perhaps rashly, as a term that can capture a range of widely debated and controversial themes in feminist thought, including illegitimate generalizations, ahistoricism, and certain understandings of "identity politics." No less vague and all-encompassing are those positions labeled "anti-essentialist," which comprise numerous overlapping theses, including the death of metaphysics, social constructionism in general, the death of the subject, the end of history, and descriptive and normative claims about personal and political identities. Thus a feminist theorist's immunity from essentialism—real or alleged—in one sphere does not preclude its occurrence in another.

Essentialism in feminist theory, furthermore, is defined not by its alleged defenders but by its "anti-essentialist" critics. Essentialism is presented as a *concern*, a feature of *bad* feminist theory, any one of a multitude of sins, "lingering" even where it is supposed to have been eradicated. Chantal Mouffe captures the tone of this general attack: reflecting in 1990 on ten years of feminist theory, she writes that "the struggle against essentialism is far from having been won."[7] Yet the pejorative use and broad interpretation of essentialism makes it difficult to detect what is to be avoided, or even if essentialism, in some form or another, can ever be avoided. Many feminist commentators use "essentialist" as one of a string of critical adjectives directed at other feminist work, yet in order to make that accusation stick, they frequently attribute forms of essentialism to their opponents that are not obviously philosophically unjustified or politically dangerous.

My recognition of the limitations of the charge of "essentialism" is not a novel one, and I concur with those theorists who have emphasized the inhibiting consequences of using "essentialist" as a pejorative adjective rather than a substantive term of critical assessment.[8] Just as not all forms of essentialism are pernicious, certain forms of anti-essentialism are politically limiting for feminists. If essentialism were taken genuinely to encompass all the philosophical sins attributed to it, then its meaning would be so broad as to lack critical force. Unless we are clear about what essentialism is and is not, and what is wrong with it, the pejorative adjective "essentialist" simply wastes theoretical time and energy and obscures a myriad of methodological and political issues within feminist theory that are worthy of more differentiated critique. As one critic recently alleged, an interest in essentialism risks becoming "passé," reflecting only a continuing investment in tired philosophical questions cooked up to indulge feminist theorists who might otherwise be more gainfully employed. Yet for all the varied usages and pitfalls of the term, "essentialism" remains a live issue in feminist theory and organizing. Let me offer three examples.

It is by now a platitude within contemporary North American feminist theory that in naming and describing such things as "women's experience," middle-class white feminists have often carelessly taken their own experiences to be representative of all women's lives, because they are both sufficiently disconnected from the lives of other women and relatively more powerful than women of color and working-class women. For example, in a recent radio discussion about generational differences, a group of four men and one woman, all in their late fifties and sixties, discussed their life paths. The men were all married professionals who talked about their workplace experiences and included their wives and children only as asides to the main business of their lives. The one woman quickly picked up on this emphasis and presented a "woman's perspective," talking about her own life at home "not working" while raising children and volunteering in her community. She then added that her sanity had been saved by "having someone in once a week," enabling her to leave the house for her volunteer job. This ungendered "someone" is, of course, another woman, and almost by definition a poor woman. At the same time as the speaker resists a patriarchal construction of "life for our generation" (one inattentive to differences among men, too), she offers a homogenized "women's perspective" that does not acknowledge the experiences of different women. In her familiar and incisive critique of Betty Friedan's classic *The Feminine Mystique*, bell hooks offers a similar argument, showing how Friedan's presentation of "American women" in fact describes the oppression only of white middle-class women, while her feminist prescriptions for these women to "get out of the house and into the workplace" can be implemented, under existing social structures, only given Black women's continuing subordination.[9]

Second, Elizabeth Spelman argues that certain forms of exclusion, especially racism within feminist theory in the United States, derive in part from a philosophical imagination that fails to understand gender as a category whose meaning depends on context.[10] As I argue in Chapter 2, her account offers a persuasive anti-essentialist critique of generalizations about women, based on the claim that certain ways of doing feminist theory (especially the method she labels "additive analysis") presuppose an "essential womanness" that all women share and around which feminists can mobilize. Instead, Spelman suggests, feminists should conceptualize gender as always inflected by other differences among women. Critical responses to Spelman exemplify the apprehensions about anti-essentialism set out in my introduction: the kind of fragmentation of gender that Spelman's analysis seems to recommend generates fears of disabling relativism and contextualism.

Finally, Chapter 4 presents an extended case study of a feminist theorist and practitioner who has, in a similar vein, been "accused" of essentialism. Carol Gilligan's research on women's moral and psychological development has frequently been criticized for essentialism in that her "subjects" have been, until recently, predominantly white, middle-class, heterosexually identified women and girls in the United States. In drawing general conclusions about gendered differences in moral voice, for example, Gilligan seems to preclude the possibility that race, class, or other differences among women will significantly affect their moral attitudes. Such criticisms again rest on claims about the nature and limitations of generalizations about women.

These, then, are examples of the kinds of debates explored in this book. I argue that generalizing about gender can be implicated in a form of methodological essentialism that is philosophically and politically misguided. Avoiding this kind of essentialism does not mean giving up on generalizing about women and men, but it does require a rethinking of the bases of general categories so as both to retain the critical political force of feminist analysis and to remain sensitive to the ways power can render difference invisible.

### Essence, Metaphysics, and Biology

The feminist preoccupation with essentialism is rarely situated to illustrate any continuity with the problem in non-feminist western philosophy. In this discussion I necessarily sidestep historical examinations of specific figures (the literature on Aristotelian essences, Platonic forms, or Locke's real versus nominal distinction, inter alia, is vast). Despite my later appropriation of Wittgenstein, I do not discuss his own essentialist targets (inter-war philosophy of language and logic). Although these debates are interesting in their own right, they are tangential to the concerns placed in the foreground by feminist anti-essentialism.[11]

Metaphysical and biological essentialisms, as they appear in discourses prior to social constructionism, are doctrines incorporating strong ontological and epistemological claims. Both posit that essence is inherent in objects in the world and argue that essentialist claims are true because they correspond to a reality existing independently from social construction. Neither one of these types of essentialism is the object of criticism internal to contemporary feminist theory. Precisely because they do not understand their own claims to be socially constructed, these two forms of essentialism are at odds with otherwise diverse feminist understandings of gender. In starting from these two extreme examples of essentialism in philosophy, I am pointing both to an outdated metaphysics that feminists have long set aside and to some weapons of sexism that pre-date all feminist social constructionisms. While it is important to acknowledge the continuing rhetorical power of these essentialisms in popular conservative politics, they exist outside the space in which feminist debates take place.

Metaphysical essentialism is a doctrine about the nature of things in the world. Formally understood, it is not manifested in the work of any contemporary feminist theorists and is not at stake when feminists accuse each other of "essentialism." In fact, metaphysical essentialism has faded from sight in contemporary western philosophy more generally. This absence leaves social theorists to debate the role of essentialism in the context of social constructionist debates about the extent of the similarities and differences between human beings, cultures, or various social groups. Feminists always operate with explicit or implicit social ontologies, and my later critique of methodological essentialism challenges a particular ontological perspective on identity categories. To dismiss metaphysical essentialism, in my terms, is only to dismiss a dated position that finds no foothold in contemporary feminism. The insinuation that metaphysical essentialism is at stake nonetheless serves a rhetorical function within feminist theory, allowing the work of certain authors to be dismissed on the basis of more sweeping criticisms than should properly be allowed. Because metaphysical essentialism is an untenable position for almost all feminists with regard to gender, eliding the distinction between this form of essentialism and others gives false weight to charges of "essentialism" at the expense of analytical usefulness.

What is metaphysical essentialism in the context of the history of philosophy? Metaphysical essentialism consists in the claim that certain species or types of things (and there are different claims to be made about different sorts of categories) have an essence: namely, a certain "quiddity" or innate structure. As Locke describes his notion of real essence: "*Essence* may be taken for the being of anything whereby it is what it is. And thus the real internal, but generally (in Substances) unknown, constitution of things, whereon their discoverable qualities depend, may be called their *essence*."[12] It is not only material substances or natural phenomena that have essences, although the kinds of essence invoked for material objects may be of a different variety than the essence of other categories.[13] Socrates searches for essences with his insistent questions, "what is justice?" and "what is piety?", to which he demands unequivocal answers that clearly cannot rest on physical properties allegedly picked out by concept terms, but rather on some otherwise metaphysical construal of their nature.[14] By what process can this metaphysical property of classes of objects be attributed?

One answer is that the metaphysical essence of particular things is indeed ineffable, and that while we may premise certain conclusions on its existence, this existence can never be demonstrated. The attribution of essences may be justified in terms of inference to the best explanation. A second alternative is to look to scientific theories to provide the material basis for essence claims. If we inquire into that "being of anything whereby it is what it is," then scientific investigation into the nature of the physical world seems to offer some possible answers, contending that essence can indeed be perceived. For example, we might argue that the essence of material substances is to be found in their atomic structures. However, this solution leaves unaddressed many kinds of essence claims that do not apply to straightforwardly material objects. Even if we can discover the inner constitutions of certain things or substances, we would not be able to identify the essential structure that makes something a token of a particular type or kind. What is the essence of a game (to use Wittgenstein's famous example)? The seeming futility of the search for metaphysical essences has been partly responsible for the increased emphasis, in modern western philosophy, on essentialism as a feature of language rather than of things in themselves.

What does the above, seemingly rather arcane, philosophical problem have to do with feminism? Put briefly, it motivates the question, "could we find a metaphysical essence of gender?" Can we find an essential "womanness" by

virtue of which women are women? The history of western social and political philosophy includes attempts to offer an affirmative answer to that question, often using essentialist philosophy of gender to justify sexism. Metaphysical essentialism appears in one form as closure against the possibility
that gender is a set of variable and mutable social constructs. This a priorism
consists in the claim that women have souls of a particular kind, or that women
necessarily possess certain forms of virtue but not others, where these claims
are premised on the most counterfactual and superficial of evidence (if any).
Much feminist work in the history of philosophy critically explores this
legacy of sexism. For example, Nancy Tuana argues that religious and philosophical claims about women's inferior souls find their way into accounts of
women as being less rational than men (whether by association with the body
rather than the mind, or by association with allegedly non-rational activities
such as reproductive labor, care-giving, or housework, or by more direct assertion). This step in turn is implicated in claims about women's inferior
moral faculties, as moral action and reason are linked in the philosophies of
Kant and Rousseau, for example. Some of these diverse claims draw on so-
called empirical evidence: Aristotle adduced that women have imperfect souls
from the "facts" that their "degree of heat" is less and their contribution to
generation is less noble.[15] But such claims often also rely on ontologies that
posit, for example, a divinely inspired sexually differentiated human nature,
or other extra-social, universal, fixed truths about sexual difference. Thus, a
belief in a pure and inherent femininity outside the social realm is perhaps
the most extreme kind of gender essentialist claim.

These historical questions are the backdrop to contemporary feminist debates about essentialism.[16] The epithet "essentialist" is frequently used to
invoke the specter of these a priori, ontologically suspect claims in the philosophical canon. So, can metaphysical essentialism—as an appeal to a universal, realist, and extra-social ontological framework—ever be employed in the
interests of feminism? It seems at first unlikely that feminists would gain from
such arguments, however stated. Certainly, no modern feminist ever presents
herself as a metaphysical essentialist in such straightforward terms. In western feminist political theory, most identifiable invocations of anything ap-
proximating metaphysical essence fall into two camps: they are either strong
polemical claims made about women within radical feminist discourse that
constitute a kind of "reverse essentialism" or they are historically situated,
oriented toward demonstrating the existence of certain traits universal to human beings from which particular political conclusions can be derived. Let
me examine these two varieties in more detail.

First, no prominent theorist directly invokes a metaphysical essence of

Woman as part of a feminist politics—claiming that women possess essential qualities different from and superior to men's. When feminists do make claims about women's superiority, they are much more likely to draw on accidental properties that women generally possess, or on features of women's experiences that are clearly socially constructed. As Teresa de Lauretis says:

> Barring the case in which woman's essence is taken as absolute being or substance in the traditional metaphysical sense (and this may actually be the case for a few, truly fundamentalist thinkers to whom the term essentialist would properly apply), for the great majority of feminists the "essence" of woman is more like the essence of [Locke's] triangle than the essence of the thing-in-itself: it is the specific properties (e.g., a female-sexed body), qualities (a disposition to nurturance, a certain relation to the body etc.), or necessary attributes (e.g., the experience of femaleness, of living in the world as female) that women have developed or have been bound to historically, in their differently patriarchal sociocultural contexts, which make them women, and not men.[17]

The most plausible example in this "fundamentalist" category seems to me to be Mary Daly: in her writing I sometimes read a strongly spiritual thread, which could be interpreted as a curious mirroring of essentialist ontology in the religious doctrine that creates a backdrop to her feminism.[18] Whatever we make of this interpretation of Daly's work, when she is criticized (as she often is) for "essentialism," what is most often at stake is not an a priori form of metaphysical essentialism. Instead critics take issue with her social ontology in the sense of her overly generalizing and insufficiently grounded claims about women. For example, Audre Lorde's critique of *Gyn/Ecology* stresses both the exclusion of women of color and their depiction as "victims and preyers-upon each other:" "To imply . . . that all women suffer the same oppression simply because we are women is to lose sight of the many varied tools of patriarchy. It is to ignore how those tools are used by women without awareness against each other."[19]

Another possible example of metaphysical a priorism is Andrea Dworkin's claim in *Intercourse* that penetration of the female body in sexual intercourse constitutes an metaphoric invasion. To sustain this argument, she elides two claims. First, she implies the necessary metaphysical claim that any insertion of any external object into the body's interiority constitutes a threatening invasion of the boundaries of the self by a foreign exteriority: "In the experience of intercourse, she loses the capacity for integrity because her body—the basis of privacy and freedom in the material world for all human beings—is entered and occupied; the boundaries of her physical body are—neutrally speaking—violated." And, "can those with a metaphysically compromised privacy have self-determination; can those without a biologically based physical integrity have self-respect?" Second, she also suggests the contingent claim that sociocultural conditions make vaginal penetration (especially by a man, and especially by a penis) into an act of hostility against women: "How to separate the act of intercourse from the social reality of male power is not clear, especially because it is male power that constructs both the meaning and the current practice of intercourse as such."[20] I would argue that to sustain a feminist position, Dworkin needs the latter claim and cannot afford the former. That she implicitly appeals to the former is, I think, more an indication of the rhetorical appeal of a priori metaphysics than of her project's bankruptcy. The social ontologies that various feminist authors use in constructing theoretical accounts of women's oppression definitely matter for the purposes of anti-essentialist analysis. But while some feminist work—like Daly's and Dworkin's—is methodologically controversial, forms of metaphysical essentialism that rely solely on a priori appeals are not the problem. While some work at the margins of feminist theory may toy with this kind of metaphysical essentialism, no theorist has offered an articulated defense of it as a proper basis for feminist claims.

Second, the political strategy of invoking a universal *human* essence to argue against sexist determinism has a long and complex history. We find precursors to contemporary feminist debates in attempts to reverse the focus of essentialism so as to claim that, instead of their essence confining women to established gender roles, it provides the basis for a critique of these roles. Such egalitarian arguments are usually premised on the claim that a non-sexed human essence has more actual or potential political significance than any essential sexual difference. For example, Mary Wollstonecraft claims that both women and men are rational, and that this human "essence"—the potential for which is prior to education—is definitive of humanity. Wollstonecraft argues that:

Reason is . . . the simple power of improvement; or, more properly speaking, of discerning truth. Every individual is in this respect a world in itself. More or less may be conspicuous in one being than another; but the nature of reason must be the same in all, if it be an emanation of divinity, the tie that connects the creature with the Creator; for, can that soul be stamped with the heavenly image, that is not perfected by the exercise of its own reason? . . . [C]onsidering woman as a whole, let it be what it will, instead of a part of man, the inquiry is whether she have reason or not. If she have, which, for a moment, I will take for granted, she was not created merely to be the solace of man, and the sexual should not destroy the human character.[21]

Thus reason is God-given, an essential quality bestowed upon human beings, and consists in the power to discern truth.

What has happened to this kind of essentialism in western political theory? Essentialism as those defining qualities of human beings existing independently of any human experience (what Nussbaum calls "metaphysical-realist essentialism") represents a significant tradition in political thought.[22] Nonetheless, contemporary authors are unlikely to accept this type of appeal to a metaphysics that either permits the unmediated perception of the real or requires claims about the "ineffable," or that which is taken on faith. For example, Nussbaum's self-described "Aristotelian essentialism" is genealogically related to, yet still quite different from, Wollstonecraft's account. Nussbaum defends essentialism, which she defines as "the view that human life has certain central defining features." She argues that "the legitimate criticisms of essentialism still leave room for essentialism of a kind: for a historically sensitive account of the most basic human needs and human functions."[23] Listing certain conditions necessary for a form of life to count as human (ranging from mortality to practical reason to "separateness"), Nussbaum makes the case that her Aristotelian essentialism allows for the human values of compassion and respect, whereas the "anti-essentialism" of her opponents does not. By using deconstructive tactics and stressing thick cultural difference, Nussbaum claims, her opponents slide into a disabling relativism, on the basis of which they are unable to make moral judgments about poverty, inequality, development policy, and global injustice. She makes clear that her view of humanity is not metaphysically a priori and instead commits herself to a form of "historically grounded empirical essentialism," or to strong "internalist" universal claims, across time and culture, about the nature of human beings. Even she—a self-defined essentialist and certainly one of the theorists most wedded to universalizing discourse writing about essentialism today—is careful to eliminate a priorism in favor of a more historically grounded account.

Nussbaum's retreat from metaphysical-realist essentialism is indicative of a more general and established skepticism about the possibility of any truths existing independently of human contexts. The broad rejection, by both feminist and non-feminist political theorists, of an image of philosophy as "mirroring nature," radically independent of all human interpretation, has found a corollary in feminist theory: debates about essentialism, as all my examples suggest, are rarely carried out at this metaphysical level. Seyla Benhabib, following Jane Flax's characterization of postmodernism, points out strong and weak versions of a "death of metaphysics" thesis as they relate to feminist theory.[24] The strong version suggests that the western philosophical tradition has been dominated by a "metaphysics of presence" that has only recently faced a serious challenge in the form of deconstruction; Benhabib argues, I think rightly, that the strong thesis grossly over-simplifies and homogenizes a diverse philosophical legacy. In its weak version, Benhabib argues, the "death of metaphysics" thesis is that philosophy cannot provide criteria of validity for other discourses and must cease to be a meta-discourse of legitimation. She defines the feminist version of this thesis as "feminist skepticism toward the claims of transcendent reason." The subject of reason can no longer be cast as a "supra-historical and context-transcendent being, but the theoretical and practical creations and activities of this subject bear in every instance the marks of the context out of which they emerge." Rejecting the supposed search for the Real as a ground of Truth, Benhabib writes: "the subject of philosophy is inevitably embroiled with knowledge-governing interests which mark and direct its activities."[25]

The dialogue between Nussbaum or Benhabib and their respective opponents plays out a number of themes that recur throughout this book: generality versus specificity and sameness versus difference are the defining terms of essentialist/anti-essentialist debates, in whatever context they occur. The substantial debates surrounding their respective theses cannot be examined in more detail here. The implications of work such as Nussbaum's or Benhabib's for gender essentialism, however, lie in one central ontological shift: the acceptance even by universalists that instead of looking for a truth about subjectivity or social realities existing independently of human interpretation, feminists need to look for commonalities and differences *from within* our own socially situated frameworks of understanding. Claims about gender must be contextualized and justified by reference to material conditions, not a priori, and must be clear about their own scope and grounds of legitimacy. The precise nature of "situated criticism," and so the extent to which contextual analysis must be local and not generalized, is an issue that divides feminists. It is also the issue that is most central to feminist debates around essentialism. Rejecting a tradition of metaphysical essentialism is only to reject a narrow range of positions predating social constructionism (not to mention deconstructionism) that have little legitimacy in political theory in any case. The essentialism debates in feminist theory are situated on a terrain in which questions of social ontology persist, but are discussed in the complex contexts of women's lived experiences, material conditions, bodies, and empirical realities, not in the philosophical world of the a priori.

Popular thinking about gender very often reflects widespread adherence to views that are straightforwardly biologically determinist, and I in no way want to minimize the political significance of oppression originating in biologically essentialist views of women's functions or roles. Nonetheless, biological essentialism, in a manner that is analogous to metaphysical essentialism, relies on truth-claims about persons that are not self-reflexive about their socially constructed nature. In what follows I first sketch a form of anti-feminist biological essentialism that argues that women's capacities can be reduced to aspects of their biology. Feminist theorists accused of slipping into biological essentialism of this kind can be defended against the most obvious versions of the charge. But the application of the term "essentialist" to discussions of embodiment reaches beyond this simple determinism to include the wide range of feminist theories that posit a pre-social sexed body. Feminists such as Luce Irigaray have been labeled "essentialist" for attempting to ground their theories in the nature of women's bodies, for example.[26] The label "essentialist" is also used by Grosz's "sexual difference" feminists against their opponents when they argue that sex, as much as gender, is socially constructed. This questioning of the pre-social, pre-linguistic reality of sexed bodies considers itself "anti-essentialist." I do not pursue the debates surrounding this form of essentialism in any detail in this book, but I use this example as an introduction to the increasingly untenable contrast between essentialism and social constructionism.

Biological essentialism in its original form is the claim that certain anatomical or physiological features of persons define their inclusion in a certain naturally occurring category, and often the very word "essentialism" is used as a convenient, if unclear, shorthand for such views. The fact that scientific and medical thinking about femininity has often used biologically essentialist arguments to justify the subordination of women is by now commonplace in feminism. As Grosz says:

Biologism is a particular form of essentialism in which women's essence is defined in terms of women's biological capacities. Biologism is usually based on some form of reductionism: social and cultural factors are the effects of biologically given causes. In particular, biologism usually ties women closely to the functions of reproduction and nurturance, although it may also limit women's social possibilities through the use of evidence from neurology, neurophysiology, and endocrinology.[27]

Women are women, the argument runs, by virtue of their chromosomes, their hormones, their sexual organs, their brain size, their brain function, their smaller and weaker bodies, and so on. From such claims, normative conclusions about gender roles ("biological determinism") are often inferred, although such inferences do not necessarily follow. Simply because a certain biological feature is indicative of membership in a particular class does not mean that any normative conclusion about the inferiority of that class need ensue—unless, of course, normative claims are smuggled into the essence-talk itself, as is generally the case. For example, Tuana points to the notoriously circular and ad hoc theories of nineteenth century craniologists who argued that (alleged) sexual differences in skull size indicated female inferiority.[28]

Feminist objections both to this kind of biological essentialism and to the normative conclusions falsely inferred from it are well-established. Biologically essentialist claims conveniently ignore the many instances of inclusion in a class that do not in fact meet the criteria for membership, making universal claims where, at best, generalizations apply. The wealth of anthropological and sociological data on the variety of models of femininity also challenges the assumption of a universal and unchanging biological basis for both sex and gender. As with metaphysical essentialism, the feminist critique of biologism has centered on the sociology of the knowledge generated within scientific research programs, on the erasure of difference that biological essentialism both permits and requires, and on the normative claims attached to allegedly value-free descriptions of sexual difference. Methodological critique clearly does not end merely because such theories purport to be based on forms of "empirical evidence."[29]

Analogous views are put forward by essentialists with regard to sexuality: there is, they claim, some "natural," authentic sexual drive that is repressed by the social; or people have some definitive sexual "orientation" that describes the way they "really are." Popular fascination with the question of "discovering" the "gay gene" perhaps best exemplifies an extreme biologically essentialist view of sexuality. Corresponding anti-essentialist criticisms pinpoint the fact that research usually centers on gay men (erasing the experience of lesbians even as it often purports to include it) and cast doubt on the "naturalness" of these claims: sexual essentialists do not pose the question "what causes heterosexuality?," nor do they draw out the contrast between gay men and lesbians or the variety in sexual behaviors. And much queer theory makes the point that essentialism with regard to sexual "orientation" fails to acknowledge the creation of "the homosexual" as a category of analysis only within a particular historical and cultural context, and prefers to elide variations in the social construction of homosexuality, basing "scientific" arguments instead on the supposed reality of an identifiable subgroup of people who are, by nature, inevitably sexually drawn only to members of the "same sex" and ineluctably different from the heterosexual majority.[30]

Anti-essentialist critique within feminist theory, while sometimes running together different forms of essentialism, does not make its strongest and most controversial charges against this particular form of biological essentialism. While some feminist theorists have been accused of it (and I examine this charge against Carol Gilligan in Chapter 4), these accusations are most often used to dismiss rather than to offer instructive critique. Some critics have tried to argue that certain forms of "cultural" or radical feminism are biologically essentialist by virtue of their appeal to aspects of women's bodily experiences as the bases of gender difference.[31]

For example, Sara Ruddick's maternal feminism argues that the experience of mothering, culturally associated with women, provides the foundation for a "politics of peace" or a certain ethical attitude toward relations with others.[32] But even the strongest versions of such theories step back from making biological difference per se the foundation of their claims, arguing instead that it is the social structuring of women's bodily experiences that constitutes a politically salient gender difference. Ruddick is anxious to stress that were men to engage more often and more seriously in the activity of mothering, they would learn the same kinds of ethical attitudes as women who currently mother; likewise, she construes "mothering" as an activity not necessarily linked to the physical state of pregnancy or to the act of childbirth—foster mothers, adoptive mothers, and so on, learn the same ethical attitudes as birth mothers (and, indeed, birth mothers who do not go on to mother their children do not learn them).[33] Some feminists may be unreflective about their inferences from sexed bodies to social constructionist claims, and they risk naturalizing claims about women and men that are intended to indicate learned or constructed aspects of human society. They may also be wedded to a view of "women" as a natural group existing prior to the exercise of power rather than constituted through it. This theoretical move then makes the presocial body into a natural foundation upon which social constructions are enacted, rather than understanding the materiality of the body itself as a site of meaning construction. Furthermore, such feminists are often cavalier in their attitudes toward exceptions and make overly generalizing claims about women and men. However, their critics, I suggest, have been similarly careless in attributing "biological essentialism" to arguments that in fact depict certain features of persons as accidental rather than essential properties; the critics thereby fail to distinguish legitimate methodological criticisms from this easily refuted charge.

Biological essentialism, in its simple reductionist form, is not the proper target of feminist anti-essentialist critique. Indeed, feminists have devoted considerable time and energy to discrediting forms of biological essentialism that infer normative conclusions about women's subordination. I pointed out earlier how metaphysical essentialism is often manifested as a priorism, with an accompanying reluctance to engage with empirical evidence. This charge is not so straightforwardly leveled at biologically essentialist claims, which may invoke a scientific or medical empirical basis. However, the exact content of this "empiricist" claim needs to be unpacked. Merely invoking claims about the biological reality of sexual (let alone gender) difference does not allay anti-essentialist fears. What is wrong with biological essentialism is not that it fails to make empirical claims, but rather that it fails to understand these claims as themselves being shaped by specific social and political conditions. The reason that both metaphysical and biological essentialisms are inimical to feminist debate is their mutual juxtaposition to social constructionism. Recent feminist anti-essentialist critique, however, has mainly been directed at essentializing moments within social constructionist discourses.

There is a distinction between anti-feminist biological essentialism that reduces women's capacities to aspects of their biology, understood as presocial facts about the reality of sexual difference, and feminist qualms about the negotiation of embodiment in feminist theories. The use of the epithet "essentialist" by sexual difference feminists can refer to any feminist position that posits a sexed body existing in original form "underneath" the social. On such a view, the term "women" refers to a naturally occurring group of sexed individuals, described by reference to the fixed conditions of membership; thus "women" exist as a natural kind before gender is imposed, rather than being produced in various ways through differing social practices. In other words, the members of categories must have some actually existing qualities, by virtue of which they are what they are. In the case of "women," this categorization could be any set of qualities that reflects the reality (which is of course not a reality at all) of the division of humanity into two sexes, female and male. This form of "essentialism" presupposes a natural kind to which the term "women" refers. It claims to construe reality in a certain way, to describe a particular state of affairs existing before, and causally related to, the designation "women." This claim requires some qualification for almost all feminist theorists.

The assumption that the word "women" merely describes a category of sex was widespread in feminist theory before the emergence of an alternative set of perspectives, which argued that "women" could not be said to exist independently of the organization of their construction.[34] Anti-essentialist opposition here, then, is to a social constructionism that itself accepts a nonsocially constructed biology as counterpoint. These perspectives represented a challenge to the sex/gender dichotomy itself as a feminist model for understanding the putative distinction between biological sex and social gender. No longer could natural sex be understood simply as prior to cultural gender. Invoking the category "women," for example, cannot be justified if premised on the belief that women exist independently in the world and that the term "women" describes a collection of people who are marked out by biological characteristics preceding language. Rather, the category of "women" is a fully discursive one, held in place, for example, by its relation to another category, "men." Just as "masters" only exist by virtue of there being "slaves," the categories "men" and "women" are dependent upon one another for their social meanings. For example, Judith Butler argues in *Bodies That Matter* that sex does not describe a prior materiality but produces and regulates the intelligibility of the materiality of bodies: "If gender is the social construction of sex, and if there is no access to this 'sex' except by means of its construction, then it appears not only that sex is absorbed by gender, but that 'sex' becomes something like a fiction, perhaps a fantasy, retroactively installed at a prelinguistic site to which there is no direct access."[35] Feminist work in this area is supported by analyses of ways in which sexual dimorphism is compelled through a nexus of disciplinary practices, many of which work on the body itself. For example, feminist analyses of the sociomedical management of intersexed infants and transsexuals, the (self-)enforcement of female "beauty" regimens, and the institutionalization of cosmetic surgery, dieting, and other disciplining practices of body modification, strongly suggest that sexual conformity is not only a "secondary" issue, confined to the realm of "gender" as normally understood, but also that bodies are constructed as sexed through inscriptions upon flesh itself.[36] One theoretical struggle here is that of reconciling recognition of the materiality of the sexed body with its construction in dominant regimes of meaning. To insist that the body is pre-social and pre-linguistic is to be an "essentialist," but anti-essentialist positions here are criticized in turn for understating the material realities of embodiment.

The very belief in the reality of sexual dimorphism has come to be labeled "essentialist." This claim is considerably stronger than the opposition to bio-logical essentialism described above. Instead of simply challenging the infer-ence from physical sex to normative conclusion, this kind of anti-essentialism insists that "sex" is in fact a constructed, linguistic category. But this debate itself does not occur only at the level of language. The materiality of bodies here engages with disputes about meaning to displace an ontology that places bodies outside the realm of the social, while not displacing the very idea of material realities. While this issue is bracketed in the argument that follows, this example reveals the appearance of the label "essentialism" within a dis-course (feminist talk of the distinction between sex and gender) that is puta-tively social constructionist. This is the theoretical move I want to investi-gate in more detail in what follows.

## Essence and Social Construction

Within social theory, essentialism is most often juxtaposed to social con-structionism. Yet the essentialist–constructionist dichotomy has clearly out-lived its usefulness as a way of understanding social and political identities. While popular sexist and homophobic discourses still trade on strict forms of metaphysical or biological essentialism, these latter are peripheral to almost all political theoretical approaches. Increasingly, the dichotomy between es-sentialism and constructionism falls away as essentializing moments are iden-tified within constructionist arguments. Thus, when feminist theorists crit-icize "essentialism," they most often target perceived faults within feminist accounts that are avowedly and overtly constructionist. Let me spell out the content of this dichotomy, before offering an account of forms of essential-ism that emerge within social constructionism.

A traditional understanding of the distinction characterizes essentialism as depicting social identities as fixed, immutable and universal, whereas so-cial constructionism emphasizes contingency, context, and cultural varia-tion. Constructionism "insists that essence is itself a historical construction":

> Constructionists take the refusal of essence as the inaugural moment of
> their own projects and proceed to demonstrate the way previously assumed
> self-evident kinds (like "man" or "woman") are in fact the effects of com-
> plicated discursive practices. . . . In short, constructionists are concerned
> above all with the *production* and *organization* of differences, and they
> therefore reject the idea that any essential or natural givens precede the
> processes of social determination.[37]

---

In relation to feminism, any argument that posits that gender roles are learned, that sexed bodies do not necessarily correlate with gendered behavior, or that the variation in understandings of femininity and masculinity across time and place can be explained only by examining local social structures and attitudes can be labeled "social constructionist." Differences between men and women are explained by social contexts rather than essential natures. Likewise, in relation to sexual identities, "'essentialists' treat sexuality as a biological force and consider sexual identities to be cognitive realizations of genuine, underlying differences; 'constructionists,' on the other hand, stress that sexuality, and sexual identities, are social constructions, and belong to the world of culture and meaning, not biology."[38] In my typology, a priori metaphysical essentialism and anti-feminist biological essentialism are opposed to social constructionist arguments. Both look for pre-social truths about personal identities, and in that strict sense they are generally inimical to feminist theorizing and political organizing.

This dichotomy, however, has been subjected to extensive deconstruction in recent feminist accounts. For example, Diana Fuss argues that "essentialism is essential to social constructionism."[39] Arguing that the terms of any binary opposition are dependent upon and implicated in each other, she suggests that social constructionism is not the antithesis of essence but rather its deferral. Merely invoking the category of "the social" does not rule out the possibility of essentialism in a different form:

> The constructionist strategy of specifying more precisely these subcategories of "woman" does not necessarily preclude essentialism. "French bourgeois woman" or "Anglo-American lesbian," while crucially emphasizing in their very specificity that "woman" is by no means a monolithic category, nonetheless reinscribe an essentialist logic at the very level of historicism. Historicism is not always an effective counter to essentialism if it succeeds only in fragmenting the subject into multiple identities, each with its own self-contained, self-referential essence. The constructionist impulse to specify, rather than definitively counteracting essentialism, often simply redeploys it through the very strategy of historicization, rerouting and dispersing it through a number of micropolitical units or sub-categorical classifications, each presupposing its own unique interior composition or metaphysical core.[40]

In a poststructuralist vein, Fuss then argues that every invocation of a category, no matter how it is inflected, reintroduces essentialism by presupposing commonalities among the members of that category. Recognizing the potential slippery slope in this argument, she claims that the crucial question to be posed of such categories as "women" is not whether essentialism, thus defined, can be avoided, but in what way it is used.[41] This claim is central to the account of essentialism in the chapters that follow, as I ask where essentialism can inhere if not in opposition to social constructionist accounts of gender.

Increasingly, as a variety of strands of western philosophy have turned away from metaphysics and toward language, forms of essentialism premised on metaphysically realist claims about pre-social truths have been marginalized within the typology of essentialisms. Essence is more and more likely to be considered a feature of language, and theories of essentialism become accounts of meaning.[42] Linguistic essentialism is the belief that the definition of a term provides the necessary and sufficient conditions of membership in its extension.[43] We take different instances of the same category term and abstract from them certain fixed common properties, which are then the defining characteristics of that concept. For example, Locke's nominal essence is found in the *idea* that we form from such defining characteristics—i.e., the nominal essence of a triangle is the idea of a three-sided shape. This account of meaning presupposes a fixed core of features that all members of the relevant class possess. Nominal essences provide constant standards by which to make claims about instances of a category term; namely, whether they do or do not count as examples of that term.

Feminists, then, are faced with a series of questions in the philosophy of language: To whom does the word "women" refer? Can we offer a set of necessary and sufficient conditions of being a woman? How do we make decisions about which similarities between women count as such conditions and which differences are irrelevant to uses of the term? Must women have something in common merely because they are called "women," and must the term refer to a bounded set of identifiable individuals? Should part of the task of feminist theory be to define the parameters of the concept "women" or to "get it right" about who women are? How is the materiality of sexual difference constructed through language? We might ask analogous questions about other central categories of feminist analysis, including "lesbians," "families," even "feminists."

If we reject the essentialist metaphysics that understands women to be women by virtue of physical sex, to claim that women are women by virtue of *any* fixed set of features of gender is still a *linguistically* essentialist claim. That is, it takes the term "women" to refer to a group of people united by the socially constructed aspects of their femininity: i.e., their common traits resulting from socialization (for example, caring), their shared oppression under patriarchy (for example, femininity as subordination), or their collective experiences qua women. Linguistic essentialism consists in the claim that any definition of "women" must assume certain necessary and sufficient conditions of membership in that definition, whether or not those conditions are biological attributes. There is one glaring prima facie difficulty with this form of essentialism: if we look for a finite set of characteristics that define each member of the set "women," we are always going to find exceptions to every possible candidate. If we say, for example, that women are women because they have XX chromosomes, female primary sexual characteristics and the experience of oppression on the basis of gender, then we can easily find an individual who is considered by all to be a "woman" but who does not have all of these qualities (an individual with XXY chromosomes, for example). Any list of candidates for the essential attributes of "women" seems to fail because exceptions can always be found.

It seems, on this account, as if *any* general account of membership in the class "women" is "essentialist," but it is not clear that this is a problem for feminism or even that this form of essentialism can ever be avoided. Many influential feminist theories build their conceptual frameworks around particular general claims about the defining characteristics of being a woman, even as they include provisos about the scope of such claims. How could feminists possibly be "anti-essentialists" with regard to linguistic essentialism? Poststructural feminists have offered trenchant critiques of linguistic essentialism, showing the contingencies and exclusions necessarily built into any system of categorization. As my argument in Chapter 3 shows, I endorse this critical move. But what are the *politics* that follow from this epistemological critique, based on skepticism about and subversion of the very categories we employ as feminists? Butler again offers the most fully developed critique of linguistic essentialism in relation to feminist politics. She argues that contesting any descriptive content of "women" is a more progressive tactic than assigning any particular content to the term. The latter strategy merely factionalizes feminists and generates the illusion that the very identity that is contested can be a solidifying ground for feminist mobilization, when in fact the notion of a pre-discursive feminine identity is precisely what needs to be undercut. Identity categories are normative, never merely "describing" a preexisting group but also offering ideal-typical characterizations of its members, a process that excludes those who do not match the conditions of membership. Rather than search for "foundations"—for the correct content of the term "women," for example—its constant rifting is the very ground of feminist theory. Recasting the term "women" as a signifier rather than as a referring expression expands the possibilities of being a woman and leads to enhanced agency: "women" are no longer a determinate set of members of a class with a fixed identity but can contest both that identity itself and the terms of membership.[44]

Viewed this way, a central task of feminist theory becomes the subversion of sexual binarisms by challenging the prevailing social meaning of gender categories—which, of course, is what most feminist theories seek to do— but without replacing them with other difference-denying constructs. The "strategic displacement" of gender categories, and poststructuralist feminism's refusal to reaffirm any specific content to the category "women," sets it apart from other feminist theories, as does its desire to multiply gender formations rather than accept status quo accounts of gender, even if these accounts are feminist. As Butler describes her early project in *Gender Trouble:*

> This text continues, then, as an effort to think through the possibility of subverting and displacing those naturalized and reified notions of gender that support masculine hegemony and heterosexist power, to make gender trouble, not through the strategies that figure a utopian beyond, but through the mobilization, subversive confusion, and proliferation of precisely those constitutive categories that seek to keep gender in its place by posturing as the foundational illusions of identity.[45]

Feminists wary of this radical anti-essentialism, however, argue that rejecting essentialism even in language leads to the conclusion that there can be no basis to feminist mobilizing, i.e., that if the very category "women" is ungrounded, then feminist activism cannot proceed. I am sympathetic to those feminists who have argued that to fully implement anti-essentialism may be disabling for certain feminist projects and disconnect feminists from useful humanist discourse that makes connections across difference, and I return to the limits and dangers of anti-essentialism in this context.[46] But here let me defend Butler's position against a straightforward reductio that I think obscures more significant objections to her linguistic anti-essentialism.

Is *any* invocation of *any* category "essentialist"? An affirmative reply might be elaborated by claiming that language itself erases difference and homogenizes in ways that must be resisted with the recognition that any counter-category will similarly exhibit a "contemptuous attitude toward the particular case."[47] Of course, there is a reductio here: if language per se essentializes, then essentialism is unavoidable if we are to speak at all. This is the reductio that anti-feminists are employing when they refuse to allow talk of "women" in order to disallow radical analysis. Some feminists have been somewhat truistically criticized for essentialism by others using exactly this premise. For example, Fuss criticizes Monique Wittig's argument that "lesbians are not women" on exactly the grounds that her "strong constructionist perspective" collapses back into essentialism.[48] Wittig argues that the linguistic categories of "men" and "women" do not pick out an independent reality but rather derive their most widely accepted social meanings from a patriarchal society that defines a dominant ideal of masculinity and a subordinate ideal of femininity: "For there is no sex. There is but sex that is oppressed and sex that oppresses. It is oppression that creates sex and not the contrary. The contrary would be to say that sex creates oppression, or to say that the cause (origin) of oppression is to be found in sex itself, in a natural division of the sexes preexisting (or outside of) society."[49] Wittig places the "heterosexual contract" at the center of the social meanings of gender, arguing that lesbians, by escaping the heterosexual order, form a third category with revolutionary potential outside sex.

Fuss's response trades on the reductio: "The weakness of [Wittig's] analysis lies in her own tendency to homogenize lesbians into a single harmonious group and to erase the real material and ideological differences between lesbians—in other words, to engage in essentialist thinking in the very act of trying to discredit it."[50] While differences among lesbians may well be salient to any analysis of their political role, it does seem that the mere use of the term "lesbians" as a category of analysis is unavoidable if Wittig is to make her point. Rather than highlighting the specific ways in which "material and ideological differences" might actually nuance or subvert Wittig's argument, Fuss goes on to offer a critique merely of the use of general categories. If we were to accept this argument, feminist theory would be unavoidably implicated in essentialism, and to use "essentialist" as a pejorative would be entirely lacking in critical import.[51]

To avoid this reductio, we can modulate our critical response to linguistic anti-essentialism: instead of all language being unavoidably essentialist, we could argue, as Butler does, that anti-essentialism consists merely in the self-reflexive recognition of the erasure of difference by language and of the contingency of categories. All categories are relative features of language, and all categories obliterate cross-cutting differences or alternative ways of describing those within the category. In this way, no one whom we might include in the category "women" fits only into that category—she is also old, Black, heterosexual, francophone, able-bodied, a survivor of sexual abuse, or any other combination of a myriad of descriptions. Likewise, if the term "women" is "only" a linguistic category, it follows that a redefinition of its boundaries is permanently possible, to include, for example, transgendered or intersexed people who elect (or are compelled) to identify as women. The facile response to the Butlerian critique of categories is to claim that if all linguistic categories are suspect then feminists are tongue-tied, unable to invoke the very labels—"women" and "men"—that first gave rise to the feminist movement and politics. A more nuanced understanding rejects the reductio and so accepts the political necessity of ongoing recognition of the contingency of categories, their perpetual tension with difference, and the need to parody and subvert terms like "women" even as we invoke them. Yet even given this acceptance of aspects of linguistic anti-essentialism, we can still challenge certain political directions that this challenge to fixed categories and awareness of contingency can take.

There are three familiar objections to the ways this variety of linguistic anti-essentialism can play out in political contexts. What would a political practice look like that refused to affirm any fixed content to our political identities? The first is merely a strategic argument: apart from being a novel and somewhat counter-intuitive form of organizing (although one that now has recognizable precedents), anti-essentialist politics may play into etiolating liberal (or conservative) accounts of social realities.[52] That is, continually to deny the salience of gender, thus refusing to affirm any specific content to women's identity, is often to conform to dominant understandings of social organization that simply erase gender. Many forms of feminist separatism are sustained by the notion of a continuous and resistant counter-hegemonic identity, and objections to separatism often try to attack the legitimacy of, for example, women's insistence on separate space, such as festivals, self-help groups, and so on. The identities that are invoked to justify separatism may be problematic (later I consider the furious debates surrounding the exclusion of male-to-female transsexuals from women's music festivals, for example), but to point to their contingency may also fuel anti-feminist demands for a return to "human" identities that have already been the subject of extensive feminist deconstruction.

This leads into a second point: many women, including many feminists, experience their identities as women (in whatever way they understand this assertion) as deeply authentic. Being a woman is not something to be treated "playfully," to be parodied or subverted. Rather, it is a deeply personal understanding of one's self. Feminist thinking, of course, has never been loath to challenge women's own self-understandings, refusing to accept the psychic inheritances of patriarchal societies. Nonetheless, the demand that we undercut every oppositional identity at the same time as we construct it may feel to many of us to be a kind of betrayal of ourselves. Skepticism about affirming identities that are premised on "states of injury" notwithstanding, the vacuum left by the refusal to fall back on discourses of authenticity is psychically abhorrent to many gendered subjects. The need to ground one's identity surfaces in transsexual theory, too: Henry Rubin, in his study of FTM transsexuals, discusses conflicts between his own Foucauldian analysis of the genealogy of trans-subjectivity, and the claims to authenticity made by his research participants.[53] Anti-essentialism in these contexts has yet, I think, to be fully worked through as a stable, constructive, and livable way of being in the world.

Third, this strategy does not take seriously enough the possibility that some aspects of women's identities, even while avowedly socially constructed artifacts of oppression, may nonetheless be ethically or politically valuable. Thorough-going anti-essentialism toward identity tends to diminish the normative claims available to feminists in presenting alternative visions of relationships, organizations, or social structures (and I take up this objection in Chapter 4 when I discuss critical responses to Gilligan).

Throughout this book I am as concerned with showing the dangers of anti-essentialist positions as with attacking essentialism. On the one hand, essentialist feminist theories unreflexive about the construction of "women" (whether in their assumptions about language or material bodies or both) are over-reliant on the notion that there are certain fixed properties definitive of membership in the category "women." While much more needs to be said about how to avoid this fixity and the extent to which it can be avoided, it is conceptually and politically problematic in many of the ways Butler suggests. On the other hand, the anti-essentialist alternatives offered by theorists like Butler seem to diminish the political resources available to feminist activists. In pursuing such questions about "women" using epistemological assumptions derived from linguistic essentialism or linguistic anti-essentialism, we feminists have painted ourselves into a corner. Forced to decide what the term "women" means prior to its use, we have alternately accepted linguistic essentialism and presented generalizing accounts of gender to which exceptions and exclusions can easily be found, or fragmented the category of gender in ways that seem to undercut the very use of generalizations for political purposes. My argument in Chapter 3 is that both of these issues can be side-stepped by a Wittgensteinian critique of essentialism. But first, I pull together these issues to present a detailed account of a final, related type of essentialism, one that is less about the exclusions inherent in the very use of language than about the methods we use to support our uses of particular categories or generalizations.

While debates within metaphysics and philosophy of language have an impact on feminist theory, the feminist literature on essentialism focuses primarily on method. That is, it stresses politically motivated arguments about how best to do feminist theory or practice, rather than truth-claims about the realities of sex and gender or claims about the nature of linguistic categorization per se. Many feminist anti-essentialists are concerned with the ontological bases and political consequences of various social construc-tionist arguments. While accepting that sex and gender are not metaphysical or biological truths about persons, they look for different ways of under-standing the differences and similarities between women and men. In con-structing these debates as methodological, I want to draw attention to the confluence of questions of materiality and meaning. To highlight essentialism as an issue in language is not to dismiss or erase the material conditions that construct sex and gender. In focusing on questions of method, and specifically of practice, I emphasize the importance of the "empirical" in constructing claims about women. Positing essentialism as a methodological problem brings together the material and the semiotic to ask how the realities of women's lives should best be described, and how those descriptions in turn shape our experience. Elizabeth Spelman has argued persuasively that the most politically powerful critique of essentialism comes from examining how generalizations about women are constructed within feminist theory so as to exclude some women, and I examine her argument in depth in the Chapter 2. First I define methodological essentialism and map out the surrounding ter-rain by looking at two exemplary methodological controversies in feminist theory: those over historiography and "women's experience."

I take "methodological essentialism," in its most general formulation, to be any way of doing either philosophy or social science that illegitimately pre-supposes the significance of some general category of analysis. Here the re-ductio comes into play again—all political talk (including feminist talk) must of necessity use general categories. So methodological essentialism is only an interesting mistake if the application of those general categories obscures di-versity in some particularly significant way. Again, for a feminist who is writ-ing today to be described as a methodological essentialist is seldom, if ever, a compliment. What is the content of the charge? Presumably, we can safely allow that no feminist thinker ever applies a general category with explicitly metaphysical intent, deliberately imposing a false generality on a diverse group of people. Those feminists who have been labeled "essentialists," whatever they think of the accusation, usually believe that their theories are, put naively, accurate descriptions of a material reality (although they may adopt different epistemological frameworks in justifying this belief). Essentialism of this particular form is a bad thing; a normative claim about the undesirability of methodological essentialism is written into my definition. The question I find interesting, however, is not whether general categories themselves present a challenge given "the problem of difference," but, given the necessity of general claims both to feminist research and feminist politics, *what methods of inquiry can legitimately be used to justify general claims about women, and what methods merely serve to impose false uniformity?*

I shall give two examples of areas of feminist debate where essentialism has been central to methodological discussions. What are the common threads in these cases? As should be clear by now, essence-talk is primarily identified with sameness, and anti-essentialism with difference. Critics of those authors accused of methodological essentialism argue that certain ontological claims mask difference. Instead of arguments that generalize across time and place, these critics want instead to insist on contextual and specific investigation and demand a renewed attention to situated differences. Where linguistic essentialism raised analogous epistemological questions about the legitimacy of general claims, here I stress method. If feminists were to engage in scholarly and political projects while bearing in mind the debates outlined so far, how would they justify historical continuity and shared understandings of women's experiences?

*Historiography and Continuity*

Essentialism raises methodological issues for feminist history and historiography. As Martin points out, the claim that feminist analyses are "ahistorical" often accompanies (and is philosophically connected to) the claim that they are essentialist. An analysis that fails to situate itself, or that employs analytic categories divorced from time, place, culture, and so on, is taken, by default, to reify or idealize concepts that in fact take their meaning from a specific historical context. As Martin says, "the trouble with an ahistorical approach to sexuality, reproduction, gender, mothering, domesticity, and the family, then, is not simply that the resulting account will be incomplete but that findings that actually hold for one time period are apt to be projected onto other or even all time periods."[54] Ahistorical theorizing then comes to be a form of methodological essentialism through its reliance on the a priori and failure to contextualize. Rather than understanding particular concepts as historically embedded, local, and liable to change, some feminists, the argument runs, have been too hasty in assuming that their analyses are transferable to other contexts. This is a charge that has been made, for example, against Gilligan's ethic of care. In Chapter 4 I look at the implications of essentialist method; here let me turn to a different example to illustrate the tension between essentialism and anti-essentialism in historiography.

Lesbian history is methodologically fraught with the ambiguities and shifts in meaning inherent in the term "lesbian." In contemporary North American contexts, the term "lesbian" already has numerous contested meanings. When a lesbian-hating man talks about "lesbians," for example, he has a very different understanding of the term than does a lesbian-feminist or a "lesbian" who understands her sexuality as a natural "orientation" rather than a political identity. Even individuals within each of these different subgroups are unlikely to agree precisely on a definition of the term "lesbian." In historical terms these ambiguities are even more striking: how can a historian write a "lesbian history" without transposing a contemporary understanding of lesbianism onto historical periods and places where that understanding does not fit with extant categories or conceptual schemes? What do we *mean* when we refer to "Boston marriages" and "romantic friendships" as "lesbian relationships"? These questions have many answers, and numerous methodological strategies are employed by various scholars of lesbian history to explain various similarities and differences between members of the central term of analysis and to justify narrative links.[55]

Feminist critiques of essentialism motivate the question, "what can justify the use of terms like 'lesbian,' or even 'woman' to refer to unchanging concepts?" In a sense this question challenges a straw person: no historian would get away with treating midwives in modern England, for example, as members of exactly the same category as midwives in England during the witch-hunts. While we might want to trace a narrative that connects these two groups, we cannot claim that they are exactly the same kinds of people. A more sophisticated challenge is raised by the example of the category of "women" itself as an historical constant. If we take seriously the anti-essentialist claims I raised earlier about the socially constructed nature of sex itself, then the historiographical challenge is not only to ask, what do Renaissance Italian women have in common with enslaved Black women in 18th-century America, but also, how do we justify the claim that those people who were counted as "women" in Renaissance Italy are members of the same category as 18th-century Black American "women"? Once the appeal to "sex"—to women's bodies as evidence of their fixed membership in a stable class—is discounted, we are left with a more fundamental philosophical challenge to the historiography of "women's history" and questions about the justificatory strategies employed in establishing narrative links. To understand the category "women" as constructed through relations of power, in Foucauldian terms, rather than prior to them, for example, introduces a more profound skepticism about the continuity of social groups.[56]

The question of historiography in feminist studies highlights the significance of *context* for the epistemological framework of a feminist theory. The vice of "ahistoricism" is a form of essentialism insofar as it represents a failure to articulate important social, political, and economic (as well as historical) background that would serve to illustrate the contingency and the mutability of feminist analyses. The demand that feminist analyses be placed in context has its origin, I would argue, in a philosophically significant and politically indispensable response to essentialism that recognizes the dangers of abstraction. Essentialism is therefore an issue both to feminist historians, concerned with how to justify historical (dis)continuity, and to feminist philosophers concerned with the justifications and consequences of different methods of social inquiry.

Feminist dissent from a dominant anti-essentialism that challenges historical continuity focuses on the need not to give up entirely on uninterrupted narrative about, for example, the history of women's oppression. For example, Benhabib expresses disquiet with what she, again following Flax, labels the "Death of History" thesis. In its weak form, she says, "the Death of History . . . could be understood as a call to end the practice of 'grand narratives' which are essentialist and monocausal."[57] Benhabib assesses the political significance of this weaker thesis for feminist theory. The arguments against meta-narratives based on deconstructing "false extrapolations" from the experience of dominant women have in turn altered "the preferred conception of theory." "It has become clear that quasi-metanarratives hamper rather than promote sisterhood, since they elide differences among women and among the forms of sexism to which different women are differentially subject."[58]

In its strong version, Benhabib claims, the Death of History thesis requires that we reject any historical narrative concerned with the *longue durée* or with macro- rather than micro-social practices. Benhabib depicts the strong thesis as encouraging the most extreme kind of historical fragmentation. Instead of "global history," the strong thesis instead demands *petits récits:* local stories about particular contexts. Benhabib objects to this kind of anti-essentialism on the grounds that it diminishes the critical resources available to disempowered groups seeking to make political demands based on a long history of oppression. Furthermore, the reappropriation of history—in the form of uncovering previously ignored or suppressed historical information and perspectives—is undercut by historiographies that treat agency as constructed through top-down mechanisms of social and discursive control. Benhabib argues that Butler's Foucauldian paradigm, for example, clashes with "the social history from below paradigm . . . the task of which is to illuminate the gender, class and race struggles through which power is negotiated, subverted, as well as resisted by the so-called 'victims' of history."[59] In this way, an anti-essentialist historiography both delegitimates grand historical narratives that may benefit oppressed groups and erases the autonomy and agency of the historical subject. Benhabib fears that for both of these reasons, a strong version of the "death of history" may "eliminate . . . the practice of legitimation and criticism altogether," reducing historical argument to local stories about subjects entirely constituted by and reduced to an effect of social control.[60]

But how local? How circumscribed must the context be? What criteria do we use in assessing how widely applicable historically located concepts are? Few feminists sit down with the express intention of writing a "metanarrative," so it is not immediately clear which feminist theories are ruled out by this strong thesis. While the historiographical debate provides a useful theoretical framework for thinking about what is at stake in revising feminist methods so that they become "anti-essentialist," it can be resolved only by attention to particular cases where different degrees of generality are differently justified with reference to the social realities under scrutiny. In this respect, the debate around essentialism and historiography is representative of many methodological controversies in feminist scholarship. The contrasting arguments of Benhabib and Butler in *Feminist Contentions*, for example, while theoretically sophisticated, do not offer criteria for assessing the validity of any particular claim about women. They illustrate a major aporia in the feminist literature touching on essentialism—the lack of tangible examples of feminist praxis and how they might be changed by anti-essentialism.

## Interpreting Experience

"Experience" is a key category of feminist thought, often taken to provide the epistemological basis of feminist theorizing, especially in radical feminist thought and practice. "Essentialism" with regard to experience has been characterized as the claim that women's experiences as they articulate them yield a single, privileged feminist interpretation. As I discuss in Chapter 5, this is the claim that Catharine MacKinnon makes for her theory, and is one of the bases on which she is labeled "essentialist." Feminist critics of this form of essentialism claim that there is no single "objective" description of any life-event, but rather alternative narratives are always already constructed with the discursive resources available.[61] All explanations of "women's experience" are power-laden and must forswear claims to truth. To privilege particular interpretations of a particular experience is to "essentialize" it, where the pejorative force stems from the failure to incorporate the possibility of other accounts. For example, Fuss argues that "the problem with positing the category of experience as the basis of a feminist pedagogy is that the very object of our inquiry, 'female experience,' is never as unified, as knowable, as universal, and as stable as we presume it to be." And, "the appeal to experience, as the ultimate test of all knowledge, merely subtends the subject in its fantasy of autonomy and control. Belief in the truth of Experience is as much an ideological production as belief in the experience of Truth."[62]

In response, hooks argues that this perspective may fail adequately to recognize the particular contexts of oppression that make it harder for some groups to speak out:

> Now I am troubled by the term "authority of experience," acutely aware of the way it is used to silence and exclude. Yet I want to have a phrase that affirms the specialness of those ways of knowing rooted in experience. I know that experience can be a way to know and can inform how we know what we know. Though opposed to any essentialist practice that constructs identity in a monolithic, exclusionary way, I do not want to relinquish the power of experience as a standpoint on which to base analysis or formulate theory.[63]

This exchange illustrates the tension in many feminist debates about essentialism between the political exigencies of fostering counter-hegemonic accounts and the demand for their critical deconstruction. We know that all explanations of experience are partial, interpretive and contingent, but if feminists reject *any* criteria for privileging one account over another, they risk playing into forms of subjectivism or extant dominant accounts that will only weaken feminist political goals.

One example from feminist practice is the construction of narratives about acquaintance sexual assault: female survivors often move from a widely available patriarchal story of self-blame and sole responsibility for the "sex" that occurred, to a less accessible feminist story about coercion, power, and exploitation in the context of male violence. They may also develop other accounts of the experience at different times in their recovery process: occasionally coming to label the assault as basically trivial or developing compromise stories wherein they ascribe some blame to themselves and some to others, for example. Each of these stories may well be profoundly influenced by other aspects of the survivor's experience: whether she was sexually abused as a child, whether she identifies as straight, or whether she has also experienced racism, for example. The same "event" can be described within radically different frameworks that not only take the same "facts" and apply different "angles" but which are also normative to the core. Anti-essentialists like Fuss are presumably not entirely neutral on which of these stories to prefer (if they were, they would hardly be feminists). But they are more likely to suggest that the preferable interpretation depends on the context of the assault rather than on a predetermined structural explanation that labels one form of explanation as "correct." And they may also allow that some of these narratives may be more emotionally or politically strategic than others, even if they are not necessarily more "objective."

In a context in which particular interpretations of experience, especially those coming from members of marginalized and oppressed groups, are trivialized and suppressed, to insist upon the epistemic significance of such accounts is a radical move; indeed, it is one of the central goals of feminist epistemology and pedagogy. With regard to the example of acquaintance sexual assault, as a feminist activist I want to respond that the acknowledgment of the possibility of multiple interpretations of a rape is scarcely the point; in many cultural contexts, a woman will be blamed for the rape, told that she asked for it, must have wanted it, or brought it upon herself. These messages are not only reinforced by direct responses offered to the survivor but are also concretely played out in the criminal justice system, in therapeutic discourses, and other institutional contexts. Whatever story about her own experience a survivor finally accepts, feminist analyses of dominant cultural messages about sexual violence show how some interpretations are afforded far less legitimacy than others. Political struggle to have feminist renderings made more accessible does not have to impose them on every individual survivor; rather, it has to make available alternatives that do not impose misogynist narratives on women.

Feminists who base their theories on "women's experience" may have been too hasty in assuming a single privileged interpretation for experiences that are complex and subtly differentiated. In this sense, Fuss's anti-essentialist strategy is useful in reminding us of the fluid, contingent, and diverse nature of testimony. Her approach is less useful, however, in offering strategies for negotiating power structures that systematically silence certain social groups. Questions about the importance of essentialism and anti-essentialism in this context have political consequences, consequences again occluded by a contrast between (bad) essentialism and (good) anti-essentialism that is too simple. In this example, both Fuss and hooks recognize the dilemma, but do not go on to offer an alternative. Again, good feminist practice requires a more nuanced set of criteria to distinguish methodological essentialism from the well-grounded use of generalizing claims.

This chapter illustrates the variety of ways in which the term "essentialism" is used in contemporary feminist theory. Few, if any, feminists use a priori metaphysical essentialism in their arguments; criticizing feminist theorists as essentialist in this way often distracts attention from subtler and more significant political tensions. The shape of social ontology is at stake here but not in the sense of metaphysics existing outside language or culture. Instead, feminists debate essentialism from within constructionist paradigms that understand social group membership in divergent ways. Similarly, few, if any, are implicated in biological essentialism in the traditional anti-feminist sense. "Essentialism" instead comes to the fore in debates about embodiment that focus on the sexed body, where anti-essentialists understand the body's materiality to be itself constructed rather than pre-social or prelinguistic. I do not take up these latter questions in this book, but this framing of the problem helps to locate live debates about essentialism within social constructionist discourses rather than in contrast to them. Linguistic essentialism takes its place as an exemplar of the tensions between generalizations within feminist theory that risk reifying their central categories and that underestimate politically significant exceptions, and anti-essentialist methods that seem to undermine feminist political analyses and goals.

All of the tensions outlined in this chapter are more often stated than resolved in feminist theory. Essentialism and anti-essentialism tend to be pitted against each other in ways that reiterate rather than move beyond the dichotomy. At the center of the political salience of essentialism are questions about the category "women." The essentialism debates around this category challenge feminist thinking on many levels: our philosophy of bodies, our use of language, our political identities, our methods, and our practices. I want to frame all of these types of essentialism in terms of questions of method: how can feminist theorists bring together social ontology, epistemology, and political philosophy to justify claims about women? The next chapter establishes a perspicuous problem-space for this question, using Spelman's anti-essentialist critique of exclusion in feminist theory as a starting point.

# Chapter 2

## Feminist Method and Generalizing about Women

 

From my discussion of methodological essentialism we can see that making unfounded generalizations—for example by presuming rather than demonstrating an essential "womanness" that all women share—is a strategy that masks diversity in ways to which anti-essentialists object. But is essentialism merely a problem in language or ontology? Why is essentialism something that matters politically to feminists? In the methodological debates outlined above, we can begin to see that essentializing strategies serve to foreclose discussion of women's specificity. They tend to distance us from more fully contextualized and precise theoretical accounts, offering what Spelman calls "short cuts through women's lives." [1] These forms of methodological essentialism are politically exclusive and insensitive to power differences among women. Conversely, it already seems as though an insistence on fragmenting the category "women" could weaken the terms of feminist politics. Some methodological anti-essentialisms seem to undercut generalizations about gender that sustain crucial feminist political claims.

This chapter spells out the political implications of various methodologically essentialist and anti-essentialist positions. I return to the impasse between the two, showing how dialogue between them has both motivated anti-essentialist claims and provoked a renewed demand for more robust theoretical uses of gender with regard to individual political identity and identity politics. I articulate Spelman's exposition and political critique of essentialism and then examine two challenges to her analysis. Such challenges fail to understand the ways a more local and contextual account of gender can be enabling for feminists. "Anti-anti-essentialism" does, however, have one worthy target: a dogmatic and politically unsophisticated fragmentation of gender. Between this fragmentation and the essentialism I contest is an under-explored middle ground.

The essentialism debates in feminism have been carried out increasingly at cross-purposes, with self-described anti-essentialists talking past the claims of their allegedly essentialist opponents, and critics who present themselves as "anti-anti-essentialist" dodging the actual views of the anti-essentialists they condemn. There is an unacknowledged consensus that feminist theory should move on from pointing out the limitations of the dichotomy between essentialism and anti-essentialism, merely reiterating the picture that "holds us captive." Instead, feminists should direct their energies toward generating novel methods that escape the terms of these polar opposites and constructively address ways of undertaking feminist political practice that are sensitive to the dangers of both essentialism and anti-essentialism. We agree that we need neither understand women as completely different from each other nor assimilate them into a single dominant identity, but we have been less successful in articulating the ontology of the middle ground, or in drawing on feminist political practice as a source of knowledge about struggles around pluralism.

In what sense is essentialism a political issue for feminist theorists? Essentialism is usually treated not as an obscure methodological mistake, but a political practice of enormous negative consequence to feminist analysis. In fact, most of the disapprobative force of being called an "essentialist" comes from its political connotations. First, essentialism raises important questions for feminist political theory about subjectivity—how we come to define ourselves as members of particular groups and how the varied contexts of oppression come to shape self-identity. Second, developing out of questions of subjectivity and bringing their own political significance are debates that locate essentialism (of various kinds) in forms of identity politics. Many feminists have been quick to accept the orthodoxy that (essentialist) identity politics are exclusionary and regressive and that some alternative (often poorly articulated) forms of political organizing are more likely to generate coalitions or other political alliances that are less essentialist. Both these sets of issues are underpinned by questions about the possibility and validity of generalizations about women.

## Subjectivity

On the first point, questions of how to identify and characterize female subjectivities are at the heart of feminist politics. There are two main forms of essentialism here: the first concerns the sense in which women's identities can be said to be more or less "authentic" and the extent to which the deconstruction of claims about women must be relentless. The danger attributed to this kind of essentialism is that whatever distinctive identities feminists articulate, these identities will become reified, taken to be natural, or "the truth" about women. By failing to explore the genealogy of particular gendered qualities, feminists (anti-essentialist critics claim) are not sufficiently aware of their contingency; we do not adequately interrogate identity claims and their processes of construction. Paradoxically, what began as an inquiry into the provisional social construction of gendered identity will fix or naturalize identity categories.

This process may occur in two ways: first, whatever positive feminist identities are presented as more truthful or authentic for women, they remain identities constructed under patriarchy, and are thus never immune from the charge that they are merely artifacts of oppression. Gilligan's ethic of care is often criticized for essentialism on these grounds: to hold that there is a distinctive "woman's voice" in moral discourse, critics argue, is to attribute an identity to women that reflects only their socialization under patriarchy and which may even serve to perpetuate their oppression. Instead of trying to discover those qualities that might make up an oppositional identity, "anti-essentialist" feminism should be concerned purely with resistance to the identities imposed on women by patriarchy, either refusing to offer a unifying picture of women's authentic selves at all, or offering alternatives that are explicitly contingent and temporary. As Julia Kristeva says: "On a deeper level, however, a woman cannot 'be'; it follows that a feminist practice can only be negative, at odds with what already exists so that we may say 'that's not it' and 'that's still not it.' In 'woman' I see something that cannot be represented, something that is not said, something above and beyond nomenclatures and ideologies."[2] Critics of feminism's emphasis on women's experience as the root of feminist knowledge and identity have pointed to the interpretive and permanently revisable nature of human recounting of experience and to the need constantly to criticize and re-evaluate our interpretations of our experience. This form of anti-essentialism rejects generalizations about women by virtue of skepticism toward all general claims about women's subjectivities, particularly toward claims of authenticity.

Second, many feminists have convincingly argued that essentialism resurfaces as the desire to have one quintessential "woman's identity" representing a variety of women (or even all women), whose experiences and interpretations of those experiences are quite different. This form of essentialism differs from, but is related to, the first. Instead of failing to make clear the continuity or discontinuity of particular concepts of gender, this kind of essentialism exaggerates or fails to specify their scope. The latter operates as an exclusionary tactic, allowing those women with the most power over feminist discourses to construct accepted feminist accounts of women's identity, to mold oppositional feminist identities in their own images. As Spelman puts it:

> It is not as if, in the history of feminist theory, just any group of women has been taken to stand for all women—for example, no one has ever tried to say that the situation of Hispanas in the southwestern United States is applicable to all women as women; no one has conflated their case with the case of women in general. And the "problem of difference" within feminist theory is not the problem of, say, Black women in the United States trying to make their theories take into account the ways in which white women in the United States are different from them.[3]

Various authors have drawn attention to the way false generalizations sometimes operate as an exclusionary tactic in much the same way as sexism. For example, by establishing a norm for humanity that is implicitly male, Woman becomes Other; once a norm for femininity that is implicitly white, middle-class, western, and heterosexual is established, women of color, working-class women, world majority women, and queers become the Others of dominant feminist discourses. These latter women need to be prefaced with adjectives in order to be identified, while dominant group women are "women" unmodified. This strategy keeps dominant group feminists at the center of speaking and writing, the authoritative voices of the feminist movement, while relegating Other women to the margins, as special interest groups.

This political imagination depends on essentialism: at the core of the group "women" are some members who epitomize "womanness" for feminist purposes, who offer a neutral and representative picture of what it is to be a woman, while other women are fringe members who bring complicating and extra-gendered identities into the category. This essentialist imagination is also oppressive, denying the racial identity of white women, for example, in such a way that women of color become the focus of analyses of racism, and the initiators of racism remain uncriticized. When Sunera Thobani, a Canadian "landed immigrant" and woman of color, was elected President of the National Action Committee on the Status of Women, for example, many commentators saw no apparent inconsistency or racism in claiming that while white women could quite adequately represent women of color (and had supposedly been doing so in this job until Thobani's election), the reverse could not hold. Women of color were too "biased," concerned only with "their own" interests, or not sufficiently knowledgeable about the "majority of Canadian women."

Feminists skeptical of generalizations about women are not necessarily objecting to generalization on principle. Rather we may be pointing toward trends in the history of political thought and in the structuring of academic feminism that "ought to encourage us to look at the degree of metaphysical and political authority presupposed by those who claim the right to point out commonality, who assert or exercise the privilege of determining just what it means in terms of others' identities, social locations, and political priorities."[4] Relations of power are at the center of any explanation of this form of essentialism. I want to criticize two related strategies here, both of them mistaken and politically regressive: the first is the tendency for "dominant group" feminists to conjure up an "ideal woman," a mental picture of the woman they see as epitomizing the subject of feminist theory. This Woman is then put to use in winning rhetorical victories in political debates. Invoking "sisterhood," dominant group feminists have sometimes made overly grand claims about what "women" need or want. It is worth noting that this strategy frequently carries weight with non-feminists, who, as part of the same power structures, are often most likely to respond favorably to feminist claims implicitly made on behalf of dominant group women. The modernist rhetoric that dominates in public political forums is not amenable to radical postmodern claims that stress complexity, contingency, or deny any foundation in extra-linguistic reality. Second, by homogenizing women's experiences and identities, some feminist campaigns or targets are made to seem more clearcut. The sexist denial within patriarchal cultures and institutions that *any* women constitute distinctive constituencies or have legitimate particular political priorities and demands can lead dominant group feminists to invoke an unnuanced political agenda.

There is an important and obvious distinction, however, between generalizations and universals. When feminists claim, for example, that "women generally have lower incomes than men," they are not necessarily committed to any of the following claims: "all people with low incomes are women," "all women have low incomes," "all men have high incomes," or "no men have low incomes." It is perfectly possible to make a generalizing claim that relies on observed connections, statistical significance, or another measure of a particular trend, without being committed to universal claims about all members of a particular category (and in my experience, a common anti-feminist rhetorical ploy is to attempt to undermine such general claims by treating them as if they were universals). While some essentialist strategies may be methodologically suspect, furthermore, to equate essentialism unmodified with false generalization is to imply—falsely—that the same criticisms that can be made of other essentialisms apply equally to all generalizations about women.

Something about the essentialism debates has encouraged feminist theory to stagnate around ontological and epistemological issues without examining more carefully how generalizations are constructed and used in feminist practice. Generalizing categories are both a necessary feature of language and of social investigation. Every category in political theory picks out aspects of membership in a group to highlight as politically significant and sidelines others. Feminist theory, in choosing gender as salient, constructs claims about women and men in particular contexts (whether context is explicitly acknowledged or merely implicit in the theory's claims). The ability to use and to challenge gender categories is the root of feminism's rhetorical power. In particular, it provides a language with which to respond to patriarchy. One of the most disturbing aspects of anti-essentialism is the potential weakening of those challenges to dominant understandings of gender that propel feminist activism. So much useful feminist cultural criticism rests on recognizing moments in dominant cultures where gender operates dichotomously. Gender dichotomies are imposed and policed in ways that do not reflect the diversity of gendered persons. But all sides in the essentialism debates have often failed to capture the distinctions between gender as a set of cultural stereotypes, as lived experience, and as feminist reconstructions.

For example, eating problems disproportionately affect women, in part because of the disciplinary effects of cultural injunctions about the female body.[5]

Merely stressing the multiplicity of forms of bodily expression or other fragmentation of categories does not capture the overwhelming gendered force of body images. This is a context where we need to be clear that gender is a very significant structural force. But attention to this dichotomizing structure might also require close attention to particular constructions of gender: while the beauty ideal that is imposed on women in contemporary North America is hegemonic—closely associated with whiteness, youth, and heterosexuality—the ways that different women experience eating problems will vary according to their race, class, sexual identity, age, family dynamics, and other distinctions. Feminist theories of the body have, until recently, tended both to minimize these differences and to erase them by positing a dominant experience of eating problems as universal.[6]

Thus just because generalizations are based on measures of a particular trend, they are not for that reason unproblematic. Who establishes the measuring standards? What common features of the members of the category will we select? Who has control over those similarities that are counted as significant and those that are dismissed as irrelevant? The mere observation that generalizations must obscure some differences while stressing some common thread does not provide criteria to justify any particular generalization over others. Sensitivity to how the power of those constructing feminist accounts tends to obscure some differences while stressing other similarities provides the basis for answers to these questions.

Essentializing strategies have long and dishonorable histories in feminist politics, and I in no way want to minimize the extent of racism, heterosexism, or other forms of exclusion within western feminist movements. However, the dogged self-criticism of white feminist theorists in particular often seems merely to repeat familiar fault-finding arguments, without creating space for the recognition of common interests and the development of respectful alliances. It also risks replicating the very phenomenon it claims to decry: when white feminists persistently point out, for example, that we have placed ourselves at the center of feminist theory, we paradoxically reinforce that position. If we examine different instances of feminist political organizing, the ways in which feminists, especially feminists from nondominant groups, actually use "women" are often both more nuanced, and more attentive to shared interests among women, including women of quite different class, race, and other backgrounds. The recognition of politically pernicious forms of essentialism should obscure neither the constructive attempts within feminist practice to overcome them nor the danger of becoming preoccupied with a particular theoretical construction of the "problem of difference."

The second general area in which essentialism becomes a political issue is in the practice of identity politics. As forms of political mobilization based on membership in racial, ethnic, cultural, gender, and sexuality groups rather than on traditional left–right axes have become more politically significant, the epistemological questions about the construction of those identities that define group membership have become more pressing. What implications does asserting a common identity as the basis for political mobilization have? Forms of political practice that implicitly adopt a unitary women's identity, or that perpetuate separatist self-understandings or exclusionary group identities, have been both adeptly scrutinized and unfairly dismissed as "essentialist." Such criticisms are analogous to analyses of the identities of individual women: assuming an identity for any particular group may reinforce the notion that this identity is fixed, not mutable, and erase diversity among the members of that group, as well as hindering cooperation with related constituencies.

The association of essentialism, identity politics, and exclusive feminist practice is well-founded in some cases, yet as a blanket analysis it oversimplifies a complex feminist history. The Combahee River Collective, for example, in their "Black Feminist Statement," articulate a form of identity politics founded in Black lesbian socialist feminist identity—hardly an exclusive or dominant standpoint: "This focusing upon our own oppression is embodied in the concept of identity politics. We believe that the most profound and potentially the most radical politics come directly out of our own identity, as opposed to working to end someone else's oppression."[7] Much of the history of feminist identity politics can be traced to women already marginalized by popular liberal feminism. Criticisms of paradigms of identity politics, however, point to the perhaps inevitable construction of core and peripheral versions of the mobilizing identity. Even when the core members of any group are themselves already sidelined in dominant feminist discourse, critics claim, appeals to identity create a new periphery. Thus there is a tension for the Combahee River Collective between their insistence on the primacy of identity as the foundation of consciousness-raising and political mobilization, and their ambivalent desire for analysis and action premised on coalition-building rather than separatism: "Although we are feminists and lesbians, we feel solidarity with progressive Black men and do not advocate the fractionalization that white women who are separatists demand."[8]

This same fear of racial fragmentation motivates hooks to articulate the familiar claim that feminist separatism implicitly draws on a single exclusive female identity. Separatists, she argues, often assume that gender is a more salient feature of political identity and interest than race, and many arguments for "woman-identified" feminist organizing that exclude men have been premised on the experiences and identities of white women. In political terms, she argues, Black women organizing in the United States (particularly, I would add, heterosexually identified Black women) have good reason to be suspicious of white feminists and to identify with Black men. Thus separatist demands for the exclusion of men from feminist contexts neglect the intersection of race and gender interests and benefit white women more than Black women.[9]

In a related example, Shane Phelan argues for the recognition of difference within queer identity politics. Instead of stressing difference by setting "our" group apart from others, she argues, lesbians should "resist the impulse for total separatism and for purity in our allies in favor of workable coalitions and porous but meaningful communities."[10] Highlighting the way lesbian-feminist separatist arguments have tended to reinforce rather than undermine the "otherness" of lesbians (at the same time as they were a crucial factor in forming group solidarity) Phelan recommends an approach that makes gains and reinforces identity through coalitions of groups claiming different queer identities. This is a widespread claim in "postmodern" queer politics: instead of identifying as lesbian "woman-identified women"—an allegedly narrow, demarcated subject-position with a heavy ideological burden— the category "queer," which may include bisexual women, male-identified butches, woman-loving FTM and MTF transsexuals, and so on, is more enabling. While all members of such groups are unlikely to understand their own identities in the same way, they may share common political goals (such as particular challenges to heteronormativity) and should form political coalitions on this basis.

Illustrating the tension between core and periphery that identity politics may generate, Henry Rubin argues that the emergence of lesbian-feminism and the "woman-identified woman" squeezed out those butch dykes and male-identified women who were no longer included in the category "lesbians."[11] One consequence of this new lesbian political identity was to force the creation of a new category—"female-to-male transsexuals"— who over time have created both a personal identity and a political movement distinct from lesbian-feminist organizing. Thus, according to this Foucauldian analysis, the identity on which any particular political movement is based creates conditions for the possibility of new subject-positions while it closes off others. One task for political theorists is thus to trace the genealogical processes by which this transformation of identity occurs (thus raising important his-

toriographical questions about which "lineages" will demonstrate the continuity of group identity).[12] However, different political practices also raise
both normative questions and questions of strategy. Again, who defines the
identity on which political mobilization is based? Who judges whether or not
those on the margins of this identity should be included or excluded? How
is the identity policed? What implications does the assertion of a particular
identity have for the popular or self-perception of members of that group?

Thus feminist "anti-essentialists" argue against the assertion of a fixed
identity as the basis of political mobilization. Fearing that adopting a political identity based on group membership will reify that identity, as well as exclude groups and individuals with relevantly connected but not identical self-
descriptions and political goals, many feminist theorists have reached the
conclusion that "coalitional politics" is a more appropriate form of organizing than conventional "identity politics." For example, Fraser and Nicholson
conclude their articulation of a postmodern feminist theory by arguing:

> The most important advantage of this sort of theory would be its useful-
> ness for contemporary feminist political practice. Such practice is increas-
> ingly a matter of alliances rather than one of unity around a universally
> shared interest or identity. It recognizes that the diversity of women's needs
> and experiences means that no single solution, on issues like child care,
> social security, and housing, can be adequate for all. Thus, the underlying
> premise of this practice is that, while some women share some common
> interests and face some common enemies, such commonalities are by
> no means universal; rather, they are interlaced with differences, even with
> conflicts. This, then, is a practice made up of a patchwork of overlapping
> alliances, not one circumscribable by an essential definition.[13]

Stressing the limitations of politics founded on a "universally shared interest
or identity" such theorists argue for the joining together of individuals or
groups with related identities or political objectives around a common goal.

One of the frustrations of the essentialism debates is the way such appeals
are generally presented as the conclusion of argument rather than as openings
to discussion of the actual shape of "anti-essentialist" feminist organizing.
Making normative assessments of different political interventions—whether
they are firmly identity-based or loosely "coalitional"—surely cannot be
merely a theoretical project based on general arguments about the (un)ac-
ceptability of identity claims but must also include strategic concerns. When
feminists appeal to "women's identity," they never do so in a vacuum: the particular women they describe or hope to mobilize, the kind of political goal

they hope to achieve, the type of opposition they anticipate and experience, and the way their identities are shaped by the very process of organizing— all of these aspects must affect political-theoretical evaluation of different political practices. A few feminist political theorists have defended various forms of "strategic essentialism," arguing that exclusion is an unavoidable and necessary aspect of political organizing.[14] If we iteratively challenge any claim to identity, then how can feminists operate in contexts where dominant claims about gender dichotomies require an unequivocal response? Or how do organizations make those decisions about inclusion and exclusion that are likely to form the basis of their political projects? Both anti-essentialist claims about feminist praxis and "strategic essentialist" responses often fail to provide concrete examples of the implications of their analyses. This discussion amply illustrates the need for criteria for assessing the legitimacy of identity claims that are more or less essentialist. An analysis of the debates surrounding identity politics and essentialism can suggest certain criteria for good feminist practice, and, in turn, experiences of feminist organizing might provide useful interventions into the philosophical debates.

### General versus Specific: *Inessential Woman* and the Slippery Slope

The connection between false generalizations, exclusion, and essentialism is most thoroughly drawn out by Elizabeth Spelman in *Inessential Woman*. The book argues against "a tendency in dominant Western feminist thought to posit an essential 'womanness' that all women have and share in common despite the racial, class, religious, ethnic, and cultural differences among us."[15] Spelman shows both how feminists have inherited from a significant thread in western philosophy a way of thinking that obscures the effects of race, class, and other aspects of identity on gender and how that thinking is perpetuated in contemporary feminist theory. Generalizations that presuppose a common and separable gender identity possessed by all women in fact often reflect only the experience of gender of women with dominant identities. Thus the "essential womanness" that has been used by feminist theorists in contemporary North America generally reflects the identity of white, middle-class women. Spelman is concerned primarily with revealing essentialist practices, and pointing out how in fact we are often required to categorize ourselves and others in ways that both establish and reinforce certain similarities and differences that seldom reflect the lives and experiences of nondominant women.

Chapter 1 highlighted how essentialism has been linked to the obliqueration of difference. Recognizing the limitations of mutually exclusive, bounded categories leads to two questions about political identity: on the one hand, can (or should) we separate one axis of political identity from others (for example, by claiming that all women share certain experiences that are "the same" regardless of their race and class)? How might talking as if this were possible perpetuate forms of exclusion and thus oppression? Spelman uses the term "additive analysis" to describe any theory that operates under the assumption that gender oppression is separable from other forms of oppression. She has three criticisms: First, additive analyses of sexism and racism, for example, distort the reported experiences of many feminists of color, who do not conceptualize themselves as "part woman, part person of color" when thinking about who they are and how they have been oppressed. Second, additive analyses suppose that I can subtract that part of personal identity that is gendered from other parts of my identity, yielding a "pure" gendered part that I bring to bear on my feminist analyzing and activism. However, "this does not leave room for the fact that different women may look to different forms of liberation just because they are white or Black women, rich or poor women, Catholic or Jewish women."[16] Furthermore, additive analyses contribute to the erasure of women of color by setting up mutually exclusive, bounded categories of "women" and "people of color." Neither one of these arguments is merely an ontological thesis about the need to understand gender as always inflected by other aspects of identity and oppression. Third, Spelman argues that additive analyses trade on the invisibility of dominant identities to make that architypal identity that allegedly represents "all women" most representative of white, middle-class women. To understand gender identity as epitomized by those women whose identities are "unmuddied" by race or class is to put white, middle-class women at the center of feminist analysis. In this way, Spelman argues that no individual should be conceptualized merely as the sum of discrete elements of her identity, be these race, gender, class, sexuality, or any of a host of characteristics that are more or less important to a person's self-description.

On the other hand, how, if at all, can (or should) we justify subsuming some characteristics under others (for example, by stressing the primacy of gender in explaining oppression)? Spelman offers various characterizations of the claim that sexism is a more fundamental form of oppression than racism. In the history of U.S. feminist theory, she argues, feminist analyses based on all versions of this claim have ignored the status of both Black men and Black women. For example, Spelman points out how Kate Millett's radical feminism is premised on the pervasiveness of institutionalized male power over women (via property ownership, economic dominance in the nuclear family, the professions, and even the police) but ignores the fact that Black men often do not possess such power, and particularly not over white women. Spelman goes on to develop an analysis of this question using an analogical argument about proceeding through labeled "doors." For example, if we choose to classify people (by asking—or requiring—them to walk through different doors into separate rooms) as either "women" or "men" and thereafter as "homosexual" or "heterosexual" (problematic categories in any case), then we end up with categories that prioritize gender, and lesbians and gay men appear to have less in common than if we had first ordered people according to sexual identity and then gender. This illustrates the problems inherent in both the very possibility of subsuming some characteristics under others, and in the decision-making processes that build and order the "doors."

This account demonstrates how decisions about the significance of similarities and differences among women are not merely ontological, nor are they just a matter of "getting it right" by doing empirical research. The axes of power that give some women definitional control over feminist goals and descriptions of women's identity shape how those goals and identities are formed. Sometimes claims to similarity can be arrogant, appropriative, assimilationist, or deceitfully selective. And claims to difference can obscure common struggle, sustain an image of women different from myself as radically Other, or serve merely to underscore the importance of my own political objectives rather than genuinely taking account of diverse interests. Lugones points out, "White women theorists seem to have worried more passionately about the harm the claim [that some feminist generalizations are exclusionary] does to theorizing than about the harm the theorizing did to women of color."[17] Thus when we white feminists say "feminist theory should be more inclusive," which kind of theory do we have in mind? And how does that place a certain kind of theory at the center of feminism while other kinds are made peripheral? When we talk about the "problem" of difference, how are those differences cast? As a problem for white feminist theory? As an irritation generated by those tricky "Other" women who get in the way of smooth generalizations? By slipping into a philosophical jargon that etiolates the political significance of essentialism, dominant feminists have often managed to take the challenges raised by multiple oppressions away from the "rough ground" of political engagement with racism, class oppression, heteronormativity, and other forms of exclusion.

Spelman's account of essentialism is convincing more as a critique of existing tendencies than as a constructive alternative. In the next chapter I build on her analysis to offer a Wittgensteinian feminist method that avoids the essentialism she highlights. Before I do so, however, I want to turn to two connected critical responses to Spelman, which set up a useful counter-weight, defining a position hostile to anti-essentialism—a kind of "anti-anti-essentialism." Natalie Stoljar takes up some of the philosophical objections to Spelman's theory of identity, while Susan Moller Okin challenges her method on the basis of empirical evidence. Both critiques miss the mark. However, the questions they raise do point to an untenable form of anti-essentialism that I want to examine and dismiss. Some forms of anti-essentialism are as disabling as those forms of essentialism under critique, so before turning to my own "middle ground" I define the limits of useful anti-essentialism.

Spelman's critics stress the dangers of relativism. If gender has meaning only in particular contexts, they argue, then how can feminists justify any claims about what women have in common? For example, Stoljar argues that Spelman adopts an "extreme relativistic account of gender."[18] Spelman, she claims, fails to specify whether women constitute a "type" (that is, a genuine class the members of which are linked either by universal properties, or "nominally" by falling under the same predicate or being part of the same resemblance structure). Stoljar takes Spelman's point that to know what "women" means is to be able to use the term correctly, as evidence that she endorses predicate nominalism. Thus she argues that Spelman claims that

> the type "woman" is no more than an ad hoc collection of women in different racial and cultural contexts that is a collection simply in virtue of the arbitrary designation of the word "woman." Predicate nominalism provides no principled reasons for collecting women into a type, and hence cannot provide a justification for feminist action on behalf of women, nor an explanation of the similarities between individual members of the type.[19]

Stoljar seems to base her argument on the observation that Spelman recognizes that we are able to distinguish, albeit not without controversy in some cases, between people who do or do not merit the label "woman." Spelman thus allegedly assumes that all that women share is the linguistic designation "women." This claim is odd in the light of her extensive, if largely critical, comments on the need to establish criteria for assessing the salience of certain actually existing similarities between women.[20] I take it that Spelman does *not* think that essentialism is a problem only in language; her "principled reasons" for stressing any difference or similarity between women concern the political contexts in which those differences and similarities emerge. In fact, in Wittgensteinian fashion, Spelman's argument is fully compatible with the "resemblance structure" account that Stoljar herself favors.

Spelman argues that the meaning of the term "women" derives from its multiple uses, and that investigation of particular uses reveals exclusionary practices. Self-conscious analyses of these practices, furthermore, may "help us to be more willing to uncover the battles among women over what 'being a woman' means and about what 'women's issues' are. It may make us more ready to recognize that our engaging in these battles is a sign of our empowerment, not something that stands in the way of such empowerment."[21] Thus, far from endorsing an extreme relativism that precludes feminist action, Spelman's argument provides the foundation of a better feminist method. Stoljar may be dissatisfied with the lack of concrete examples in Spelman's work of generalizations that are justifiable, of similarities drawn between women that are accurate and not exclusionary. This constructive work is absent from *Inessential Woman;* it is, after all, not what the book is about, but Spelman is not susceptible to criticism on the basis that she understands "woman" to be an arbitrary designation.

Okin also argues that Spelman's analysis evinces a "slide toward relativism" that makes it inadequate to the exigencies of a theory of justice.[22] Claiming that Spelman provides a "paucity of evidence" for her claims that "women's experiences of oppression are different," Okin argues that Spelman merely asserts the existence of radically different contextual meanings of gender, and needs to demonstrate the reality of such difference more thoroughly. She proposes to put "anti-essentialism" to the test by applying it to a comparison of the oppression of women in the "Western industrialized countries" and in "poor countries." Okin claims that this comparison will yield a result precluded by Spelman's analysis: that the situation of the latter group relative to the former is "the same, only more so." Thus Okin picks up the same criticism as Stoljar, but she argues against the alleged consequences of Spelman's theory of identity.

Aside from the simple retort that *Inessential Woman* is packed with concrete empirical examples of instances where essentialist accounts of gender have oppressive effects, many of them contemporary, Okin mistakes Spelman's exposition of the contingency of generalizations about women for necessary claims about differences among women. Spelman's method would itself affirm Okin's project of "testing the empirical evidence," and would not necessarily rule out her conclusion that she has found more similarities than differences between women in the "Western industrialized countries" and in "poor countries." Spelman's analysis does highlight the need to attend to the contexts that make such claims useful and legitimate, to other schemes of categorization they rule out, and to relations of power that make white middle-class feminists (for example) predisposed to generalize in particular ways. Okin claims to refute Spelman's argument that unless a feminist theorist perceives gender identity as bound up with other aspects of identity she ignores the effects of these other differences. Her counter-argument runs: "One can argue that sexism is an identifiable form of oppression, many of whose effects are felt by women regardless of race or class, without at all subscribing to the view that race and class oppression are insignificant."[23] But this response is equivocal: by reducing sexism to a single "form of oppression," Okin sidesteps Spelman's point that the (many) forms of gender oppression vary and that women do experience oppression differently according to race, class, or other politically salient differences.

In missing all of these issues, Okin's own argument ironically becomes susceptible to Spelman's critique. Okin offers very broad analyses of various inequities that supposedly exist in the same form in a variety of contexts, differing only quantitatively, not qualitatively. On what basis does she claim these inequities are "the same"? To take one example, in describing social and economic inequality and injustice within families, Okin asserts that: "The comparison of most families in rich countries with poor families in poor countries—where distinctions between the sexes often start earlier and are much more blatant and more harmful to girls—yields, here too, the conclusion that, in the latter case, things are not so much different as 'similar but more so.'"[24] The dubious link between degree of poverty and sexism within the family aside, Okin seems in such examples to exhibit precisely the kind of disdain for context to which Spelman objects. We might ask: What, or whose, definition of family is being deployed here? Which families are being compared with which, and why is that comparison chosen? What, or whose, definition of work is used to arrive at measures of inequality? How does unjust gender socialization differ in a wealthy Bangladeshi and a poor American family?

Any claim about women, if couched in sufficiently vague terms, can have broad applicability. I (and Spelman) would agree that, generally speaking, traditional patriarchal families are loci of gender oppression. But it raises more interesting theoretical and political challenges for feminists to ask specific questions about how that oppression is played out in particular contexts. To argue that the very same western analyses can be straightforwardly applied to Other cultures is a familiar imperialist move, no less so if the analyses in question are feminist. Understanding gender in context—a position with no necessary link to cultural or moral relativism—is a cornerstone of culturally sensitive and appropriate "development" work. Okin recognizes that the ostensible similarity of women's oppression in her analysis cannot determine the shape of "development" practice:

> As the work of some feminist scholars of development shows, using the concept of gender and refusing to let differences gag us or fragment our analyses does not mean that we should overgeneralize or try to apply "standardized" solutions to the problems of women in different circumstances. Chen argues for the value of a situation-by-situation analysis of women's roles and constraints before plans can be made and programs designed. And Papanek, too, shows how helping to educate women to awareness of their oppression requires quite deep and specific knowledge of the relevant culture.[25]

Spelman argues that the failure to understand gender in context reinscribes oppression. Okin argues that gender oppression is broadly similar cross-culturally, but she steps back from drawing firm conclusions about feminist practice from this claim, allowing that "overgeneralizing" may obscure, in this case, important cultural differences. It is unfortunate that Okin does not analyze the "we" in this quote who are helping to "educate women to awareness of their oppression." It is not clear that Spelman would disagree with Okin's claim that women's oppression has similar sites and forms across cultures, but her analysis does recommend a more cautious approach to assuming sameness across differences inflected, as are those between women in "developed" and "poor" countries, by relations of power.[26]

### "Anti-Anti-Essentialism"

These two critiques of Spelman are instructive because they highlight what "anti-anti-essentialists" most fear: the fragmentation of gender. In "Anti Anti-relativism," Clifford Geertz points out that despite the laws of logic, "anti-anti-relativism" is not the same position as relativism itself. Just as one can adopt an "anti-anti-abortion" stance without thinking that abortion is a good thing, so one can be "anti-anti-relativism" without being a relativist.[27] I suggest, analogously, that one can be "anti-anti-essentialism" without being an essentialist. In this vein, several feminists have pointed to the dangers of an a priori affirmation of difference or a principled "gender skepticism." In defense of generality, some have argued that a knee-jerk invocation of difference in all methodological contexts may operate to obscure important commonalities rather than bring salient differences into view.

Emphasizing how "essentialist" is used as a pejorative to undercut reconstructive feminist projects, for example, Jane Roland Martin asks whether "anti-essentialism" now forms a restrictive orthodoxy within contemporary western feminist theory: "In our determination to honor diversity among women, we told one another to restrict our ambitions, limit our sights, beat a retreat from certain topics, refrain from using a rather long list of categories or concepts, and eschew generalization. I can think of no better prescription for the stunting of a field of intellectual inquiry."[28] Martin's concerns highlight the dangers of critiques of essentialism that function at a theoretical level rather than taking into account the exigencies of feminist practice. What does it mean to operate against culturally dominant constructions of femininity and masculinity if invoking an alternative account of women's identities is disallowed? What if those dominant constructions have a significant impact on how men and women understand themselves and each other? Do some forms of anti-essentialism lead us down the slippery slope to naive gender relativism?

Stressing the underlying reality of connections between women across race, class and other divisions, Susan Bordo points out, in a rich and persuasive article, that radical gender skepticism does nothing to ensure that the reality of diversity is respected, and undercuts the grounds of feminist politics. Bordo identifies a new "cultural formation . . . complexly constructed out of diverse elements."[29] She argues that this formation serves to shift feminist attention from practical contexts to questions of adequate theory, placing the construction of a theory that matches certain prescribed criteria prior to the adequate understanding of such things as relationships between white women and women of color in a particular context. Bordo attributes responsibility for this gender skepticism to two phenomena: the academic elision of critiques of ethnocentrism with poststructuralist theory, and feminist appropriations of deconstructionism. Her "anti-anti-essentialist" arguments fall into two categories: first, she uncouples claims about racism, heterosexism, and other "-isms" from epistemological claims about generalizations. Second, she argues that the academic context of anti-essentialism generates qualms about its political motivations and effects.

The "dogma" of anti-essentialism—characterized here by Bordo as the claim that generalizations are in principle essentialist—fails to meet the needs of feminism for a number of reasons. First, she argues, there is no necessary connection between gender skeptical methodologism and anti-racism, for example. Simply asserting the value of fragmenting categories will not generate a better understanding of the micro-politics of oppression. Second, white feminists, in particular, seldom justify their deployment of the mantra of "gender, race, and class," which pervades recent theorizing. "Why these axes of difference?" Bordo asks. When the very ideological frameworks that originally cast these axes as politically salient are undercut by some of those theorists who invoke "gender, race, and class," what justifies their choice of these categories? Bordo poses a similar question: "Why, it must be asked, are we so ready to deconstruct what have historically been the most ubiquitous elements of the gender axis, while we remain so willing to defer to the authority and integrity of race and class axes as fundamentally grounding?"[30] Setting aside whether this is an accurate description of feminist tendencies, the question nonetheless highlights the empty nature of this form of anti-essentialism. The necessity of ignoring some axes of difference in any particular context makes hostility to generalizations a methodological dogma rather than a useful guide.

Finally, Bordo argues that we can accept the multiplicity of women's identities while still acknowledging cultural moments where gender operates dichotomously. How we conceptualize such moments is clearly open to question, and Bordo provides a complex analysis of the Hill–Thomas hearings to illustrate her point. Whatever we make of this example, it shows, I think, that feminists cannot avoid gender duality by methodological fiat.

> Assessing where we are now, it seems to me that feminism stands less in danger of the totalizing tendencies of feminists than of an increasingly paralyzing anxiety over falling (from what grace?) into ethnocentrism or "essentialism." (The often-present implication that such a fall indicates deeply conservative and racist tendencies, of course, intensifies such anxiety.) Do we want to delegitimate a priori the exploration of experiential continuity and structural common ground among women? . . . If we wish to empower diverse voices, we would do better, I believe, to shift strategy from the methodological dictum that we forswear talk of "male" and "female" realities (which . . . can still be edifying and useful) to the messier, more slippery, practical struggle to create institutions and communities that will not permit *some* groups of people to make determinations about reality for *all*.[31]

Bordo is also wary of the academic context of gender skepticism. Mere theoretical attentiveness to difference does not ensure adequate representation for members of historically excluded groups, either in theory or in academic communities. In fact, insisting on the primacy of "difference" merely constructs radical Others and may actually preclude useful dialogue between women; it also occurs in academic contexts that are closed to actual difference, and rarely presents the often privileged academic with the more immediate challenges that arise from working within a diverse group. Generalizing hypotheses are not necessarily silencing or exclusive, Bordo argues; in fact, they may invite dialogue, when deconstructive readings refuse to assume a shape for which they must take responsibility. The intense hostility of many feminists to positive constructions of the feminine (Bordo cites Gilligan, I think correctly, as an exemplary target of such hostility) may come less from concerns about their "essentialism" than from a fear of infection by the inferior female otherness they allegedly depict. The professionalization of feminist philosophy, Bordo argues, works against the counter-hegemonic categories deployed by feminist activists:

> In this institutional context, as we are permitted "integration" into the professional sphere, the category of female "otherness," which has spoken to many feminists of the possibility of institutional and cultural change, of radical transformation of the values, metaphysical assumptions, and social practices of our culture, may become something from which we wish to dissociate ourselves. We need instead to establish our leanness, our critical incisiveness, our proficiency at clear and distinct dissection.[32]

I am sympathetic to the tenor of Bordo's argument here. The level of abstraction at which the essentialism debates have been carried out has often seemed to me far removed from the exigencies of feminist political practice. And I often have to resist the temptation to let my own writing slip into a jargon-laden technical style that dissociates itself from the emotive political issues at stake. Bordo's claim that some anti-essentialist arguments tend to create distance rather than encouraging dialogue resonates for me as well: I have often experienced white women students using classroom discussion of some of the contentions loosely grouped under "postmodern feminism" to construct an image of "women of color" as radically different from themselves. (A Black acquaintance once remarked to me wonderingly, after auditing a series of classes on "feminist theory and women of color" in which white female students had made strong claims about the Otherness of women of color, "Who do they think I am? I grew up in the West Island! [a middle-class suburban area of Montreal]".) This both obviates the need to answer such questions as "how can we work together respectfully?" and is a form of racism symmetrical with Spelman's "boomerang perception." Just as Spelman points out how "well-meaning white parents," in encouraging their children to overcome racist prejudice, used the ploy "they are just like you" (never, "you are just like them"), so the claim "we are *nothing* like them" encourages solipsism rather than reciprocal dialogue.[33] It also represents what Lugones calls a "failure of love": "there is a complex failure of love in the failure to identify with another woman, the failure to see oneself in other women who are quite different from oneself. . . . [White/Anglo women's] world and their integrity do not require me at all. There is no sense of self-loss in them for my own lack of solidity. But they rob me of my solidity through indifference, an indifference they can afford and which seems sometimes studied."[34]

I agree with Bordo, furthermore, that unqualified anti-essentialism, in particular with regard to theories of subjectivity, has no necessary connection with the arguments concerning false generalizations or multiple identities I have been addressing. In fact, some feminists have argued that these two strands of anti-essentialist influence have conflicting political goals. For example, in "The Race for Theory," Barbara Christian argues that in the context of literary criticism, "deconstruction" of literary traditions perpetuates the very exclusions it purports to undercut.[35] Many women of color writing today about their racial and cultural identities in feminist contexts both challenge monolithic, white-identified, accounts of womanhood and reaffirm another devalued, marginalized, or suppressed identity. For example, bell hooks's work on Black women and self-recovery specifically appropriates the modernist language of self-help for radical political purposes, to argue that

> Black female self-recovery, like all black self-recovery, is an expression of a liberatory political practice. Living as we do in a white-supremacist capitalist patriarchal context that can best exploit us when we lack a firm grounding in self and identity (knowledge of who we are and where we have come from), choosing "wellness" is an act of political resistance. Before many of us can effectively sustain engagement in organized resistance struggle, in black liberation movement, we need to undergo a process of self-recovery that can heal individual wounds that may prevent us from functioning fully.[36]

By stressing the suppressed and previously distorted experiences of Black women in the contemporary United States, hooks's account offers hope of a more authentic, "healing" self-identity. Such work may rediscover old subjects or define new ones, or point to the complexity of cross-cutting axes of identity within all subjects. It does not, however, suggest that experience has no one privileged interpretation, or that the subject is dead—far from it, in hooks's case. In other words, many of the methodological insights contained within critiques of essentialism are not derived from postmodern philosophy, nor even from postmodern feminism, however loosely these terms are understood. Thus a feminist theory such as Spelman's can offer anti-essentialist views of subjectivity—for example a view that sees every invocation of identity as contextual and historically situated—without being committed to some of the bolder claims of anti-essentialism.

Bordo is far more cautious and more nuanced in her critique of anti-essentialism than is Okin, recognizing her own location and the political dangers of dismissing anti-essentialism too casually. My reservations about Bordo's argument center on her construction of the position she is attacking. The dogmatic view she calls "anti-essentialism" verges on being a straw person, representing, at best, moments in some authors' work rather than a fully articulated programmatic approach. She is careful to characterize gender skepticism as a convergence of trends rather than a solid stance. This depiction itself, however, elides "anti-essentialist" arguments that are very different from each other. When Bordo argues against principled gender skepticism, does her argument apply with equal strength to Butler's account of gender as performativity and to Spelman's contextual method? Is there no important difference between objecting to a particular generalization because it is exclusionary, for example, and objecting to generalizations in general? Bordo recognizes these distinctions, but, like Spelman, her account is critical rather than constructive. Where does this leave my own project?

### From Theory to Method

This chapter expands on the connection between false generalizations about women and methodological essentialism. While feminism needs general claims, often these claims are constructed to reflect inequalities of power among women that allow dominant group feminists to define identities and political interests. In the course of my defense of Spelman, I pointed out how "anti-anti-essentialists" identify a position wherein feminists object to generalizations about women per se. This "principled anti-essentialist" position is incoherent; I have some doubts, furthermore, as to whether any feminist theorist consistently adopts it. It nevertheless defines one end of a spectrum, with metaphysical essentialism at the other. Along this spectrum are a variety of positions: from extreme a priorism about the Form of Woman to a principled rejection of all generalizations about women. Just as in Chapter 1 I suggested that metaphysical essentialism is a straw person for feminist anti-essentialists, so here I am suggesting that principled anti-essentialism is both an untenable position in itself, and a straw person for anti-anti-essentialists.

To motivate later chapters, I want to argue that despite the ostensible differences between the texts discussed, there is an unacknowledged consensus in the literature on essentialism. First, Spelman, Okin, and Bordo would all agree that feminism needs generalizations and that a position rejecting all general claims is untenable. The existence of false generalizations, however egregious, does not necessitate avoiding *all* generalizations, and indeed, as these authors concur, to do so would be to commit a kind of methodological suicide, since all social theory rests to some degree on generalizing categories and theses, however carefully nuanced these may be. Recognizing that the category "women" is too crude to be of real methodological use, we might substitute "working-class women" in a particular analysis. This becomes "white working-class women," or "white working-class married women," or "white working-class married women in Michigan in the 1980s," and so on down the slippery slope. Yet we do not have to commit ourselves to ending up at the bottom. Some of these adjectives may well enhance our analysis, making it more precise and informative; others may turn out to be less relevant, obscuring commonalities rather than highlighting important differences. To insist ahead of time that only difference is to count is to re-adopt a kind of methodological narrowness that inhibits productive feminist investigation. Such an a priori affirmation of difference may block the discovery and investigation of commonalities, and we cannot tell a priori which commonalities and differences are relevant to the political issue at hand. Likewise, to reject all criticisms from exclusion on the grounds that these will provoke an infinite proliferation of analytic categories in one's scholarship is to foreclose recognition of the importance of particular objections. A critical race theorist who is asked to account for his lack of explicit attention to gender, for example, does not answer the objection by pointing out that he also elided class relations, regional differences, and varied ethnic identities within a racial group, and that it would have been too challenging a project to include all these axes of difference in his work.

Feminists are familiar with negotiating these methodological paradoxes. For example, in my own work against sexual violence I am often struck by the straightforwardly radical effects of asserting women's commonalities against sexist efforts to fragment women as a group. Of those individuals who are adult victims of sexual assault, at least 90% are women, which is a startling figure by any sociological standard. These women may be young or old, rich or poor, black or white, fat or thin, survivors of other sexual abuse or not, self-defined lesbian, heterosexual, bisexual, and so forth. The consequences of the assault will be very different for these different women: an elderly woman with few financial resources leaving her abusive husband has her life changed by sexual violence in quite a different way from a young college student whose blind date rapes her. Yet there are significant theoretical connections between these two occurrences in feminist analyses, in the emotional responses of the two women, in the attitudes and actions of their aggressors, in their healing processes, and in other respects, which make it both politically useful and useful *to these women* for feminists sometimes to campaign in relatively generic ways against sexual violence perpetrated against a wide range of women. Indeed, the strength of feminist organizing against sexual assault resides in the creation of a general connecting discourse. If these two women find themselves in the same support group, their experiences, while very different, may resonate with one another, and they may find important common threads in the fabrics of their lives.

If the support group wants to avoid being exclusionary, of course, it will address in its meetings how poverty, age, cultural background, and other variables that are relevant to its members have affected their experiences of sexual violence. The group may decide to split into separate subgroups at different times for different women. On a structural level, it will have sliding scale or no fees, it will offer childcare services, and it will schedule meetings at times and in locations that make it accessible. Yet members of the group may choose to march together on a "Take Back the Night" demonstration under a banner proclaiming "Women: Safe, Strong, and Free," or they may lobby for changes in the law surrounding sexual assault. Thus this example demonstrates that feminist practice can often make use of general categories, women's common experiences, and relatively uninflected political analyses, while still avoiding exclusionary traps. This is not to deny that many feminist actions have been, and continue to be, exclusionary in practice. The extent to which uninflected categories should be discarded because essentialist, however, is a question that seems to speak to issues in feminist theory rather than to the pragmatic issues confronted by feminist groups in responding to oppression.

Thus all feminist theorists with any commitment to making their analyses relevant to feminist activism, of whatever kind, must be committed to allowing some sorts of generalizations about women. Crucial questions revolve around the nature of these generalizing claims, how they are used politically, and how they are justified. Put simply, illegitimate generalizations are also bad because they are illegitimate, not merely because they are generalizations. It often seems to me that the allure of anti-essentialist discourses has immobilized feminist political theorists. We need not be committed to any form of essentialism when we identify commonalities among women, and these commonalities might still be accurate explanatory frameworks for oppression, or be experienced as deeply authentic identities. General claims about women are not necessarily essentialist, although they may misrepresent their alleged constituency, make false assumptions about "women's lives" or "women's experience," or make numerous other mistakes. Keeping this debate at the level of ontological questions about generality and "difference" sidesteps analyses of power that offer criteria for understanding how homogeneity comes to be imposed and when "strategic essentialism" might be most useful.

Thus we cannot arbitrate between different claims about what women have in common without giving examples of particular contexts where such claims apply. Some generalizations, it seems reasonable to assume, will be justified and others will not. All the authors I have been discussing draw this conclusion in one way or another. But the feminist philosophical literature on essentialism has tended toward internal dialogue, often at cross-purposes (as in the case of Okin on Spelman), and has not effectively demonstrated that much is at stake for feminist practitioners in discussions of essentialism. This is one of the reasons Wittgenstein's "back to the rough ground" is epigrammatic in this book. If we keep the debate at the level of ontology, we run the risk of being trapped in an idle dichotomy: either we continue to be excited by anti-essentialist examples, seeing exceptions to every general claim, or we impose preconceived ideal-types onto women in ways that matter politically for those women.

Reclaiming the term "essentialist" may have important critical force in a discipline that has failed to interrogate its own professed "anti-essentialism." However, both accusations and allegiances, as Spivak says, often merely give information about "what color cockade you're wearing in your hat."[37] "Essentialism" and "anti-essentialism" are not two discrete and juxtaposed positions, but terms describing multiple positions complexly located on a spectrum. Neither end of the spectrum represents a viable position for feminist theorists. Therefore, we need to look to the middle ground between essentialism and gender skepticism to find ways of talking about women that neither do violence to our diversity, nor represent us as inconsolably different.

In Chapter 3 I will find a perhaps unlikely ally in Ludwig Wittgenstein, who offers a critique of essentialism that can be appropriated in order to perform precisely this task. Wittgenstein's anti-essentialism recommends that we "look and see," an injunction motivated by concerns connected to my own evolving argument. Instead of trying to "get it right" about who women are, we can give examples of contexts where different claims are justified. However, this exercise still requires criteria of justification; it still demands that we define which similarities and differences among women are to count. In Chapters 4 and 5 I take up the challenge of giving such examples, using my Wittgensteinian feminism to develop an anti-essentialist feminist research method and organizing strategies.

# Chapter 3

## Philosophical Investigations (in a Feminist Voice)

And we extend our concept of number as in spinning a thread we twist fibre on fibre. And the strength of the thread does not reside in the fact that some one fibre runs through its whole length, but in the overlapping of many fibres.[1]

1. Let us consider the construct that we call "women." I don't just mean white, middle-class, heterosexual, able-bodied, young, attractive, western women, but all women. What is common to them all? Don't say: "*there must be something in common or they wouldn't be called 'women.'*" Likewise, don't say: "*If women have nothing in common, then how can feminism form a political movement?*" Look and see what the construct of women consists of, and what women might have in common. For, if you look, you will not see something that is common to all, but similarities, relationships, and a whole series of them at that. Look, for example, at heterosexual women. They are attracted

to, and may form sexual relationships with, men. Now pass to bisexual women: some features drop out and others appear! Think now of a woman of color (if you haven't already). How is she like a white woman? And what is the relationship of a Jewish lesbian to a straight Chicana? Does a poor woman in England have anything in common with a wealthy one in South Africa?

> And the result of this examination is: we see a complicated network of similarities overlapping and criss-crossing: sometimes overall similarities, sometimes similarities of detail [PI § 66].

2. Furthermore, even when I talk about one woman it is not correct to find the logical sum of these individual interrelated concepts: if I am white, anglophone, middle class, young,. . . , then the concept of "me" is not an additive analysis of these different parts [PI § 68]. I cannot abstract from the rest that part of me that is race, that which is sexuality, and so on. (Yet obviously I can still *use* the concept of myself.) Likewise, when I compare myself to a woman of color, whom I resemble in many other respects, I cannot say "add some color, and we are the same."

3. "*So how can you talk about 'women' at all?*" Well, when I talk about them, I give examples that I intend to be taken in a particular way, so that the examples may be *used* (in the game of politics perhaps). The danger of this is that we may not recognize that these are just examples and not an ideal, an inexpressible common thing that represents all women. For what does the mental picture of a woman look like when it does not show us any particular image, but what is common to all women? I think that if you see "women" in a certain light you will use the term in a certain way, and because your account does not apply to all women, but only to those you are thinking of, in using an ideal you will be guilty of a generalization that is quite unjustified:

> The idea now absorbs us, that the ideal '*must*' be found in reality. Meanwhile we do not as yet see *how* it occurs there, nor do we understand the nature of this 'must.' We think it must be in reality; for we think we already see it there [PI § 101].

4. "*So what is the purpose of this ideal, if it is not found in reality?*" In this case, the ideal comes to serve a political purpose for you, as my examples serve my political purposes. The ideal woman can be held up as a metaphysical necessity that comes to legislate my identity. So when we identify similarities and differences, we must be quite clear that this is a pragmatic exercise: "How should we explain to someone what a game is? I imagine that we should de-

scribe *games* to him, and we might add: "This *and similar things* are called 'games'" [PI § 69].

5. "*But if you are a feminist, then you need to make generalizations about women, for this is the essence of feminist politics!*" Exactly. I have never denied that. When I look around a classroom, for example, I see women having common experiences of being excluded and trivialized. But that is not to say that even we are all the same. I can draw a boundary around us, for a special purpose. (Perhaps I want to demonstrate something for you.)

6. The ideal becomes an empty notion, which muddles me, and prevents me from seeing what I have to do. What feminist action should I take if I am in pursuit of a chimera? We have taken out all the substance of "women" and are left with a vacuous concept: "we have got onto slippery ice where there is no friction and so in a certain sense the conditions are ideal, but also, just because of that, we are unable to walk. We want to walk: so we need *friction*. Back to the rough ground!" [PI § 107].

7. Sometimes you draw a boundary around concepts to use them yourself. (This may be called a stereotype.) What matters is that you look and see whether or not you have drawn the boundary self-consciously. Sometimes the boundary is oppressive; sometimes it acts as an object of comparison:

> For we can avoid ineptness or emptiness in our assertions only by presenting the model as what it is, as an object of comparison—as, so to speak, a measuring-rod; not as a preconceived idea to which reality *must* correspond. (The dogmatism into which we fall so easily in doing philosophy) [PI § 131].

8. But now you will say: "*This is nonsense. All women do have something in common; namely, their bodies. Do you want to deny that?*" All right, the concept of "women" is bounded for you by the physical reality of sexed existence. It need not be so. You have given the physical character of "women" particular limits, but I can use the term so that its extension is not closed by the same frontier.

9. This much I will allow you: some aspects of some male and female bodies are different. But why have we drawn the most important boundaries there? Why do we not draw them around other differences between us? Certainly it matters that some women menstruate, have breasts, vaginas, bear children. But do all women share these features? And how will we describe them? The physical boundaries of sex are elective foundations, supported by the walls of social practice. The discourse we weave around our bodies creates what we think of as a reality in correspondence with nature.

10. So now you agree: "*bodies don't matter*" (on this I am still only partly in

agreement) and ask again, *"if bodies aren't exactly real, how is the social construct of 'women' bounded?"* It is bounded by a set of rules that regulate it very well, yet which leave some gaps.

11. *"Essence* is expressed by grammar" [PI § 371]. The category of "women" has been confirmed by language—such as the gendered pronouns some languages use to divide the world in two. This obscures the contingency of that division and leads us to assign it more importance than we otherwise might: "Philosophy is a battle against the bewitchment of our intelligence by means of language" [PI § 109].

12. The category of sex is created and defined by a fluid boundary. For what matters about being a woman? Look and see. We can claim things in common, like perhaps motherhood, or sexuality, or emotional sensibilities, but that is not to say that we will all, always, have these things in common. I use my own experience to find out what the women I know have in common. The construction of gender identity is a complex thing, and it varies among people; that is to say, it is mutable. (We have approached the problem from the other side, and now we know our way about!):

> One might say that the concept "game" is a concept with blurred edges.— "But is a blurred concept a concept at all?"—Is an indistinct photograph a picture of a person at all? Is it even always an advantage to replace an indistinct picture by a sharp one? Isn't the indistinct one often exactly what we need? [PI § 71].

13. So, perhaps we do not need to specify what the concept "women" is at all. In fact, specifying might not be to our advantage. Rather we need to take the longer path toward discovering who we are and who we are not.

14. We extend our concept of women as in spinning a thread we twist fiber on fiber. And the strength of the thread does not reside in the fact that some one fiber runs through its whole length, but in the overlapping of many fibers.

What does the preceding Wittgensteinian conversation tell us about feminist theory? First, it elaborates a familiar stalemate: namely, that any feminist theory that tries to incorporate the multiplicity of differences among women will not be able to make the generalizations required for feminist politics. This leaves feminist theory trapped between an acute gender skepticism and the use of crude and exclusive generalizations. These polar accounts are sometimes presented as the only options for feminists, yet by enquiring both into meaning and into feminist method, a Wittgensteinian feminist critique of essentialism helps us to locate ourselves outside the terms of the dichotomy. This chapter uses my own *Philosophical Investigations* to show how to continue with feminist theory and practice without falling into methodological essentialism. By paying close attention to Wittgenstein's remarks in a central section of his *Philosophical Investigations* (roughly §§ 66–131), we can undermine the theoretical bases of essentialism through his challenge to one traditional philosophical picture that "holds us captive."

I proceed by briefly locating Wittgenstein's critique of essentialism before showing how it connects to feminist anti-essentialism. Wittgenstein's later philosophy offers a solution to certain methodological problems within feminist theory. In particular, I present an articulation of the connection between Wittgenstein's notion of family resemblance and his critique of ideals, on the one hand, and problematic forms of essentialism with regard to the category "women," on the other. I indicate how this relates to Spelman's analysis in *Inessential Woman* and point out how Wittgenstein's arguments for purposive line drawing and his notion of "objects of comparison" provide insight into contemporary feminist theorizing about sex and gender identities, making the case that conceptual delimiting is a matter of political strategy, not of ontological necessity. Finally, I indicate that Wittgenstein's injunction to "look and see" might constitute more than just a slogan for feminist social theory, and I outline the contours of a feminist method that offers a way to go on using anti-essentialist insights. Wittgenstein's skepticism toward theory moves our attention away from the "problem of difference" as a philosophical trope, toward questions about feminist practice. If we accept the Wittgensteinian argument that meaning is constructed through, rather than prior to, our use of language, then an anti-essentialist method must look at deployments of the term "women" and their political implications.

### Wittgenstein, Essentialism, and Feminist Theory

In debating the inter-relation of canonical twentieth century philosophy and feminist thought, Wittgenstein is often mentioned, usually in the context of the epistemological consequences of his private language argument.[2] Little of the feminist literature, however, takes up the challenge of weaving his later philosophy into feminist political critique in an explicit fashion (although more are now doing so).[3] Indeed, Wittgenstein's philosophy, especially his later philosophy of language, is often presumed to be at odds with agendas for social change. Wittgenstein himself was no feminist, and I bracket here any epistemological or political issues raised by appropriating for feminist work the ideas of canonical philosophers hostile to feminist politics.[4] I shall argue that Wittgenstein's intentions notwithstanding, both linguistic and methodological feminist anti-essentialist arguments find a useful philosophical toolkit, and a way to go on, in his anti-essentialist arguments in the *Philosophical Investigations*.

My goal in this appropriation of Wittgenstein is to offer neither an exegesis of his views nor an analysis that is "faithful" to the *Investigations*. A wave of recent Wittgenstein scholarship takes at face value his oft-cited remark from the preface, "my goal is not to spare other people the trouble of thinking. But, if possible, to stimulate someone to thoughts of their own." This new genre of scholarship in ethics and political philosophy deploys Wittgensteinian frameworks in wide-ranging contexts only loosely tied to the details of Wittgenstein's arguments: for example, Peta Bowden makes Wittgensteinian method the basis of her analysis of ethical activities of caring, Theodore Schatzki moves from language games to a study of social practices, and James Tully uses Wittgenstein as a motif for his work on constitutionalism and cultural diversity.[5] Wittgenstein's critique of essentialism and his admittedly opaque remarks on theory and practice serve here only as backdrops to the debates in feminist theory that interest me.

Wittgenstein's conception of essentialism was primarily linguistic, his targets being contemporary philosophy of language, logic, and metaphysics. (Among these targets was, of course, his own early work, the *Tractatus Logicus-Philosophicus*.)[6] He viewed essentialism as a linguistic phenomenon entailed by the claim that members of a particular class share a common key property by virtue of their common name. He rejects the notion of a single "essence" to these classes, where "essence" implies a statement of the necessary and sufficient conditions for the application of a particular term. Wittgenstein conceives many of the linguistic "mistakes" associated with essentialism as arising from misguided metaphysical assumptions (for example, the assumption that terms in aesthetics and ethics can be conclusively defined [PI § 77]), and from the characteristics of logic [PI §§ 107–8]. He thus seeks to undermine linguistic essentialism by challenging both an account of language whereby terms refer to things existing as "natural kinds" in the world, and the belief, in its various forms, that meaning is constructed prior to the use of language. He raises two implicit objections to linguistic essentialism: first, that it relies on a priorism at the expense of empirical enquiry, and second, that linguistic essentialism is a theory that does not reflect our actual use of language.

General claims made about women that are based on the experience of only some women often exhibit the same a priorism and failure to examine empirical evidence that Wittgenstein criticized. An essentialist ontology that takes the use of the word "women" to represent a collection of people with specified characteristics existing prior to the application of the term erases both the diversity of women and the fact that women's identities as women emerge from their particular social locations. Thus linguistic essentialism encourages us to assume, on the one hand, that all women are women by virtue of fulfilling a finite set of necessary and sufficient conditions, thereby inviting the assumption that the word "woman" describes merely an instance of these general conditions.

On the other hand, it obscures the varied contexts of the social construction of gender identity, encouraging feminists to posit a general definitional account of "women" that is allegedly specific to no particular woman. Not only is this latter story epistemologically problematic in Wittgensteinian terms, but it also is susceptible to sustained feminist political critique. In the absence of linguistic and methodological essentialisms, there is no reason to suppose that the experiences of some women can represent those of all women, and the picture that has held (some of) us captive is revealed as a political strategy rather than "the truth about women." In the *Philosophical Investigations*, Wittgenstein makes the case that the meanings of words are determined by an examination of their use, rather than their use being determined by pre-existing ideals. More radically, he argues that we can use words without being able to specify precise criteria for their application. One concept that elucidates this theory of language is Wittgenstein's notion of "family resemblances."

### Additive Analyses and Family Resemblances

Spelman employs a philosophy that is implicitly Wittgensteinian, and an explicit rendering of the connections between *Inessential Woman* and the *Philosophical Investigations* offers a powerful language for navigating our way out of the labyrinths she describes. Wittgenstein articulates an anti-essentialist method more scrupulously than Spelman, gives a more detailed sense of how the philosophical "therapy" works, and demonstrates how to carry on given the recognition of essentialist errors. Most notably, Wittgenstein's concept of family resemblances is an alternative to certain kinds of mistaken additive analyses (the phenomena Spelman criticizes). Rather than offering an account of the linguistic essence of any particular term, he points to a variety of connected ways the term is used in language, none of which is definitive [PI §§ 65–67]. If we adopt the notion that women bear family re-semblances to one another, we can avoid a misleading ontology that sets up mutually exclusive, bounded categories.

On this account there need be no definitive set of characteristics that all women share, but rather we can understand ourselves as connected to each other by a network of overlapping similarities, some of which may be bio-logically real—like breasts, a vagina, a uterus, the capacity to conceive and bear a child, XX chromosomes; others of which may be more obviously con-structed—like a particular relation to one's mother, ethical attitudes, expe-riences of subordination, and so on. But no *single* characteristic is necessary to make an individual a woman, and none is sufficient.[7] Thus, on this view, it is perfectly possible to make sense of the fact that two "distantly related" individuals can both be women and share none of the same characteristics except that they are called "women." A male-to-female (MTF) transsexual woman, for example, might have XY chromosomes, experience of being raised as a boy in a white, urban bourgeois nuclear family, and convention-ally feminine self-presentation. A butch woman might have XX chromo-somes, experience of being raised as a girl by lesbian parents in a small Northern community, and conventionally masculine self-presentation. On my Wittgensteinian-feminist view, it is not "wrong" to call them both "women" even though they do not share any common features potentially definitive of womanhood. This is not to suggest that linguistic usage can never be changed (the argument commonly leveled against Wittgenstein's account of meaning as use). In what follows I develop the feminist possibili-ties for this view of language in the context of the need both to change con-ventional sexist meanings and to offer justifications for political decisions about inclusion and exclusion.

Wittgenstein anticipates several objections to these considerations, all helpful for my anti-essentialist feminism. First, he argues that all instances of concepts like "game" (or, we might add, "women") do not have a disjunctive shared property—some characteristic(s) we can identify as being common to all games—but rather the common term gathers together multiple in-stances that have overlapping similarities. Our attempts to find common properties are examples of our being led astray by the single word that links these family resemblances. Second, a concept is not the logical sum of sub-concepts, each of which can be rigidly defined—board games, card games, Olympic games, etc.—since we can, and often do, use it in a way that is not bounded. That is, we invent new games, or make the case that something not previously thought of as a game should be included in that concept. Witt-genstein rejects the idea that a concept without rigid boundaries is useless, and he shows us a variety of ways in which we use concepts despite the openness of their frontiers. Thus explanation of a particular phenomenon by example is not necessarily subsequent to explanations that posit essences, but rather may be a better strategy for articulating the use of a particular term.

This attack on linguistic essentialism has important implications for methodological essentialism. It provides an alternative ontology that sidesteps the view that there is an essential womanness, separable from class, race, and other contexts, that all women share. This approach also sidesteps the ontological (if not the political) need to have people pass through classifications of the sort Spelman describes. However, we can still use the term "women," make generalizations about women, and engage in feminist politics. Wittgenstein's notion of family resemblances offers not only a supplementary ontological critique of essentialist practices, but also a solution—a new way of thinking about the similarities and differences among people. Of course, to describe women as bearing family resemblances to each other only constitutes an ontological therapy, or a way of freeing ourselves from the misleading philosophical picture that holds us captive, not necessarily a riposte to those (myself included) who see political reasons for positing gender commonality. It does, however, reveal these reasons as purposive rather than predetermined, and therefore as carrying a concomitant demand for justification. The practice of becoming self-conscious and self-critical about the bases of one's own classifications is, I think, a crucial part of feminist consciousness-raising in the current political climate.

Rather than considering language as revealing truths about the world, we are urged to examine linguistic usage. Thus instead of assuming a quintessential "womanness" that all women share because they are called "women," we should look more closely at the applications of the term. Then, to understand what "women" means, we would have to give examples of different people called "women," and if feminists wanted to describe a particular social phenomenon as, for example, "a women's issue," we would have to justify that label by pointing to the ways it affects (and sometimes, constructs) people we call "women" and stipulate the women to whom it applies. In addition to preventing some women from simply ignoring the experiences of others, this method would also de-legitimate the claim that the experiences of nondominant women do not actually count as "women's experience."

The way the stale debate surrounding essentialisms in feminist theory "holds us captive" is similar to the problems the *Philosophical Investigations* sets out not to solve but to dispel. Feminists of many kinds seek a way of thinking—a philosophical imagination—that embraces plurality, starting from the realities of women's lives, not from the exigencies of a theory unselfconsciously trapped in essentialism. Wittgenstein's later work is one of the most profound modern sources of skepticism toward "philosophy" for its detachment from the world, offering a critique of theory that resonates with much contemporary feminist writing. His own conception of philosophy is one of the most vexed questions in scholarship on Wittgenstein, not least because the answers must be sought in some of his most perplexing aphorisms. Primarily Wittgenstein rejects a Cartesian philosophy of doubt and certainty (the aim of philosophy thus being to discover what we can *know*).[8] Rather, he examines problems in language and seeks to demarcate sense and nonsense: "My aim is: to teach you to pass from a piece of disguised nonsense to something that is patent nonsense" [PI § 464]. Philosophy offers only new insights into old facts, clarifying and describing rather than explaining: "Philosophy simply puts everything before us, and neither explains nor deduces anything.—Since everything lies open to view there is nothing to explain" [PI § 126].

Philosophy does not help us progressively to accumulate knowledge but rather becomes a skill for dealing with illusions stemming from those fundamental features of language and structures of thought that shape the way we look at things. For those who sense here a kind of conceptual chaos, Wittgenstein offers carefully justified footholds. Adopting the family resemblance approach does not preclude a systematic description of conceptual phenomena or rule out generalizations: "What, then, are the criteria for possession of philosophical understanding. . . ? . . . The skill manifest in marshaling analogies, disanalogies, and actual or invented intermediate cases that will illuminate the network of our grammar."[9] Wittgenstein seems to envisage philosophy as thus entering a new paradigm—a kink in the development of human thought analogous to Galileo's revisions—where it no longer mimics science and struggles with metaphysics; instead: "[Philosophical] problems are solved, not by giving new information, but by arranging what we have always known" [PI § 109].[10]

In reflecting on recent feminist theory we can immediately see some points of connection. Certainly feminists have placed minimal emphasis on uncovering a priori truths, and feminist philosophy has in general been imbued with a keen sense of theory as deconstructive, with the recognition and incorporation of previously silenced or unheard voices, and with philosophy as the investigation of diverse (and often marginalized) lived experiences. Philosophical language has featured in this project as a significant limitation to the free expression of women's voices: in critiques of sexist and phallocentric discourse, in creating new, gynocentric forms of philosophical expression, in challenging narrow parameters of what is to "count" as philosophy, and in confronting language as a tool of oppression. Wittgenstein's strategy also undermines a phallocratic conception of philosophy that posits "hard" disciplines such as logic and epistemology as the "core" of philosophy, while "soft" areas—like ethics—remain peripheral, and in so doing echoes his concept of the "democratic" "body philosophical."[11] For feminist philosophers, too, philosophy is a skill and an activity, a way of challenging conceptual dogma through the affirmation of different experiences and realities. And Wittgenstein helps us to see the limits of narrow concepts, essences, and ideals and to find a philosophical therapy that frees us from them.

This description highlights the anti-philosophical nature of the Wittgensteinian feminist view and, indeed, its opposition to any philosophy that seeks to identify metaphysical truths. It does not preclude, however, a kind of philosophy that attempts a careful picking apart of damaging philosophical pictures and a better kind of thinking that recognizes its own location. The project of "feminist theory" should proceed with caution, avoiding the total fragmentation of its central categories. If "difference" is pursued with too much zeal, then one conclusion is that the only interests I can intelligibly have are my own (and they too disintegrate), and feminist politics descends into solipsism. It is impossible to imagine a world without theory, in the broadest sense of the term, where people did not enquire into different conceptualizations and seek to explain a variety of events within a single framework. This process itself is rightly prized, moreover, as one of the attributes of a self-determining individual or community, and the analyses offered by feminist theory are both liberating and part of a legitimate strategy for resisting oppression.

The focus on essentialism as a *theoretical* problem is nonetheless an example of the kind of philosophy Wittgenstein's critique is directed against. To talk about essentialism as a purely ontological or linguistic problem can be a distancing strategy, a way of removing oneself from the particular and focusing on the general. Echoing Wittgenstein's remark, "instead of 'craving for generality' I could also have said 'the contemptuous attitude towards the particular case,'"[12] "theory" undermines specificity, not only by denying difference in language, but in reality. Lugones pinpoints this sentiment when she says:

> The white woman theorist did not notice us yet, her interpretation of the question placed the emphasis on theorizing itself, and the generalizing and theorizing impulse led the white theorizer to *think of all differences as the same*, that is, as underminers of the truth, force, or scope of their theories. Here racism has lost its character and particular importance—a clear sign that we have not been noticed. This trick does not allow the theorizer to

see, for example, the need to differentiate among racism, colonialism, and imperialism, three very different interactive phenomena.[13]

The verbal sameness of the term "difference" and the multitude of arguments feminists have advanced under its banner again direct attention to linguistic uniformity rather than to the many political issues surrounding "different differences" that exist in real lives. A philosophy of generality serves to delegitimate the needs of particular women. If we have a simple theory that explains sexism in one tidy slogan, then why look for different realities? The most crucial lesson is that the prerogative to define identity is not equally shared. Decisions about which similarities are to count (and which differences really do not matter) are usually made by those with the most power.

## Line Drawings

Apart from looking at diversity within the group of people usually referred to as "women," we can challenge essentialism by examining some more or less successful attempts to defy conventional boundaries around the term. In locating feminist theorists between methodological essentialism and principled anti-essentialism, a Wittgensteinian approach gives us reason to see the decisions we make about definitions as deeply political. In Wittgenstein's remarks on the possibilities of setting the boundary of a concept in many different places, and further on the need to set a boundary at all, I see radical possibilities for feminism. It might initially seem as if I am ignoring my own advice and using philosophy to obscure biological difference, if the word "women" actually corresponds to the category of women bounded by the physical reality of the female body. Indeed we do need to recognize the reality and significance of biology, not as pre-social or extra-linguistic "facts" about chromosomes or genitalia, but as lived experience of embodiment with politically significant cultural meaning. Others have argued in more detail that the female body has been erased both from canonical political theory and from certain feminist theories, and that both feminist and non-feminist discourses make uncritical assumptions about the natural reality and necessity of sexual dimorphism.[14] Simultaneously afraid that our bodies would be erased, that we would be reduced to our bodies, or that our bodies would over-determine our selves, we have struggled with how to locate the sexed body in feminist philosophy.

The specific contribution of a Wittgensteinian feminism to these debates lies in the argument that where we draw the boundary around the category "women" constitutes a political act, and one that should be scrutinized for its particular purpose, no less when biological characteristics feature on one side or the other of the boundary. "To repeat, we can draw a boundary—for a special purpose. Does it take that to make the concept usable? Not at all! (Except for that special purpose)" [PI § 69]. Thus feminists can aim for semantic influence over the category "women" and redefine its boundaries with the explicit acknowledgment that this is a political activity (not an unproblematically "objective" scientific or medical one) within which power differentials affect the semantic authority of the participants, including different women. Perhaps we can also take up the Wittgensteinian notion of foundations as axes: "I do not explicitly learn the propositions that stand fast for me. I can *discover* them subsequently like the axis around which a body rotates. This axis is not fixed in the sense that anything holds it fast, but the movement around it determines its immobility." [15] If we posit "women" as that bounded group of people held in place on its axis by various popular, medical, and scientific discourses, not fixed in the sense that a pre-existing reality "holds it fast," we can also see how adding feminist challenges to "the movement around" women might lead to further displacement of those who are accepted as women, by way of an alteration in the meaning of that term.

Such methodological possibilities for the subversion of sex and gender identities form a key part of undermining simplistic and rigidly imposed binary definitions of "women" and "men"—an integral part of the task of any feminist theory. It is also a task that makes especially apparent the necessary connections between feminism and queer theorizing and activism: any feminism that fails to understand itself as deeply implicated in the struggles of all those who are oppressed by normative heterosexuality—not only lesbians and not only women—will miss a key facet of gender oppression. So how can feminists allied with queer activists challenge oppressive sex and gender binarisms while justifying strategic line drawing around particular groups of people for the purposes of oppositional politics? The notion that male and female bodies create two discrete groups that are biologically bounded and exist prior to any use of category labels is both empirically inaccurate, and obscures the fact that the terms "man" or "woman," "female" or "male," and "boy" or "girl" are not attributed by unequivocal reference to primary or even secondary sexual characteristics. In fact, to the extent that physical sex cues are real, they can be overridden to a remarkable degree by social context. [16] The crucial exception here is, of course, the classic delivery room question, "is it a boy or a girl?," an attribution that obscures the existence of intersexed infants, who cause discursive chaos for medical practitioners and others intent on imposing and constructing human sexual dimorphism. [17]

Thus some of the deepest challenges to the boundary of the term "women" in western societies come from those whose gender presentation does not conform to their birth sex (or perhaps to any commonly understood category), who alter the physical sex of their bodies, or those who have sexual characteristics that fall outside the terms of the conventional binary. While an obsession with genital status can serve merely to reinforce the myth that gender collapses into sex, critical histories and theories of transsexuality and intersexuality are important.[18] They offer openings to dialogue for all feminists thinking through the political effects of binary conceptual schemes, and opportunities for building political coalitions with those who have related but not identical experiences of sex–gender oppression. The extreme reactions of confusion, distaste, and violence toward those whose bodies do not accommodate sexual dimorphism, or whose gender identity deviates from their sex assignment, demonstrate the deep psychological and political dependence within dominant western cultures on sex–gender conformity. An emerging body of work thus offers a clearer perspective on the historicity, contingency, and oppressive force of existing categories of sex and gender for all feminists.[19]

For example, non-transsexed feminists have had ambivalent attitudes toward the inclusion of MTF transsexuals in feminist community that deserve further political scrutiny. Janice Raymond's classic hostile analysis of the politics of transsexuality, along with highly publicized essentialist transsexual memoirs (of which Jan Morris's *Conundrum* is perhaps the most highbrow), has contributed to a thread of feminist skepticism about the politics of transsexuality.[20] One major source of this skepticism has been the deployment of essentialist accounts of sex and gender in theories of transsexuality. Raymond, for example, stresses the conservatism of the then-dominant medical model and makes the case that transsexuality (and, by default, transsexuals themselves) reinscribes oppressive patriarchal sex and gender binarisms, and both reflects and generates popular support for metaphysical and biological essentialisms.

Likewise popular discourse around transsexuality in modern western cultures has clung to a metaphysical essentialism both historically specific and in denial of its own historicity. For example, Morris remarks at the beginning of her autobiographical narrative: "I was three or perhaps four years old when I realized that I had been born into the wrong body, and should really be a girl." And later: "I believe [the 'conundrum' of 'transsexualism'] to have some higher origin or meaning. I equate it with the idea of soul, or self, and I think of it not just as a sexual enigma, but as a quest for unity . . . In my mind it is a subject far wider than sex: I recognize no pruriency to it, and I see it above all as a dilemma neither of the body nor of the brain, but of the spirit."[21] Here in its most extreme form is the idea that one's soul is sexed and must conform to its sexed body. Biologically essentialist claims have also been embedded in medicalized understandings of transsexuality as a "disease" caused by, for example, hormonal imbalance.

Thus feminists such as Raymond point to the essentialisms implicit in medical and popular models of transsexuality, and have constructed MTF transsexuals in particular as reinforcing politically suspect line drawing between female and male. Raymond's interpretation of transsexuals' testimony reinforces an understanding of MTFs as mimicking and reinscribing a patriarchal construct of femininity. Thus, the argument runs, dominant accounts of transsexuality reify a binarism that should properly—in the interests of both adequate explanation and effective political strategy—be deconstructed. The paradox of this position is that similarly located feminists have also been critical of transsexuals for the latter's failure to recognize the *inflexibility* of gender boundaries. Arguing that MTF transsexuals are not "real women," many radical feminists have resisted including MTFs in the category. Border wars over the admission of MTF transsexuals to women-only festivals and organizations, for example, continue to divide feminist communities.[22] Such arguments for the exclusion of MTFs shy away from explicitly essentialist claims about the biological basis of femininity, claiming instead that they do not have the experience of childhood female socialization in a patriarchal society, or that transsexuals will contaminate women's hard-won separate space with their "male energy" or desire to appropriate. Nonetheless, the use of the euphemism "womyn-born-womyn" to characterize those who *are* counted seems to belie this claim. (One cannot, surely, since Beauvoir, be "born" a woman?)

This contradictory feminist position relies on a partial account of transsexed identities that is rarely in keeping with transsexuals' own understandings. As I have shown, there exist numerous dominant essentializing models of femininity—each endorsed by some anti-feminist women—alongside diverse feminist alternatives. Likewise in transsexual theorizing, the conservatism of a Morris can be juxtaposed with more radical and politically astute accounts of trans-subjectivity, such as those offered by Kate Bornstein, Leslie Feinberg, Jay Prosser, and Susan Stryker.[23] Many of these theorists are themselves critical of the essentialisms in medical discourses, but they point out that conformity to medical gatekeepers' expectations is a central criterion for gaining access to surgeries or hormone treatments. Surgeons, physicians, and psychiatrists persistently reinscribe oppressive gender scripts and construct normative heterosexuality when they insist on pre-op transsexuals living *as a man*, or *as a woman*, in their most patriarchal and essentialist senses, or demand that MTF transsexuals endure more pain or surgical intervention in the interests of, for example, acquiring a vagina "deep enough" for penile penetration.[24] These treatments are important in a culture that demands that one's sexed body minimally conform to one's gender presentation not least for personal safety and legal purposes. Changing information technology has made critiques of medical practices more accessible and thus more widely integrated into transsexuals' constructions of their own needs, and some are organizing against certain medical and psychiatric norms. Again, different trans-theorists have different attitudes to body modification, and a growing movement among transgendered men in particular argues against it, partly in light of the poor aesthetic and functional quality of phalloplasties, but also on political grounds.

The arguments I have put forward against the reduction of the category "women" to any set of necessary and sufficient conditions provide compelling philosophical reasons against the methodologically essentialist view that MTFs cannot count. The appeal to "womyn-born-womyn" first fails as a biological criterion: it seems also to exclude intersexuals who have been surgically constructed as female perinatally and lived their lives as girls and women, while including FTM transsexuals who are living as men. Politically speaking, too, the exclusion of MTFs from women-only space relies on a blanket characterization of the motivations and histories of a diverse group. Furthermore, this is a group whose members are systematically stigmatized and harassed for gender trangressions and who struggle for recognition as "women" in a culture that insists on a conformity that for most will only ever be partly achieved. MTF transsexual narratives frequently dispute the presumed trajectory of a male-privileged life prior to transition, instead positing a turbulent and silenced experience of gender ambivalence, accompanied by attempts at gender discipline and abuse from others.[25] These experiences of gender oppression seem to provide a useful basis for alliance with non-trans-feminists. That some MTFs do not have feminist consciousness, or have self-understandings with which some radical feminists disagree, hardly distinguishes them from "womyn-born-womyn."

The advent of queer theory, the genres of postmodern politics, and burgeoning political movements that give voice to trans-activists have led to new and subtler feminist questions about trans-identities than Raymondian positions allow. What are the lived realities of being neither woman nor man, as some radical transsexuals now describe themselves, and what can non-trans-feminist theorists learn from them? What insights into the political consciousness of gender can trans-feminist theorists offer other feminists?

How does the historical and sociological study of the changing shape of trans-identities make visible the cultural politics of gender ambiguity? How can non-trans-feminists locate themselves in relation to trans-theorists in ways that avoid appropriating or colonizing trans-lives as a curiosity or theoretically "useful" case study? What is required of me, ethically and politically, in order successfully to build solidarity with transsexed and transgendered activists who not only differ from me but whose self-understandings I sometimes find theoretically and politically troubling (as they sometimes do mine)? How can pro-feminist theorists of transsexuality integrate the ambivalence of transsexuals themselves toward essentialist and social constructionist discourses?[26] Rubin writes of his struggle to accommodate the reactions of his FTM research participants to his initial historical analysis. His account did not jibe with the discourse of authenticity preferred by most of his interlocutors.[27] While all radical political theorists must deal on some level with this gap between testimony and interpretation, in the case of an already vilified and silenced minority group (such as FTM transsexuals) the methodological dilemma is particularly acute.

In posing these large questions I want to indicate, first, the connections between trans-theory and critiques of essentialism; second, I want to endorse the extension of the border of the concept "women" to include MTF transsexuals, suggesting that this move is supported by my Wittgensteinian feminist approach. The question "are MTF transsexuals women?" is not well-formed in the absence of a fixed set of criteria of womanhood to which we can appeal. I suggest that MTF transsexuals bear family resemblances to those people conventionally labeled "women" and that there is no mistake entailed in calling them women. This endorsement, however, need not imply that all claimants to the title "woman" need be uncritically embraced by any coalition of feminists struggling to carve out a space of resistance. The term does not lose all meaning merely because a novel contested use has won the battle for acceptance. Again, which uses should be accepted by any marginalized group is a contextual and strategic question. The criteria of difference offered by some feminists, (for example, the experience of what Naomi Scheman calls "perinatal pinking"—that is, "having been named female around the time of birth"[28]) may mean that in some contexts there are good political reasons for stressing that transsexed women are distant rather than close relations of the women making the judgment about inclusion or exclusion. Thus part of the challenge of my analysis comes from its insistence that deciding whom to exclude (or include) in a given political context is a power struggle, in which the dominant members of an existing group vie with the peripheral members, rather than an exercise in ontological correctness.

To make this clear, let me give another example in which my judgment is that *exclusion* is most politically appropriate move. Jacquelyn Zita, in her widely cited article, "Male Lesbians and the Postmodernist Body," poses the question "can men be lesbians?"[29] Zita asks whether a theory of the postmodern body might allow men to occupy the subject-position of women-loving-women. If this subject-position is an historical construction, a place-holder in a range of identities rather than a natural kind, then a given body may merely occupy that space rather than define it. Clearly there is something Wittgensteinian in this: "The 'male lesbian' is not saying that occupants of this category are not lesbians, but that the category needs to be stretched—not by adding men, but by adding men who happen to be lesbians."[30]

The central drawback to this suggestion is that the theory works to its logical conclusions by focusing on subjectivity as a linguistic space rather than on the politics of the bodily experience of the agent and how she is located in a material context of oppression. There are reasons for drawing the line around the concept "lesbian" in such a way that it includes those who have lived experience of desiring women while occupying a female-coded body, given the deeply significant social and political ramifications of this experience. Furthermore, the appropriation of the term "lesbian" by male-bodied, male-gendered men—not all of whom, in my experience and as my prediction, are or would be even minimally well-intentioned or politically astute—would result in tangible political losses: less "female lesbian"-only space, a fading of the distinct character of lesbian communities, or a weakening of the ability powerfully to name oneself "lesbian," for example. The central difference between this case and the MTF transsexual example is that the use of the term "lesbian" to apply to men fails deeply to challenge conventional understandings of sex and gender boundaries: a person with a male body who changes her gender presentation to female, feminist caveats notwithstanding, is disturbing an established frontier around the concepts "women" and "men." She will likely struggle for a recognition that will never be comfortably attained in a trans-phobic and essentialist culture, and will often be punished for her transgressions. The straight man dating women who suddenly renames himself "lesbian," no matter how astutely he reworks his own subjectivity, however, is unlikely to be recognized as a gender outlaw unless he also modifies his gender presentation. Lesbianism is not only a state of mind. The more radical move for the woman-identified man, it seems to me, would be to remain nominally heterosexual, but to show by example the (admittedly constrained) progressive possibilities for that subject-position.

Thus it is often the case that, even as we accept the radical ontological consequences of an anti-essentialist Wittgensteinian approach, we must pay careful attention to the political consequences of where we draw lines around terms. Zita's discussion points not to an affirmative answer to the question "can men be lesbians?" but to the need for justificatory strategies that emphasize the material political gains and losses of line drawing in specific contexts. Ambiguously sexed bodies, trans-identities, the case of the male lesbian, and other examples illuminate the politically salient, as well as the variously constructed, qualities of sex and gender boundaries. These examples highlight the fluidity of the boundary around the concept "women," and the possibilities for challenge to conventional usages. While our ontological concerns give us some freedom in leaving terms open, however, the strategic imperatives of politics require objects of comparison; they demand that we draw boundaries around terms to use them as "measuring rods." As Linda Zerilli says,

> Politics consists precisely in the making of claims, which being claims, are inevitably partial and thus exclusive. . . . That the claim "we women demand x" excludes some women turns not on the theoretical insight (in the study) into the exclusionary character of the category of women but rather on the political character of making claims (in a public space).[31]

Making a concept comparatively useful might entail that its boundary be firmly, albeit not immutably, fixed. Wittgenstein recognizes the need for some conceptual delimiting; however, he urges us to acknowledge the contingent nature of our terms, and to view them as purposive tools rather than "a preconceived idea to which reality must correspond."

None of the foregoing implies that all categories are oppressive and that women should therefore cease to lay claim to gender as an explanatory element of social theory. The excessive reluctance to draw lines around terms can be just as ontologically misguided and politically unhelpful as essentialism, not least because I sometimes suspect that this kind of theory is written by those who can afford to let their philosophical imaginations run away with them, leaving more prosaic politics behind for the less privileged. Some anti-essentialist philosophical strategies give the impression that their exponents toy with, or are titillated by, the kind of examples that make an anti-essentialist case, rather than examining how, in the light of anti-essentialism, we can move on and construct useful feminist theory. To claim, for example, that "woman can never be defined" may constitute a valuable critical contention within an existing philosophical discourse yet does not obviously further feminist projects that must draw on the notion of specific groups of women, united in some identifiable set of experiences or political objectives.[32]

I have come up against a familiar paradox: namely, that at the same time as feminists try to subvert the stereotypical categories established by patriarchy, we may wish to defend the conceptual limits of the categories women create for ourselves. Otherwise everything becomes available for co-optation, and in the process feminist claims lose their political saliency. Overcoming the "bewitchment of our intelligence by means of language" is not simply a matter of opening every conceptual boundary and inviting everybody in. It consists in careful attention to the political and ethical implications of where we draw lines around terms, not on philosophical well-wishing.

Between the poles of radical deconstruction and rigid essentialism lies a large philosophical terrain, and it is here that Wittgenstein sets us down. His choice is plain: we can leave a concept open (using it in the knowledge that its constituents have no common disjunctive property), or we can draw a line around it for a purpose. Here there is a case for taking very seriously the possibly negative political implications of that boundary, yet even a concept with "blurred edges" is identifiable. In some cases refusing to allow any politically motivated limits of meaning might have negative political connotations, as I showed above. Some commentaries on categories like "women" and "lesbians" seem excessively reluctant to draw boundaries, and in leaving terms gaping risk political vacuity and ineptitude. There are good political reasons for being inexact about what we mean in many cases, yet at other times philosophy must not be allowed to run ahead of the political reality with which it contends, lest it participate in the creation of deconstructive theories that are as far from usage and experience as the metaphysics they seek to undermine.

### From "Slippery Ice" to "Rough Ground"

Implicit in my argument so far is the belief that anti-essentialism, in all its versions, has become a set of key insights into "difference," exclusion, and feminist theoretical method. These insights, co-opting Judith Butler's words, are "notions [that] have entered into an historical crisis that no amount of reflection can reverse." [33] Few feminist theorists, however, have taken up the challenge of exploring how anti-essentialist philosophy might relate to empirical social research paradigms, or to political practice—that is, what to *do* with anti-essentialism. And while feminist political practices have engaged with exclusion, difference, and power in numerous sites, this engagement deserves to be articulated in closer connection with anti-essentialist feminist theory. These are strange lacunae in light of the fear of vapid generalization and the desire to contextualize that supposedly characterize all forms of anti-essentialist feminism. We know that "there are no short cuts through women's lives," but where are the better paths? [34]

In the following two chapters, I examine the implications of my anti-essentialist account for feminist practice and point out ways in which practice may shape anti-essentialism. Part of my overall argument in this book is that anti-essentialism gains its critical force by bringing to feminism a contextual critique of power relations among women. Philosophizing about "difference" may well make clearer to us how oppression is reinscribed by certain theoretical moves. But, as my Wittgensteinian analysis highlights, moving toward the "rough ground" of feminist practice is an essential part of formulating a feminist theory that incorporates plurality in ways which respond to the exigencies of, for example, feminist research and feminist activism.

Any anti-essentialist claim is under-determined by feminist theory. In this case, any account of the similarities and differences among women must be informed by some empirical considerations: which group of women do we mean? At what time? In what place? And the materiality of sex and gender oppression constrains and directs legitimate generalization. But these questions cannot simply be labeled "empirical" or "material" without further investigation into the social construction of material reality. After all, Friedan's *Feminine Mystique*, one of the Second Wave texts most widely criticized for falsely generalizing, is avowedly "empirical," based on numerous interviews with women "all over America." [35] Despite its claims to universality, Friedan's method is nonetheless vulnerable to criticism for extrapolating from her own experience, for constructing "women" in her own image. As a feminist investigator,

> I have to have decided what kind of similarity or difference I am interested in. It makes no sense to ask simply whether women are similar or different—I have to specify in what way they might be similar or different. Moreover, I have to employ criteria of sameness and difference—I have to use some measure by which I decide whether they are the same or different in the specified way. And finally, I have to determine the significance of the similarities and differences I find. [36]

The Wittgensteinian injunction to "look and see," occasionally invoked by philosophers as the last word, seems to me (as a political theorist with training in social science, sometime activist, and reluctant philosopher) to be only the beginning of feminist investigation into anti-essentialism.

In putting forward "anti-essentialist" ways of thinking about feminism, I have interdependent philosophical and political reasons for avoiding the purely critical project of pointing out homogenizing tendencies in political theorists' invocations of social groups. I am concerned that "accusations" of essentialism are not only theoretically confused, but also politically stifling. For example, two well-known feminists who are among those most often labeled "essentialist," both in published critiques and in academic conversation, are Carol Gilligan and Catharine MacKinnon. Anti-essentialist challenges to their work have, in some cases, been both theoretically sophisticated and politically compelling, bringing out buried assumptions about gender and hidden exclusions that require correction. I cannot help noticing, however, that both women are feminists deeply concerned with political action: in MacKinnon's case, as a feminist litigator and anti-pornography activist, and in Gilligan's, as a social psychologist involved in the empowerment of adolescent girls. As I will discuss with regard to Gilligan in Chapter 4 and MacKinnon in Chapter 5, this very concern with political action leaves them open to charges of essentialism. Feminists should be worried about a theoretical trend that risks undermining feminist political action rather than making it more just.

In what follows I develop anti-essentialist claims about power and exclusion, while sounding a note of caution about the implications of a principled anti-essentialism. As Kathy Ferguson says, "Genealogy ruthlessly pursued tends to avoid the problem of political action, not because it is incapable of allowing for political distinctions and moral claims, but because the evocation of difference does not in itself tell us which differences are most worthy of our attention." [37] This latter project requires criteria; it will not be enough to list "differences" without offering specific analyses or weightings of their significance. Thus the common objection that anti-essentialism necessitates the endless proliferation of categories of analysis, requiring an impossibly complex and analytically vacuous social theory (or, simply, "a very long book" that regretfully cannot be accomplished), falters here at the first hurdle. This refusal to engage anti-essentialist critiques, however, in part reflects the lack of available methods for justifying particular analytical choices, and the preeminence of certain social theoretical categories that are themselves taken to require no justification or nuance. We need feminist methods for implementing anti-essentialism since neither the interminable deconstruction nor the uncritical reification of the category "women" is adequate to the demands of feminist practice. Philosophical aims do not have to dictate conceptual categories any more than matters of direct observation. As Martin argues:

> While a person engaging in feminist scholarship is guided by both political and intellectual purposes and values, these no more dictate one's the-

oretical categories than do one's data. Just as different sets of categories will be consonant with a given body of data, alternate conceptualizations will be compatible with a given set of values and purposes. The question of which categories we should choose cannot be answered in advance of inquiry or decided upon once and for all because the contexts of our investigations change over time and so do our interests and purposes. Further, everyone need not choose the same categories. Indeed, if the categories that feminist theorists have been recommending seem to fit some research interests and purposes, the general categories that feminist theorists have told us to shun may turn out to be appropriate to other projects.[38]

Thus it strikes me that debates about anti-essentialism are in fact often making normative claims about *how to do* feminism. That is, arguments that feminist theory should be contextual, or should pay attention to differences between women, or should use generalizing categories only with the explicit recognition that they are contingent constructions, are claims not only about how to construct new and more sophisticated theoretical accounts of women's oppression, but about how more obviously empirical feminist goals should be met. This seems to me a point where the professed interdisciplinarity of women's studies might most fruitfully be developed. For surely questions about the nature and legitimacy of generalizations about women are *empirical*, however we understand this term?

Part of this concern with the "empirical" (a favored social scientific term) is also a concern with the *material* (the term of choice of many social theorists). Iris Young, in her treatment of the same philosophical problem I have been discussing in this chapter, proposes that Sartre's notion of "seriality" provides a useful way of thinking about women as a social collective. The term "series" describes a social collective "whose members are unified passively by the objects their actions are oriented around and/or by the objectified results of the material effects of the actions of the others."[39] One of the main attractions of seriality as regards "women" is thus the relation of a series to "practico-inert" objects: "as a series *woman* is the name of a structural relation to material objects as they have been produced and organized by a prior history, which carries the material necessities of past practices congealed in their matter."[40] Young is concerned to identify the background constraints against which "women" come into being, and to decouple gender from identity in order to avoid imposing homogeneity. I think the concept of seriality is useful here, but it does not obviously negotiate a path between the Scylla of false generalization and the Charybdis of gender skepticism. What it does do, however, is draw attention to the sometimes competing theoretical demands of the material conditions that constrain individuals in ways that bring "women" into existence, and the desire to articulate an identity-concept "women" that captures women's experiences. To be a woman is neither merely to occupy a subject-position over-determined by structures of oppression, nor to understand oneself as possessing an originary, authentic identity. Thus in thinking about "women" we need constantly to maintain a dual perspective, looking at the larger social relations that constrain identity construction, and at the phenomenology of women's experiences. The family resemblance concept "women" describes interconnecting identities that are experienced and constructed in the context of a material history. Thus to "look and see" requires attention to both the structural relations in which "women" are embedded, and women's identities as they emerge from those relations. Neither of these perspectives alone will be adequate to the task of understanding women as a social collective.

We draw boundaries around "women" in order to use that category for a specific purpose. I take a corollary of this to be an important anti-essentialist point; i.e., that we deconstruct and reconstruct meaning *through* our use of categories. Such feminist processes, however, also take place in patriarchal contexts where ideas about "women" are constructed through the material conditions of different women's lives. The justification of boundaries around the use of terms will never be a purely abstract linguistic undertaking. The points that anchor these boundaries are themselves defined by the material conditions and lived experiences of women, as in the examples above. But these conditions and experiences (including lived experience of the female body) are always already socially constructed. The fragility of resistance can be exacerbated by theoretical and political insistence on the rejection of those categories that enable us to make sense of our opponents. Thus to fail to give examples of my anti-essentialist feminism in action, on the rough ground, would be to reinscribe those relations of power that my arguments aim to make visible.

Within this book, the move to examine some of the practice-oriented ways in which anti-essentialism might be relevant is in direct response to my exegesis of the tail-chasing that dominates the essentialism debates, as well as a Wittgensteinian skepticism toward theory. Divorcing claims about generalization from concrete political contexts within which those claims are relevant puts us onto "slippery ice." That is, when we talk about the pitfalls of making generalizations, or the need to emphasize difference over sameness, we run the risk of privileging abstract philosophical discussion over the "rough ground" of practice. Again, there is no straightforwardly accessible truth about the right kinds of categories to invoke; we cannot simply point to reality to make objective claims about the similarities and differences that unite and divide women, as the following discussions of research methods and activism will illustrate.

My own experience as a feminist theorist, teacher, and activist gives me personal reason to be concerned with the failure of feminist theory to connect with practice. I take seriously the contributions of feminist theorizing both to changing the academy and to informing feminist practice, and I want to avoid the potential anti-intellectualism of a naive flight from theory. But activism yields a certain kind of knowledge about particular social contexts that is often erased within feminist theorizing. For example, when I first started to organize against sexual violence, as a feminist who does not identify as a survivor of sexual abuse, I realized that I had seriously under-estimated the pervasiveness and the social significance of myths about incest. Observing how individuals, many of whom have quite "progressive" politics in other respects, reinscribe both crass and subtle stereotypes and fallacies made me realize that popular conceptions of childhood, power, "the family," and sexuality combined in potent ways to undermine women's credibility and confidence, including their ability to speak authoritatively in classrooms on unrelated topics.[41]

First, the knowledge I have gained through activism makes feminism seem much more beleaguered in the world at large than it does in some academic contexts (although it is beleaguered enough in those).[42] This knowledge reveals the continued dominance of sexist, dichotomous understandings of gender, and the need for oppositional discourses that take a clear and unambivalent form. Second, it brings into focus the imperatives of practice, including the material conditions that sustain patriarchy. I am not suggesting that the relative privilege of feminist theory can or should simply be replaced with the privileging of practice, and any attempt to fix this distinction will always ultimately be untenable. I do not want to assume a moral high ground, where "activist" concerns are arbitrarily distinguished from "theoretical" issues. But the respectable salaries, relatively comfortable working conditions, and social prestige accorded to securely employed academic feminists create standpoints quite different from the standpoints of feminists working in sexual assault centers, women's centers, feminist bookstores, and so on, in ways which need to be more explicitly acknowledged in academic feminist writing.

Finally, the project integrating activism and theory mapped out here offers a partial resolution of the dilemma that plagued Wittgenstein in a different context. He believed that the dissolution of conventional metaphysics and of the "bewitchment of our understanding" by language leaves no justifiable role for the "armchair philosopher." Hence he enjoined his pupils to be actors in the world and to abandon academic philosophy. What he leaves is a "therapy" in philosophy that can itself serve educational goals, but which, maybe more importantly, de-legitimates the search for a single truth and sends us out instead to investigate multiple language games. Thus addressing essentialism requires a change in the role of the philosopher, by identifying the rough ground as a domain of thought and engagement.

I have sketched the usefulness of Wittgenstein's philosophical method to anti-essentialist feminism, showing not only how it offers a critique of certain ways of thinking, but also a way to go on, a philosophical therapy. His notion of family resemblance provides a way of reconceptualizing the similarities and differences among women, and his account of purposive line drawing provides a tool for halting the extreme fragmentation some forms of anti-essentialism seem to recommend. Wittgenstein's skepticism toward philosophy and his injunction to "look and see" are part of what motivates the interdisciplinary feminist project I have outlined here. From a vantage point outside the disciplinary boundary of contemporary western philosophy, many of my arguments seem self-evident, and the rough ground appears as familiar terrain. "Of course," many feminists might say, "when have we ever done anything but start from women's lives?" But for those who remain "bewitched" by essentialism, whether as reluctant advocates or as stalwart critics, a developed Wittgensteinian feminism could offer a methodological path between two extremes: one extreme affirms the unity of women in ways that are inattentive to difference and reify artifacts of oppression, while the other toys with the philosophical limits of categories in ways that discredit valuable generalizing analyses of the oppression of women and undermine unifying feminist political goals.

With these concerns in mind, in Chapter 5, "Between Theory and Practice," I examine in more detail the claim that feminist analyses can avoid essentialism by basing themselves in practice. In particular, I challenge MacKinnon's claim that her theory of women's oppression is not essentialist because grounded in empirical reality, women's experience, and feminist practice, arguing that she begs the crucial question of how essentialism is inscribed in all these categories. Wittgensteinian feminism offers important insights into the fragmentation and consolidation of "women" in activist sites, and I examine some specific examples of power and exclusion that might dictate the terms of our purposive line drawing around categories such as "women." Before that, I turn in Chapter 4 to feminist research methods and examine the potential for essentialism and anti-essentialism in Gilligan's developmental model of girls' psychology.

# Chapter 4

## "Look and See": Gilligan and Feminist Research

What does the injunction "look and see" actually demand? Which practical contexts might we choose to rework in the light of the tension between essentialism and anti-essentialism, and how might our theories be shaped by the exigencies of practice? Recall that at the end of Chapter 2 I pointed to an unacknowledged consensus among anti-essentialist authors that feminism needs generalizing claims but that neither the a priori affirmation of sameness nor that of difference is adequate to the task of constructing feminist theories. In Chapter 3, I argued in a similar vein for a return to the "rough ground" of feminist practice as a means of ending the tail-chasing of the essentialism versus anti-essentialism debates in feminist philosophy. To elaborate variations on this theme is a major and under-explored interdisciplinary project in feminist studies, which has been framed in the abstract but not made concrete by feminists concerned with the set of issues surrounding essentialism.

"Look and see" cannot be merely a philosopher's gesture, a recommendation for a kind of naive empiricism, nor can it be a simple appeal to materiality or "material conditions" as the foundation of feminism. Feminist philosophies of science and social science have revealed the political complexities of our investigations into natural and social worlds as well as the ways in which these investigations are shaped by our epistemological inheritances, cultural and historical specificity, and social locations. And far from methodological a priorism, most feminist philosophy has always understood itself as based on the realities of women's lives. Thus there is no clear distinction to be drawn between "the empirical" (or "the material") and "the philosophical" in this debate, and indeed the crux of my own argument is that this very distinction is untenable. The potential of interdisciplinary work across those broad and diverse fields commonly distinguished as "philosophy" and "social science," however, has been under-explored with regard to the essentialism debates. This chapter redresses, on the one hand, the lack of feminist philosophical examination of specific attempts to justify empirically based generalizations about women. On the other hand, it points to the under-theorizing of some feminist commentary on social research methods, which serves to divorce the insights of feminist philosophers into the epistemology of generalization and difference from the insights of feminist social researchers engaged in particular projects that aim to analyze (and sometimes to change) oppressive social contexts.

I proceed by articulating, first, the connections between feminist research and the methodological problem to which my Wittgensteinian feminism provides a solution: namely, how to avoid falsely generalizing claims at the same time as we construct empirically based accounts of women's oppression. I ask how false claims about the "sameness" of women's experiences and identities can enter research processes, obscuring relations of power, as well as how over-eager "anti-essentialist" criticism can diminish the value of research and undercut attempts to investigate and change instances of gender oppression. One way to explore the implications of this tension, recommended by a Wittgensteinian method, is to offer examples of research that engage it. Second, therefore, in this chapter I present a case study of a feminist theorist and researcher widely censured for essentialism who has attempted to respond to methodological criticism without letting go of the political aspects of her research.

Carol Gilligan's analyses of women's and girls' distinctive voices are an example of both the limitations and the necessity of generalizations about gender. I introduce her work to highlight how feminist theorists have failed to move on from dismissive anti-essentialist critique to more nuanced, practical engagement with her political projects. I delineate criticisms of Gilligan's earlier work for its essentialism, and interpret her most recent book, *Between Voice and Silence: Women and Girls, Race and Relationship*, co-authored with Jill McLean Taylor and Amy Sullivan, as her attempt, in part, to respond to charges of methodological essentialism.[1] This book revises her original method and thereby escapes those charges of essentialism leveled at her earlier work.

Feminist theorists who claim that Gilligan reifies femininity and draws overly general conclusions about women from the experiences of only a small group, I argue, are often cavalier in their dismissal of her political projects. They fail to recognize both the political value and the nuance of her work. This argument is not intended as a straightforward defense of Gilligan's theses in moral psychology or of the ethic of care in feminist moral philosophy; indeed, I find much to disagree with in these theories. Instead, it aims to articulate the conditions that would have to be met for Gilligan's method to evade charges that it is "essentialist." Gilligan meets surprisingly many, although not all, of these conditions. Although she does show an attentiveness to key axes of difference among girls and women that her critics have not recognized, her method fails fully to meet anti-essentialist challenges, in large part because she lacks certain methodological resources needed to make adequate contextual judgements about power. Thus her new work ultimately remains open to criticism for failing fully to incorporate the insights of a more practice-oriented anti-essentialism. I present these criticisms as conversational openings that suggest useful revisions to Gilligan's method, rather than as evidence that her project can be simply dismissed.

"Feminist research" is an essentially contested concept. I bracket here the debates about whether feminist research currently has any one distinctive method and assume that feminist research across humanistic and social scientific traditions draws eclectically on various epistemological frameworks and techniques.[2] By "research" I mean any form of structured inquiry into any social context, whether it is performed by outside investigators — such as professional academics or consultants — or by members of the group or community under investigation, or both. Feminist researchers employ a diversity of techniques, from statistical analyses of large data sets to the ethnography of everyday life. This chapter examines how and why Wittgensteinian anti-essentialism might be incorporated into qualitative research settings, in particular in contexts where dialogue between researcher and participants are the main research method. In order to be "feminist," such research should at least be methodologically motivated by the interests of oppressed and marginalized groups, with an integrated account of how gender contributes to oppression and marginalization. Different feminist methodologists interpret such definitional requirements in different ways, and it is beyond the scope of this book to summarize the existing literature on feminist critiques of social science and feminist research methods.[3] Here I want to focus on how feminist empirical inquiry, broadly construed, might be inflected by essentialism and anti-essentialism.

Early theoretical discussions of research methods by white, middle-class, and "First World" feminists brought feminist political movements into academia to challenge the literal and implicit exclusion and derogation of women in the theories and categories of the humanities and social sciences. Most of these commentators on social research took men as a group whose interests were served by conventional methods, and invoked "women" as a counter-category. Prior to around 1980, much feminist discussion of nonfeminist research methods thus engaged largely in a response to the exclusion of any women or of women's interests from methodological concerns. This literature situated itself primarily in opposition to a practice of social science that invokes a familiar agenda of objectivity, detachment from research subjects, transparently knowable social truths, and the virtues of generalizability and quantifiability.

Its neglect of power differences among women notwithstanding, much of this methodological writing and actual research was essentialist in ways that enabled privileged feminists to attain significant, albeit partial, political goals. Bringing falsely general claims about "women" into contexts where all women are excluded does not constitute an adequate feminist politics, and certainly much feminist research both created and perpetuated overly general claims about women's oppression. It also opened up, however, a critical space for counter-hegemonic objections to conventional, sexist social scientific inquiry. These objections center on both the content of social research and on method: not only are research results about "people" often drawn from all-male subject groups, but the very "ways of knowing" that characterize malestream social inquiry have been brought into question. For example, when women have been studied, they have often been relatively powerless within the research context and their lives not understood as enmeshed in a system of gender oppression. Traditional research has seldom viewed political change as one of its goals; women have frequently been exploited by researchers prying into their lives with no aim of reciprocity or support.[4] This approach, while limited in its ambit, nonetheless created the conditions of possibility for a more thoroughgoing feminist critique of some of the categories employed by feminists themselves. The feminist anti-essentialist challenge has therefore been to question, in ways by now familiar, the category "women." This challenge has been a necessary corrective, given the growing recognition that much academic feminist research, while often marginalized in social scientific disciplines, has been implicated in the same forms of essentialism I have been discussing with regard to feminist philosophy.

More recent work in this area therefore takes up questions of power relations among women, pointing toward new epistemological and methodological frameworks. Many feminist researchers are at pains to inflect or contextualize the category "women" in methodological discussions. References to "women" researchers and "women" subjects must be understood as appeals that are themselves cross-cut with other axes of power. Likewise, an initial contrast with sexist research that assumes or argues that "women" have different interests in the process and outcome of research projects than "men" has been qualified by the recognition that women have different interests from each other, or different interests from different groups of men. For example, feminists have criticized Maria Mies's widely cited discussions of action research in a battered women's shelter, which construct the goal of feminist research as "collectivizing" women's experiences through identification of the researcher with the researched.[5] This approach may homogenize the experiences of significantly different women, where the power of the researcher enables this process. As Diane Wolf asks:

> Can we truly offer the view from below, when we are far above it, looking down? Can middle-class women actually "drop down" in class status, even temporarily? [Mies'] approach may emphasize activism and may point to certain differences between the researcher and the researched, but the assumption is still that such differences can be bridged in a meaningful manner. The power differentials that exist in the research hierarchy are not problematized as posing an insurmountable problem. Finally, the role of the researcher as an initiator or catalyst for change in the lives of disadvantaged women is encouraged by Mies rather than critically questioned as a foreign, neocolonialist intrusion.[6]

Methodological discussions have sometimes been inflected with essentialism in part because of the familiar assumption that diversity among women "subjects" makes it hard to generate feminist theory. For example, Cannon et al. point out, "To generate theory, it is much more useful if the small samples under study are relatively homogeneous, since extreme diversity makes the task of identifying common patterns almost impossible. Unfortunately, *as a result*, much of the newly emerging scholarship on women excludes women of color and working-class women of all races."[7]

This "result," however, clearly does not emerge only from a desire to keep samples homogeneous, but also from the predominance of certain identities among feminist researchers and certain relations of power within research processes. Explicitly recognizing, theorizing, and accommodating these relations constitutes an important direction for the maturing field of feminist methodology.[8] For example, the falling out of favor of the term "subject" and its replacement with less objectifying terms such as "interviewee" or "participant" demonstrates feminist recognition of this problem, albeit offering only a semantic solution. While a premise of early feminist research was that of "identifying with" "subjects" (i.e., seeing in the situation of one's participants something of one's own identity or experience of oppression), this premise has been challenged by asking which criteria make such identification possible or desirable. An uncritical assumption that one has a particular identity or experience of oppression in common with one's participants reflects an implicit additive analysis made possible by the power of the researcher over the subject. The belief that "as a woman" one shares some particular set of experiences or identity with the women whom one is researching may be realistic in some cases. Yet to presume that there is a more general form of identification with women "as women" is an essentialist claim of the kind I have been criticizing. The fact that, in most cases, the researcher shapes the terms of the research gives her the power to cast the research experience as one of feminist "identification," using her categories to make the participant's identity or experience conform to hers, rather than vice versa.

For example, Catherine Riessman analyses the interview transcripts of an Anglo middle-class and Hispanic working-class woman, each speaking to a white middle-class woman interviewer about her separation from her husband. Riessman argues that the Anglo woman organizes her narrative temporally and is well understood within the gendered framework familiar to the feminist interviewer:

> This collaborative [interview] process was aided by gender, class, and cultural congruity, which produced the unspoken but shared assumptive world of the two women. They implicitly agreed about how a narrative should be organized and about the content that was relevant to an account of marital separation.[9]

The Hispanic woman's narrative is episodic, but, Riessman argues, this is not grasped by the interviewer, who repeatedly tries to make her narrative fit the temporal framework with which she is more familiar:

The interviewer and the narrator struggled over who would control the topic and what constituted an adequate answer to the items on the schedule. . . . [D]espite gender congruity, the joint construction of an account of marital failure was hindered by the lack of shared cultural and class assumptions. The interviewer held onto the white, middle-class model of temporal organization and thus could not make sense of the episodic form that Marta used—the dramatic unfolding of a series of topics that were stitched together by theme rather than by time.[10]

Similarly, essentialism may be played out in the assumption of "trust" as a defining feature of feminist ethnography. Older discussions of feminist research are replete with claims about the self-evident "rapport" that develops between woman researcher and woman participant. While in many cases this kind of emotional bond may exist, it seems more likely to develop where there are small power differences and personal similarities between researcher and "subject." And this construction cannot make sense of situations in which the researcher is "studying up" or faces insider or outsider dilemmas that extend beyond gender.[11] These concerns about the fundamentally power-laden and exploitive nature of even the most methodologically cautious and overtly political feminist research have led some to ask whether truly feminist ethnography can *ever* be possible.[12] This is an important question, but ultimately I disagree with Judith Stacey's conclusion that the term "feminist research" is necessarily an oxymoron. There are too many areas of social life that are currently defined by patriarchy and where no feminist knowledge exists to guide our actions, as I illustrate later in this chapter in my discussion of Gilligan.

Thus I want to develop methods of feminist research that are capable of gendered critique and of highlighting the salience of gender in a particular research context, at the same time as they recognize other cross-cutting axes of difference and how power relations tend to reify certain accounts of gender. A Wittgensteinian feminist need not suppose any particular criteria of relevance when formulating or investigating any locus for research. She need not suppose, for example, that her participants will fulfil any necessary and sufficient conditions of womanness, nor that race, class, or any other differences will be more or less significant than gender in particular research contexts. Furthermore, in investigating the multiply nuanced meanings of gender in specific contexts, she can conceptualize similarities and differences among women as family resemblances rather than as identity relations or Otherness. Thus she avoids the dangers of universalizing from one group to another, and the familiar charge of relativism with regard to gender. Feminist researchers thus would not approach research contexts looking to find out what all women have in common, but looking for resemblances between their identities and experiences. Rather than posit an ideal type to which those identities and experiences do or do not correspond, they would be tentative about the significance of gender and its implications. Family resemblances thus offer feminist researchers a way to generalize without making sameness claims or asserting radical difference. The kinds of conclusions we will draw about women will be neither reductive nor theoretically significant solely in a single narrow context.

This kind of approach, however, is still in the process of being articulated. The recent response to essentialism in feminist theory and research has tended to approach essentialism as a "vice in itself," primarily representing a lack of intellectual rigor on the part of earlier feminists. We too often approach particular authors with the attitude that if essentialism can be discerned in the text, then the theorist's entire project can be discarded. Part of this intellectual trend, as I pointed out in Chapter 1, involves the fetishization of the dangers, pitfalls, and evils of "essentialism" as well as the demonization of those texts considered "essentialist." Identifying latent essentialism has all too often become critique for its own sake rather than an integral part of an ongoing constructive project. The problem-space defined by essentialism and anti-essentialism contains genuinely important ontological and political issues. But many feminists tend to throw the baby of political efficacy out with the bathwater of essentialism.

Nowhere is this trend more apparent than with regard to Carol Gilligan's projects in feminist psychology and politics over the past fifteen years.[13] Gilligan played a central role in bringing feminist analysis into the field of developmental psychology, showing how various models of "human" moral psychological development were actually premised on only one paradigmatic perspective, closely associated with masculine psychology. Her work has been unusually politically informed relative to her field, and increasingly premised on a feminist analysis that emphasizes the empowerment of girls and women.[14] Anti-essentialist challenges to Gilligan have been, in some cases, both theoretically sophisticated and politically compelling, bringing out buried assumptions about gender and hidden exclusions that are often crucial correctives. One cannot help noticing, however, that Gilligan is a feminist deeply concerned with political action. These very concerns motivate her to make claims that leave her open to charges of essentialism. Her theoretical categories, while admittedly unnuanced, provide a basis for feminist analysis and mobilization that is politically problematic at the same time as it can be enabling and galvanizing for many feminists working with girls in contexts in which the psychology of gender is under-theorized. Gilligan is certainly aware of anti-essentialist criticisms and has responded to them both theoretically and methodologically. This makes her an unusual and instructive figure in the essentialism debates. Many feminist philosophers are content to pursue the theoretical issues subsumed under "essentialism" without giving thought to how they might inflect practice, while many feminist social researchers remain intent on pursuing methods that make uncritical use of the category "women."

Thus the preoccupation of Gilligan's readers with exclusively critical analyses of *In a Different Voice* does a disservice to the increasing nuance and sophistication of her prolific work during the years since this book's first publication in 1982.[15] Gilligan has been treated shabbily by many of her theoretically inclined interlocutors, who otherwise generally espouse and practice both intellectual generosity and interpretive charity. The remarkably pervasive attitude of disdain toward her work among feminist philosophers—often, I suspect, a disdain based on a very cursory reading only of *In a Different Voice*—confirms Bordo's comments:

> I have often been dismayed at the anger that (white, middle-class) feminists have exhibited toward the work of Gilligan and Chodorow. This sort of visceral reaction to theorists of gender difference . . . is not elicited by their ethnocentrism or ahistoricism; it is specifically directed against what is perceived as their romanticization of female values such as empathy and nurturing. Such a harsh critical stance is protection, perhaps, against being tarred by the brush of female "otherness," of being contaminated by things "female."[16]

I want to make the related point that unfairly dismissive reactions to Gilligan are enabled by a theoretical orientation that does not understand itself as connected to feminist practice. My most fruitful discussions of Gilligan's work have not been with feminist philosophers but with feminist practitioners—a woman working on a children's helpline, a youth group leader, and training group facilitators at a sexual assault center, for example. Anyone who works with girls or young women, as I do, is aware of the paucity of feminist literature offering explanatory frameworks for their psychological struggles. University teachers (especially teachers of feminism), as professionals working with young women, need to invest in understanding young women's lives.

Psychology is not the only or even the best discipline within which to generate theories of women's oppression, and Gilligan's empirical work no more gives her an epistemically unassailable position than it does any other feminist. But as a perceptive psychologist who is well connected to numerous active and pragmatic feminist projects, particularly in education, she deserves our most charitable reading.

The challenge facing feminist theory thus lies in the observation that neither interminable deconstruction nor uncritical reification of the category "women" is adequate to the demands of feminist practice. The task we have inherited is to take seriously commitments entailed in anti-essentialism but to find ways effectively to incorporate them into counter-hegemonic political projects. Gilligan's *Between Voice and Silence* represents a departure from her earlier work in its explicit examination of race and class in the context of articulating girls' psychology. Yet Gilligan continues to make strong general claims about gender as a basis both for important analytical distinctions in psychological development and for feminist political mobilization. In what ways does Gilligan's method continue to be "essentialist"? What epistemological and political issues does Gilligan struggle with in trying to respond to charges of essentialism? Is this a kind of essentialism that she can avoid, and would its avoidance attenuate or advance her political goals? To answer these questions a good starting point is to articulate an example of feminist practice that understands anti-essentialism and political engagement as indispensably allied, rather than inevitably at odds.

### Carol Gilligan: The Arch-Essentialist?

*In a Different Voice* argues that conventional models of psychological development fail to understand the alternative paradigm of moral thinking Gilligan labels the "ethic of care." Existing psychological theory tends to cast women as failing to achieve separation from others, a separation attained with less ambivalence by men. Instead of labeling women as "less developed," Gilligan suggests that "the failure of women to fit existing models of human growth may point to a problem in the representation, a limitation in the conception of human condition, an omission of certain truths about life."[17] The ethic of care cannot simply be characterized as an imperative for self-sacrifice or denial. Gilligan recommends an understanding of women's psychological development as struggling to remain connected in ways that are desirable, healthy, and resistant, albeit politically laden.

Since completing the work on which *In a Different Voice* was founded, Gilligan and her collaborators have focused on qualitative research with adolescent girls in the United States. They claim that girls' crises and dilemmas offer not only a window on the systemic disempowerment of girls in "Western culture" but also potential strategies and techniques for resolving generic human problems. Although in some ways this work turns away from the ethical decision-making that was a central theme of *In a Different Voice*, it continues to ask critical questions about gender bias in psychological theory and about the value and meaning of interpersonal connection and relationship. By uncovering the texture of girls' psychologies, Gilligan wants to articulate how women can help girls to overcome disempowerment (and vice versa) and turn girls' healthy resistance into a political force rather than a form of psychological corrosion.

Gilligan depicts a turning point in girls' lives at adolescence that has profound and shocking resonances, I imagine, for many of her female readers, myself included. Gilligan perceptively describes girls' loss of self-confidence, self-esteem, and honest connection with others, at a time when they are more likely to develop depression, eating problems, and suicidal behavior and to become distanced from relationships with family, teachers, and friends. She characterizes such crises as "problems of connection" rather than as a failure adequately to separate, and by uncovering the roots of women's psychological disenfranchisement, she aims to provide an explanatory model that will offer insight into their continuing struggle as adults with problems of interpersonal (dis)connection:

> Teenage girls and adult women often seemed to get caught on the horns of a dilemma: was it better to respond to others and abandon themselves or to respond to themselves and abandon others? The hopelessness of this question marked an impasse in female development, a point where the desire for relationship was sacrificed for the sake of goodness, or for survival. Adolescence seemed to pose a crisis of connection for girls coming of age in Western culture.[18]

Gilligan locates girls' relational understandings of decision-making and moral dilemmas in contexts of oppression, arguing that girls' ethical perspectives are systematically marginalized and girls pressured to conform. "Human" problems, or at least some of the problems of "Western culture," she argues, can be illuminated by a clearer understanding of how girls negotiate disconnection, and how their understandings of relationship are obscured by patriarchy. In this sense Gilligan is avowedly feminist, her method including an explicit recognition of the devaluation and distortion of girls' voices in patriarchal culture as well as a commitment to allowing their voices to come to the fore and to incorporating them into feminist political solutions [BVS: 191]. By illuminating the developmental psychology of girls at adolescence, Gilligan hopes to make clear the transition from connection in childhood to disconnection in adulthood that both results from and reinscribes patriarchy.

The theoretical model for Gilligan's account of female adolescence continues to derive, albeit increasingly tenuously, from object relations theory. The key feminist premise of her account is that the central cause of male domination, in those societies where women are almost always primary parents, is separation of the self from the mother at a young age. This process of separation is supposedly the central cause of the masculine autonomous self with its "justice orientation" to moral problems and relationships. Girls, by contrast, retain their sense of relationship with their mothers (and others more generally) until adolescence, when they also go through a process of separation and dis-identification. Their experience, however, is complicated by patriarchy: girls are rewarded for dissociating from their desire to remain "in relationship" and are judged negatively if they fail to develop masculine attitudes to relationships and to ethical issues (as they were in Kohlberg's original psychological model). If they do adopt a masculine attitude, on Gilligan's account, they lose skills crucial to their healthy resistance to patriarchy. Thus at adolescence girls in western cultures face a double bind: they can either abandon their childhood knowledge of connection with others and lose a weapon in their struggle against patriarchy, or they can try to retain it and face being ostracized and negatively judged.

Gilligan continues to claim that her interviews illustrate ways in which girls are "out of relationship." But surely "relationship" (in the broad sense of connection with another person) is absolutely crucial to the development of all human beings at all stages of their lives? Girls who are disconnected and distant from family, teachers, and friends are obviously going to struggle psychologically. To add theoretical substance to this claim, therefore, Gilligan premises her theory of psychological development on a complex social ontology that conceptualizes healthy human lives as webs of relationships. Certain forms of dissociation or disconnection from these webs, she argues, are psychologically damaging for both women and men. Interpersonal dissociation is, however, both more typical of males, and is, in general, valued and rewarded by western patriarchal cultures. Gilligan thus implicitly characterizes as pathological certain masculine ways of not being in relationship, making the connection between these pathologies as individual dissociation, and as theorized phenomena in political and moral lives. Thus there is a normative sense in which we want to say that it is pathological for girls to become disconnected from relationships at adolescence:

> Efforts to be strong, self-reliant, and outspoken can be reasonable and effective survival strategies in a difficult, and sometimes hostile, environment. These efforts can cease to be adaptive, however, when they move to a position that precipitates disconnections from others, covering over vulnerabilities and the desire for relatedness [BVS: 68].

This theoretical framework is not always easy to detect in Gilligan's writing, which rarely contains arguments articulated in ways familiar to feminist philosophers. Gilligan's "findings" cannot be finitely and accurately catalogued and made transparent; instead, she offers an interpretive model developed through narrative, analogy, and examples. It is also a framework in a state of development and flux through her publications. Nevertheless, Gilligan does continue to draw upon all of the preceding claims even in her most recent work, arguing not only that this model is an accurate description of girls' experiences, but also that it provides a basis for feminist mobilization among older women determined to break damaging cycles of gender socialization and abandonment of girls and young women.

Given this admittedly imperfect theoretical underpinning, on what basis is Gilligan labeled an essentialist? Critics of *In a Different Voice* have implied three types of objections. Some have suggested that Gilligan's essentialism is of a particularly strong kind, claiming that in attributing the "ethic of care" to women she is reinforcing a biologically determinist notion of women's nature. For example, Linda Kerber writes:

> I agree with Gilligan that our culture has long undervalued nurturance and that when we measure ethical development by norms more attainable by boys than by girls our definition of norms is probably biased. But by emphasizing the biological basis of distinctive behavior . . . Gilligan permits her readers to conclude that women's alleged affinity for "relationships of care" is both biologically natural and a good thing.[19]

Gilligan displayed an early commitment to object relations theory and made use of Nancy Chodorow's work, which, while often subject to similar accusations of methodological essentialism, is clearly an approach that relies on socialization rather than biology.[20] Although *In a Different Voice* may be insufficiently explicit about the origins of gendered moral voices, at no point does Gilligan explicitly or implicitly argue that they are biological features of either men or women, where these features are understood as pre-social. She adopts a social constructionist model and makes quite clear that these different voices are learned, albeit at a very young age.

A second sense in which Gilligan might be labeled an "essentialist" stems from her alleged failure to place the ethic of care in its political context. She does seem to proceed with the assumption that the ethic of care represents an "authentic voice" (in an ill-defined sense) for women (or at least for some people) without adequately setting the stage to illustrate how the ethic of care is a "slave morality" formed in the limiting circumstances of oppression. Commentators have pointed out the disturbing similarities between ideologies of femininity such as the Victorian "angel in the house" and a description of women as caring and oriented toward relationship. In contemporary contexts, they argue, the "different voice" merely illustrates the survival skills women learn under patriarchy, which reflect the necessity of remaining attentive to the oppressor more than any kind of pre-patriarchal authenticity. Thus, the criticism goes, Gilligan valorizes socio-moral attitudes that are merely feminine, not feminist. Her analysis, if it is to be redeemed at all, should be more explicitly situated in a context of gender oppression and offer a transformative vision of a better, more politically challenging moral voice, not merely a description of the existing voices.[21]

A third set of criticisms stresses that Gilligan is an essentialist by virtue of her use of overly general categories. That is, critics allege she is a methodological essentialist in the sense I articulated earlier. As Fraser and Nicholson put it,

> By constructing a female countermodel, [Gilligan] invited the same charge of false generalization she had herself raised against Kohlberg, although now from other perspectives such as class, sexual orientation, race, and ethnicity. Gilligan's disclaimers notwithstanding, to the extent that she described women's moral development in terms of *a* different voice; to the extent that she did not specify which women, under which specific historical circumstances have spoken with the voice in question; and to the extent that she grounded her analysis in the explicitly cross-cultural framework of Nancy Chodorow, her model remained essentialist.[22]

Gilligan is apt to use broad general categories ("women," "Western culture," and so on). These categories are inclined to erase historically, culturally, and politically salient differences among their individual members.[23] Critics have observed that this tendency to generalize does not stress (but, it should be noted, does not necessarily deny) the socially constructed and necessarily local, temporally specific, and diverse nature of gender. These generalizations are not only philosophically undesirable because of their failure to contextualize; they are also undesirable because they are false. If feminists were to investigate the experiences of women and girls of color, working-class and poor women and girls, and so on, they would find that the model Gilligan first proposed is a less useful explanatory framework for the experiences of these "others." Thus many methodological anti-essentialist criticisms come from other social psychologists, who argue that Gilligan's two paradigms of moral thinking are present in both male and female "subjects"; that Gilligan's samples are too small; and that her analysis un-self-consciously describes a category "women" without critically examining the narrowness of her subject groups, the significant sociopolitical differences among women, or whether certain groups of men under conditions of oppression might not also systematically deploy an ethic of care.[24] By using in her original research women who are mainly white, assumed to identify as heterosexual, and mainly middle-class, her critics claim, Gilligan constructs an avowedly gendered model of moral development based only on a small group of dominant women. To the extent that the ethic of care is co-extensive with "women's moral voice," that voice is most typical of a white, heterosexual, middle-class woman in the United States of the 1980s, and furthermore is perhaps heard only in certain limited moral situations.

Published critiques of Gilligan's later work have returned to similar arguments. For example, Judith Stacey criticizes "Joining the Resistance: Psychology, Politics, Girls and Women"[25] for its undiscriminating use of humanist, universalist categories. In particular, Stacey suggests that Gilligan presents a transhistorical, transcultural, and context-free account of female adolescence.[26] While these charges seem somewhat overstated, I too was struck by Gilligan's failure even to gesture toward the concerns of feminists of color and postmodern critics. By omitting mention of the race of the girls she interviews, Stacey points out, Gilligan leaves the reader to assume that (or wonder whether) they are white. This seems to be an essentializing move of the kind I have criticized: white girls are simply "girls"—except when they are girls of color, a difference barely worth mentioning. It is remarkable that the cultural, racial, and ethnic backgrounds of the girls interviewed are briefly mentioned only in a footnote, and then with no indication of how this information might be relevant to the research process. Stacey, furthermore, rereads Gilligan's "muted attention" to social class in light of her own class autobiography, arguing that what Gilligan interprets as a gendered adolescent crisis in "Anna," one of her participants, can also be read as an ambivalent experience of social class.

Citing her own use of "dialogic," "reflexive" forms of representation, Stacey finds Gilligan's account of personal narratives simplifies the complex identities of the girls, and glosses the identity of the researcher and her role in the research process. Again, the identity of specific researchers is most often given in footnotes, without reference to their experiences of girlhood, their race, or their class. I suspect that Gilligan would abhor the forced insertion of her own and her colleagues' life stories into her texts, which remain admirably attentive to the voices of the girls. Yet it is precisely in her most elusive and fascinating methodological contribution—her thoughts on "voice"—that this information is most sorely needed: "Two questions about relationships clarified a woman's position: Where am I in relation to the tradition which I am practicing and teaching? and Where am I in relation to girls, the next generation of women?"[27] Surely the answers to both of these questions depend on which woman is asking them and on the girls to whom she wishes to relate? Thus many of the criticisms of Gilligan's work focus on her appropriation of modernist political language, and on her use of a generalizing theoretical genre that fits neatly (albeit often through distortion of her more complex and politically radical claims) with a popular rhetoric that seeks reductive, encapsulating accounts of gender difference. How does Gilligan respond to these challenges?

Her rebuttal of the philosophical criticisms of *In a Different Voice* has been brief:

> In listening to people's responses to *In a Different Voice*, I often hear the two-step process which I went through over and over again in the course of my writing: the process of listening to women and hearing something new, a different way of speaking, and then hearing how quickly this difference gets assimilated into old categories of thinking so that it loses its novelty and its message: is it nature or nurture? are women better than men, or worse? When I hear my work being cast in terms of whether women and men are really (essentially) different or who is better than whom, I know that I have lost my voice, because these are not my questions. Instead, . . . my questions are about voice and relationship. And, my questions are about psychological processes and theory, particularly theories in which men's experiences stands for all of human experience—theories which eclipse the lives of women and shut out women's voices.[28]

Gilligan claims that her argument is interpretive, based on narrative counter-examples to those examples favored by conventional psychological theory, not on generalizable or statistical claims. She unabashedly foregrounds gender in understanding relationships and adolescent crisis, although she allows that girls' and women's experiences are shaped in the context of other axes of power. Gilligan does not deny that some men use the ethic of care in thinking about moral problems or that the ethic is shaped by conditions of oppression.[29] She does not simply describe a universal and essential feminine but instead delineates a resistant and critical ethical perspective that challenges womanly self-sacrifice and unqualified caring and struggles to incorporate a self-protective attitude with the desire for relationship with others.[30] Indeed, in her later work she is increasingly explicit about how patriarchal oppression creates the necessary conditions for female crises of connection, and she construes her project as an explicitly feminist intervention.

This dialogue between Gilligan and her critics concerning her theory and methods has its frustrations. Often talking at cross-purposes and in voices divorced from actual texts, her critics have been content to style Gilligan as a hopeless modernist. And Gilligan's replies tend toward the theoretically insubstantial and defensive. So how should feminist readers understand her contribution to feminist theory and the politics of her method, and particularly the significance of this conversation about essentialism? My view is that Gilligan's rich and evocative portrayal of girls' adolescent dilemmas in her later work, and her methodological discussion, are an invaluable contribution to feminist practice and a potential framework for "action research" aimed at, as the title of one ongoing project indicates, "strengthening healthy resistance and courage in girls."[31] The significance of her contribution lies in providing a framework for understanding female adolescent psychology that is, first, not merely an amendment to existing research on boys, and second, avowedly feminist. Gilligan repeatedly stresses that adolescent girls have simply not been much studied; she attempts to explain why adolescence is the seedbed of female trauma and to document, within a theoretical framework, the processes of disempowerment that will plague girls throughout their lives.

By identifying a different way of thinking about relationships and moral dilemmas, and by telling a rich story about a time of crisis and impasse in the lives of the adolescent girls they study, Gilligan and her colleagues offer a framework for understanding the under-theorized feminist commonplace that all girls struggle psychologically in patriarchal societies. They argue that this struggle itself has produced ways of understanding connection to others that are systematically devalued and undermined by patriarchy and that meet their most serious challenge at the time of female adolescence. By retaining until early adulthood the strong sense of connection with others that boys lose as young children, girls manage to avoid processes of dissociation that are distinctively masculine pathologies and that have, according to Gilligan and other theorists who have put object relations theory or the ethic of care to feminist uses, negative ethical and political implications.[32] Gilligan allows girls' voices to take center stage in her books, and, however we criticize her method, such criticisms do not negate the path-breaking nature of her contributions to the social psychology of girls. Her work is an admirable example of interdisciplinary feminism, where insights from feminist philosophy are brought to bear on feminist research and practice, and vice versa.

Although Gilligan's critics have often treated her work rather reductively— reading her work casually and uncharitably only to attack it—criticisms that *In a Different Voice* is essentialist are significant: they pinpoint epistemological issues related to generalization, contextualism, and pluralism, and they speak to methodological concerns about how inequalities of power foster essentializing research programs. Still, the very familiarity of all these criticisms has bred a certain contempt for Gilligan—the arch-essentialist—and this has caused moral and political philosophers to dismiss her work as both inadequately theorized and insufficiently feminist. Few feminist philosophers have looked to Gilligan's more recent work for insight into essentialism and social research paradigms or for any performative response to her critics, despite the ever-burgeoning social science scholarship that applies the ethic of care to a variety of praxes and policy issues, from feminist jurisprudence and political theory, to nursing, pedagogy, international relations, and political organizing.[33]

The most effective method for reading work like Gilligan's requires feminists to examine how generalizations are used; not to reject the use of generality altogether, but to ask what is enabled and what excluded in the context in question. Without Gilligan's generalizations, we would be left to depend on psychological theories that either ignore girls' narratives or rate them as second-class. Her early interventions stressed that girls' voices had *not* been listened to; thus the political salience of Gilligan's project lay in creating a space for girls to be heard. Having identified unanticipated characteristics of the girls' and women's voices in her early studies, Gilligan clearly approaches her later research fields with a set of preconceptions that may or may not adequately interpret the voices of "different" girls. If anti-essentialist insight is applied to this work, then surely it should not be merely in the form of a set of criticisms, an interminable deconstruction, but as a route to a viable alternative method, with similar feminist goals of empowerment. Generalizations about the experiences of girls, furthermore, should not be rejected a priori. The imperative facing anti-essentialist feminists is not *whether* to make generalizations but *how* to make them. Thus in the remainder of the chapter I want to defend Gilligan against these excessively broad criticisms of essentialism in order to locate more revealing and nuanced objections that will enable better feminist research methods.

### Between Voice and Silence

In this context, the publication of *Between Voice and Silence* raises an interesting set of questions about the ability of a social researcher, engaged in fieldwork of various kinds, effectively to respond to charges of essentialism. And there is no doubt that Gilligan has taken the label "essentialist," and its political connotations of racism and exclusion, to heart:

> Tensions within feminism over the last twenty years have become heightened over the question of difference. Women who are white and privileged have been criticized by both black and white women and called "essentialist" for speaking about gender without also addressing race, class, cultural and sexual differences among women. It is a mark of a racist and class-driven society that those who are in a dominant position can easily remain blind to the experience of others and thereby to the reality of their own domination, and this blindness extends to women as well. At the same time, women often hold a higher standard for other women and are more forgiving of men. The implication that women must speak of everything or keep silent is one of the many constraints on women's voices that characterize and maintain a patriarchal society and culture [BVS: 7].

But the choice to "speak of everything or keep silent" is a false dichotomy. Feminists are not reduced to fruitless struggle with the infinite complexities of political identity or giving up the fight altogether. Although Gilligan makes useful contributions to our ability to bring anti-essentialism to bear on ethnographic problems and on the politics of feminist method, she struggles to implement fully the political theoretical concerns I raised earlier.

At the beginning of this book I pointed to the limits of wholesale rejection of feminist projects for their alleged "essentialism." I mapped out a terrain where we recognize the value of feminist political goals and use anti-essentialist insights to engage political projects that may still be invested in essentializing discourses or may manifest essentializing moments. When situated on this terrain, Gilligan's work is neither right nor wrong, neither irredeemably essentialist nor politically utopian. My counsel for anti-essentialist feminists is thus not to bring the full force of philosophical critique to bear simply in order to ferret out Gilligan's essentialism nor to step back from the political engagement of her work, but to create conversational openings for more pragmatic anti-essentialist insight. Anti-essentialist feminist analysis of *Between Voice and Silence* suggests that categories need to be nuanced and situated, but that the exigencies of advocating for all adolescent girls require that their distress and disenfranchisement be heard unequivocally. Thus in suggesting ways in which Gilligan's most recent work might more effectively engage anti-essentialist feminist theory, I want to avoid an agonistic rejection of her project as insufficiently theorized, excessively generalized, and unworthy of feminist examination and instead offer criticisms that point to ways feminist theory and practice can come together to make the study of women's moral voices and attitudes to relationship more inclusive, more self-reflexive, and more politically useful.

Gilligan argues that she need not make dichotomous claims about girls and boys and that her interpretive method merely sketches alternative ways of conceptualizing relationships rather than fixing a universal gendered schism.[34] The homogeneity of Gilligan's initial samples, furthermore, does not presuppose any kind of essentialism, including the danger of falsely generalizing from the experiences of a select group of girls to all girls. It could even be the case that girls' experiences at adolescence are sufficiently similar that the transfer of a model based on one group of girls to another group is unproblematic, and that the experiences of "different" girls merely provide more varied examples of the same general phenomenon. This prognosis, of course, continues to establish a norm that a simple "disclaimer" about the possibly limited scope of the analysis cannot undercut. As Lugones argues:

> When I read theories about mothering, constructions of the moral domain, constructions of the self, and so on, that are prefaced by disclaimers about the universality of the theoretical claims, I am left at sea as to whether I am to take what I am reading as anthropological or sociological field reports. After the disclaimer, nothing again indicates that difference has been recognized. The logic of the discourse emphasizes ignoring difference and acknowledging a singularity of practice, discipline, or construction.[35]

Therefore, Lugones argues, attempts to acknowledge difference require an *interactive* step, a move to establish real conversations that will make clear to white feminists the precise contours of the differences they investigate as well as their own implication in sustaining those contours.

In fact, Gilligan does take a version of such a step. *Between Voice and Silence* continues her original projects in the context of her growing feminist political concerns with race and class differences among women. This time, Gilligan's group of "participants" consists of twenty-six "working-class or poor" girls, of whom eight are African- or Caribbean-American, four are Latina-American, eight are Portuguese-American, and six are Irish- or Italian-American. Gilligan's method is still repeated, open-ended interviewing. The interviewer then listens to the interview transcripts according to the voice-centered method most recently formalized by Brown and Gilligan in their "Listener's Guide."[36] During the first listening, the interviewer notes the narrative content and direction of the interviewee; during the second she listens for the self—"for the voice of the 'I' speaking in this relationship"; on the third and fourth playbacks she attends to how the interviewee talks about relationships. Throughout their discussion, Brown and Gilligan stress the political nature of this listening method: "Our *responsive* Listener's Guide, in attending to realities of race, class, and sex (who is speaking, in what body, telling what story of relationship—from whose perspective, in what societal and cultural frameworks?), is therefore also a *resisting* Listener's Guide, that is, a feminist method."[37] The content of the interviews differs from previous studies in that specific questions about race were later included, whereas none had been present before. The researchers, furthermore, participated in a series of retreats designed to examine women's relationships across racial difference. The retreats, we are told, involved eleven women—five Black, five white, and one Latina—and entailed profound and painful examination of the differences and commonalities among them. Thus the research context, compared with analogous projects, is striking in the depth of its commitment to addressing the interactive understandings of the researchers with regard to race and class.

How do Gilligan's theses about girls' adolescent crises fare when narratives are collected from working-class girls of color? The interviews, perhaps unsurprisingly, did reveal differences between girls of different racial, ethnic, and class backgrounds in their discussions of the interview topics. For example:

> What Ruby does not share with most of the girls from more privileged settings is the pressure to meet idealized images of femininity that many begin to face at this time. Concerns about not expressing anger or hurting other people's feelings, which become prominent from early adolescence onward among many girls from middle-class backgrounds, are not issues for Ruby. When she discusses conflicts or dilemmas, for example, she

speaks about fairness, respect, and care, yet she does not excessively deliberate over whether or not she has hurt someone else's feelings [BVS: 43].

Ana [a Latina girl] describes a strict environment at home, where acting "like a woman" includes being discreet about her interest in boys. She often gets into trouble when she talks to her mother about boys: if her mother "feels all grouchy," she will get angry and "start saying, 'All you think about is boys.'" In fact, all the Latina girls in the study describe partial or complete injunctions against such conversations, unlike many of the African American and white girls, who say they can talk with their mothers about sex or dating [BVS: 61].

Much of Chapter 3 is devoted to talking about differences between the relationships of African-American girls, Latina girls, and white girls with their mothers, and recurrent themes throughout the interview narratives include dropping out of school and early pregnancy, topics that are absent in earlier research with more privileged groups of girls.

Gilligan is quick to stress that "difference" should not be interpreted as "lack," as implying that these girls' contributions to the researchers' understandings will be less useful:

We will struggle in this book with the word *different*, mainly to hold it apart from its common mistranslation, "deficient." Our group of twenty-six girls was so informative in part because of the cultural and racial differences among them . . . Difference, in our understanding here, is the essence of relationship [BVS: 2].

The authors thus recognize the danger of establishing a white, middle-class norm from which "different" girls will deviate, and instead cast racial and class differences as always necessarily relational. The project, however, implicitly rests on the assumption that whatever the differences between girls of different class and race backgrounds, these differences exist in the context of more significant similarities:

Amid the diversity of race and ethnicity in this study, these spontaneous narratives describe aspects of these relationships that remain insistent across differences, aspects that form an unambiguous and powerful template for meaningful relationships between women and girls [BVS: 118].

The authors rightly contest the false dichotomy that different women must be either hopelessly opaque to each other or assimilated into sameness, both in feminist theorizing and in forming political alliances. Thus overcoming difference for political unity is cast as a central goal:

> What would it mean for women to suspend the old terms of identity and move beyond the race, class, and gender divisions that cordon women off from one another in familiar ways: women of color/women of no color; women with and without privilege of class, ethnicity or sexuality? What would lead women to link arms across these categorizations? The political answer is a common vision for economic and political and societal changes. It is here that the engagement with difference becomes essential [BVS: 208].

The conclusions Gilligan draws about the experiences of non-white, non-middle-class girls seem to hinge on the claim that they will experience the same kind of relational impasse at adolescence, but that it may well be worse than that of their white and/or privileged counterparts and that it will certainly have more negative consequences. Despite these differences, Gilligan's original explanatory model for crises of connection remains the same, taking the same basic form for all girls in western patriarchal cultures, although the context and consequences differ.

How should we understand this ambiguous, generalizing account of gender? And against this complex backdrop, what kinds of anti-essentialist criticisms can be sustained? Despite its virtues, Gilligan's method does predispose the researcher to overlook how race, class, and other salient group differences shape processes of theory construction. This seems representative of those shortcomings feminists most often exhibit in trying to respond to anti-essentialist critique. "Difference" is often incorporated into feminist projects in a formulaic way, placing disproportionate emphasis on formal inclusion (adding participants from other social groups, for example) and less on examining the deeper methodological and pragmatic implications of anti-essentialist criticisms. Gilligan's epistemological framework has changed between her early work and the recognition (especially in *Between Voice and Silence* but anticipated elsewhere) that her inherited method may be inadequate to the demands of anti-essentialist feminism. Fully to detail this shift, however, is too large a project for this chapter. Gilligan's more recent work does nonetheless manifest a major conceptual and methodological transition, and she is rather disingenuous in her reiterated suggestions that it simply represents further application of the same approach.[38] Here I want briefly to give credit to how Gilligan's method has evolved to recognize more explicitly the power of the researchers to elide difference. Then I will turn to three specific examples in *Between Voice and Silence*. These examples are presented to explore the following question: How might the existing research method encourage the investigators to ignore the particular histories and unequal relations of power structured into axes of difference?

Gilligan does not simply assume that there are facts about girls waiting to be discovered and presented in the "idiom in which [reality] prefers to be described,"[39] nor is she inattentive to how her own preconceptions have shaped her past inquiry. She straightforwardly acknowledges that her method plays a central role in generating and shaping her theoretical conclusions, and recognizes that power is central to the context of interpretation. "Power differences constitute the social reality in which psychological development occurs, and these affect both development and how developmental research is carried out" [BVS: 29].

Gilligan herself points to the tension between her political goals and the research methods she has inherited from social psychology. As her work has progressed it has become more explicitly feminist, more resistant to disciplinary conventions, and more eclectic. For example, she resists traditional notions of objectivity to incorporate some of the insights of standpoint epistemology:[40]

> Listening to girls who are more on the edges of a dominant patriarchal society by virtue of race, class and cultural difference, we found their voices deeply informative; essential to composing a psychology of women and girls that is not imprisoned by the invisible racial blinder of whiteness, or by economic and political advantage, or by sexual and familial access to powerful men. Listening to girls of color, girls from different cultures, girls from families that are economically pressed, we heard relationships between girls and women, and also relationships among girls and women, described from different angles and reflecting different psychological and political realities [BVS: 208].

In Gilligan's previous studies, the emphasis on voice was unidirectional, with "the interviewer" an unnamed and undescribed presence, the medium for the questions on the interview schedule. How girls' articulations of their attitudes to morality and relationships are shaped not only by patriarchal oppression, but also by power dynamics in the context of the research itself, is left virtually unexplored. Gilligan does gesture toward these difficulties: at one point in *Meeting at the Crossroads* she describes the developing underground of girls' responses in the school to the influx of interviewers, the ways the girls rehearse each other, and prepare for their interviews.[41] She maps out how this underground is influenced by the powerful identities of the researchers and the tools of social research that they use. In *Between Voice and Silence* we are told about the glossing over of power differences in the retreats: "Related to issues of trust were difficulties in coming to terms with the existence and the effects of differences in power. Jill observed during one of the retreats that 'the less powerful in the group are very interested in having a conversation about power, but it has not always been so for everybody in the group . . . [which is why] it's got lost so often'" [BVS: 161].

In contrast with earlier work, the interviewers are sometimes named, and occasionally their relation to the participant is theorized in some way. For example,

Anita's response [as an African-American girl to a white interviewer] taps into the central question in all psychological research—can one understand another whose life experience is different? She rejects the "you can't understand anything" position with respect to racial difference, but she also suggests that the interviewer's understanding of "this stuff" is limited because of her racial difference. "This stuff" has a number of possible meanings, and as Anita elaborates further, many of them are related to race and racism [BVS: 35].

The authors raise new concerns about how interviews are shaped by the presence of different interviewers; they recognize that the tone and content of the participant's speech will change depending on who poses the questions, and that this change will be linked to differences of race and class: "The question 'Who is listening?' now became an integral part of our voice-centered, relational method—integral to our understanding of both voice and relationship. We realized that our previous emphasis on 'Who is speaking?' reflected in part our own and our research participants' class and cultural location" [BVS: 2–3].

It is not only in the interview itself that race and class differences influence the creation and interpretation of speech. In listening to tapes and reading transcripts, Gilligan enlarges the "interpretive community" to include more women of color, concluding that this change has deepened and diversified the group's understanding of the girls. For example, Anita's interviewer and those members of the interpretive community who read her transcripts have very different understandings of her situation. Jill, her white interviewer, interprets her outspoken and forthright manner as both psychologically resilient and politically resistant compared to norms of femininity. But Pam and Janie, two African-American readers, were dismayed by Anita, finding her "brash, opinionated, cocky and just a pain" [BVS: 37]. Their interpretation of Anita's words is still politically feminist, but, in Janie's view her "statements could be heard as excessively assertive and unyielding, almost belligerent, an example of 'resistance for survival,' a reaction against destructive elements in her social world and in the larger sociopolitical context of the United States," rather than as desirably assertive and self-confident [BVS: 38]. Here is a positive example of reflexivity in Gilligan's work, which allows her to escape the anti-essentialist criticism that she fails formally to include women of color in the process of interpretation, or that she fails to attach epistemological significance to this inclusion.

So what's the problem? Both the epistemology and the methodology informing the interviews, particularly the processes that generate general descriptions of female adolescent crisis are still under-theorized. To avoid essentialism, Gilligan needs to interrogate further the relevance to the research process of the identities of the interviewers, their relation to the girls they interview, the epistemological significance of the "interpretive community," the influence of the interviewing method itself on the research findings, and the ways differences may or may not emerge in the research process.

First, Gilligan seems to assume that girls who resist connection with their interviewers are manifesting an unhealthy form of resistance, dissociating from relationship in pathological ways. When the researchers perceive the girls' voices to be inauthentic, they seldom connect this lack of authenticity explicitly to the research context, but instead attribute it to more general malaise in the girls' lives. The researchers thus adopt an epistemically privileged (though ambiguous) position outside the domain of relationship. This position is made possible not by ignoring differences of identity or experience between interviewee and interviewer per se, but by failing to analyze the interviewers' power over the girls, partly by virtue of these very differences. Gilligan has a keen sense of the ways girls exhibit resistance when they negotiate relationships with friends, mothers, teachers, and so on. But she seems less insightful about the forms of resistance girls may evince toward her own research. James Scott's analysis of the public and hidden transcripts that characterize relations of power is useful here: Scott points out that subordinates rarely tell the same story to those in positions of power that they tell among themselves. Resisting the temptation to label the latter type of narrative more authentic than the former, he argues that by assessing the discrepancies between the public transcript (what subordinates say to those in power) and the hidden transcript (what subordinates say among themselves) we can better assess the "impact of domination on public discourse."[42] Power is ubiquitous, yet the differences between these "public" and "hidden" transcripts may tell us more about its operation, and about the subordinates under scrutiny, than any analysis of a public transcript that does not understand itself as such. Scott's examples of power relations (he makes much use of slaves and masters and of caste systems) are undoubtedly qualitatively and quantatively different cases than the power between researcher and "subject" in Gilligan's project. Nonetheless, his detailed model for analyzing the dialogic, scripted nature of power and resistance and his attention to the strategies employed by subordinates offer a much-needed corrective to Gilligan's analysis.

Gilligan's generalizations serve particular purposes by highlighting certain aspects of girls' experiences across difference. Because they purportedly constitute the truth about girls, however, Gilligan faces no epistemological imperative to recognize their contingency and tends to gloss over the particular cases that do not conform so neatly to the general theory. This is both a methodological and a practical problem: the tendency of dominant-group feminists to overlook difference is exacerbated by a method that does not adequately interrogate the histories of multiple axes of oppression in forming identities. In the example, Jill seems, as the authors admit, to lack the experiences shared by African-American girls, and in her interpretation of Anita's interview she falls back on the terms of a pre-existing interpretive grid to explain Anita's actions as defiant and resilient. Girls who challenge expectations of femininity are thus heard as resistant proto-feminists. Pam and Janie, on the other hand, use their own experiences (both of their own girlhoods and of work with other Black girls) to make sense of Anita even when this contrasts with the working theory of feminist resistance operative in the research context. They hear Anita's responses more as a voice distorted, railing against the limiting conditions of powerlessness. Both interpretations are feminist renderings, but the former is more susceptible to the criticism of essentialism above: namely, that in trying to make Anita's narrative fit into Gilligan's epistemological framework, an interpretation is presented (and contested) that fails to recognize how different axes of power shape the girls' narratives.

The second problem is that Gilligan has always used interviewing as her primary method, and she continues to do so in *Between Voice and Silence*. Some of the foregoing concerns become magnified, however, in the context of dyadic forms of inquiry. In particular, "difference," while overtly conceptualized as relational rather than fixed, is nevertheless constituted within a relationship between two people rather than being negotiated in a larger group. Gilligan often understates how not only "difference" but also the power embedded in differences—including the historical and social background within which differences are formed—might shape girls' responses to questions from older women in positions of authority, often of a different race, and always of a different class (in terms of present status if not background). There is a peculiar disjunction between the testimonial prose, literary references, and emotionally evocative discussions of women joining together across difference that characterize much of the text, and the glimpses into the interviews themselves, where the researchers follow "interview protocols." The valuable insight that an "interpretive community" can contribute to understanding the girls' responses seems curiously restricted to the later stages of the research. Gilligan is far less cavalier than many other feminist researchers about identification, trust, and rapport between feminist interviewer and female participant. Still, she seems to assume that the interpretive community will be able to uncover different standpoints simply by listening to the fixed results of a dyadic interview conducted in a single, power-laden context.

Third, Gilligan has taken anti-essentialist critique seriously enough to identify particular axes of difference that need to be emphasized in her revised research method. In *Between Voice and Silence*, race and class are identified as axes of difference that had been previously glossed over. But are these the only differences that shape girls' experience of adolescence? Gilligan seems to acknowledge that they are not:

> A narrative account is produced interactively, depending not only on the questions of the interviewer and the experiences of the narrator, but also on the "social location" of both. Hence, any telling of "a story" may be affected by race, ethnicity, gender, class, age, sexual orientation, religious background, personal history, character—an infinite list of possible factors that form the scaffolding of relationships between people [BVS: 14].

Which of these "infinite" possible differences will be significant emerges in the course of empirical inquiry. Of course, it is a methodological commonplace that every researcher must enter a project with preconceptions that, at least initially, privilege some axes of difference over others. The most serious anti-essentialist challenge in this case, however, lies in recognizing the contingency of those emphasized differences and remaining open to the possibility that previously recondite axes of difference will emerge. This challenge can best be met by recognizing how power operates to make difference invisible to the powerful—in this case, to the researchers. Gilligan's agenda is not sufficiently flexible in this way; the girls have to fit into the "right" differences or risk being misheard.

It is surprising, for example, that Gilligan makes no mention of adolescent sexual experiences that deviate from conventional heterosexual activity, especially given that the book contains an entire chapter on sexuality. A note to Chapter 5, however, worth quoting in full, offers the following vignette:

> When Lilian's interviewer began the questions about sexual interest and sexual decision-making, *As teenagers, boys and girls have to make decisions a lot of times when they are going out with someone . . .* , Lilian asked, "With a boy?" Her interviewer confirmed this: *Yes, with a boy. Can you describe when you had to make a decision in that relationship?* "Not really, no." *Do you go out with boys?* "No." *Not really?* "No." Lilian's interviewer again tries to ask about sexual decision-making, to which Lilian first responds, "I don't know, I don't know . . . I'm sort of lost," and then, "I understand what you're saying. I'm just sort of, I'm trying to think . . . I really don't go out with boys. I get along with boys as good friends, we're basically good friends." *I was thinking more kind of in an intimate relationship with someone, with a boy . . . just a situation with a boy where you had to make . . . a sexual decision?* "I don't know, I'd rather not talk about it." *You'd rather not.* "If you don't mind." Then perhaps in an effort to focus her interviewer's efforts elsewhere, Lilian asks, "Would you like a piece of gum?" Although the interview protocol was designed so that questions about sexual interest and experience could apply to either sex, Lilian's interviewer in tenth grade unfortunately lapsed into the general cultural assumption of heterosexuality and asked specifically about boys, thus closing off any possibility of more discussion [BVS: note 3 to Chapter 5, 221].

On first reading, I was torn between admiration for the authors' intellectual honesty in including a damning admission that could easily have been left out, and deep disappointment that the only acknowledged breakdown of heteronormativity in a girl's narrative had to be relegated to a footnote. Not only does the interviewer "ask specifically about boys," but in the authorial commentary this is attributed to a "cultural assumption of heterosexuality."

The implication here is clearly that Lilian may be trying to conceal her lesbianism from the unwitting interviewer. Whether or not Lilian is sexually attracted to other girls (we will never know, because this experience has been so thoroughly erased), the text assumes not only normative heterosexuality but also that girls will be sexually active or interested, necessarily engaged in making "sexual decisions." To assume that they are *not* would be another kind of erasure, but these interview questions fail to provide an avenue for exploring the not uncommon experience among adolescent girls of sexual withdrawal or resistance to the norms of heterosexual dating. These latter phenomena are themselves connected to institutionalized heterosexuality, which I would characterize as more than a mere "cultural assumption" and instead an oppressive system for disciplining the desires and actions of future heterosexual women.[43] Thus both the relations of power between researcher and participant, as well as the relations of power among researchers, structure the implicit theory embedded in the research questions and the construction of experience those questions permit.

It seems clear from this incident that, unsurprisingly, there are undercurrents—"hidden transcripts"—of girls' lives and aspects of their experiences that are not revealed in the interviews. Other examples are addressed more directly by the authors: for example, in her interview, Sandy hints at, but does not reveal, sexual abuse, and elsewhere Gilligan mentions that specific questions about social class must be carefully couched so as not to run into taboos about poverty and deprivation that will generate more silence [BVS: 109–15]. What conditions make it possible to erase non-conformist sexuality in the context of a method that purports to be sensitive both to differences and to silence?

Gilligan concludes, rightly, that an enlarged interpretive community, acting both as gatherers and interpreters of narratives, would offer more insights into the differences and silences that characterize the girls' speech. Part of the solution to problems like that manifested in Lilian's interview must be to prepare researchers to enter the research context with specific injunctions about difference in mind. As the authors acknowledge, dominant cultural assumptions will tend to render some differences invisible. The imperative to recognize differences and their effect on the construction of identity, however, cannot be premised only on the mantra of gender, race, and class; it also requires an understanding of the mechanisms of power which make some axes of difference more or less visible in particular contexts. Thus it would seem that the research group should not simply continually add more members, from different social groups, in order to maximize objectivity (although having just one openly lesbian researcher might well have altered the acutely un-self-conscious heteronormative understanding of sexuality presented in Chapter 4 of *Between Voice and Silence*).[44] Instead, the epistemological and methodological challenges articulated here are prerequisites for an analysis of power that lends flexibility to the research process by continually interrogating its context and categories.

## Toward Anti-Essentialist Research

Critics of essentializing discourses might still respond to Gilligan by claiming that she naively assumes that voices are more or less authentic, more or less "honed to the truth" [BVS: 11]. These epistemological premises, one argument might run, reveal both her continuing (if ambivalent) investment in a kind of objectivity that has an undistinguished genealogy, as well as her failure to attend to power-laden discourses that obscure attention to difference and reinscribe hegemonic categories. A principled anti-essentialist might say that there can be no legitimate generalizations about girls' psychology. Girls' complex identities are necessarily negotiated in specific contexts, through relations of power, and amid infinite axes of difference. One anti-essentialist argument therefore constructs an epistemological case for Gilligan's hopeless naiveté in building an uncompromisingly universal picture of girls' realities through such unrefined methodological tools.

None of the critiques of Gilligan I have considered make their case in quite such uncompromising terms. In listening to responses to her work at conferences, in classes, and in general academic discussion, however, I suspect that many feminist philosophers find much to agree with in this latter critique. Nevertheless, this is still the kind of critique that, standing alone, merely diminishes the political usefulness of Gilligan's project. It performs the act of dissociation she pointedly describes: "Learning about difference is not about epistemology, not simply about whether, or to what extent, we can know another human being or another culture. Exploring difference is about relationship" [BVS: 173].

The fact that girls' voices have not been listened to, and that Gilligan's work opens up a space for them to be heard, is part of what contributes to the political salience of her project. Nonetheless, certain implicit assumptions— that girls' voices can reflect "psychological truths" with varying degrees of accuracy and can legitimately be interpreted in terms of the same developmental model across race and class difference—predispose the researchers to emphasize certain aspects of the research context.[45] I do not want to deny that there are crucial commonalities in girls' experiences across race and class, nor do I want to perform an act of dissociation, removing real, concrete questions about the emotional well-being of girls and women and abstracting to a philosophical safe haven. Rather I want to pinpoint ways the epistemological basis of Gilligan's work inclines us to ask certain questions rather than others, and not always those that will provide the most useful political insights. So how might anti-essentialist feminism be used to make constructive suggestions that develop rather than deplete the political resources available in empowering adolescent girls? How can we do justice to the complexity of difference and power in research at the same time as we construct accounts of girls' lives that are a strong basis for policy development and political intervention?

First, although Gilligan's interviews are loosely structured and dialogical, many of the methodological problems sketched in this chapter seem most pronounced in the context of a girl participant and woman researcher dyad. A complement to open-ended interviews is Elizabeth Frazer's use, in her research with British teenage girls from a variety of class and ethnic backgrounds, of discussion groups consisting of a small number of girls, with the investigator as facilitator.[46] Such groups will inevitably also produce their own silencing effects, as some girls hold back from speaking in front of others or present themselves as they would like to be seen by their peer group. No research method can guarantee that all girls will speak with equal ease—indeed, the quest for such an elusive method is part of the epistemological framework I am arguing against. Nevertheless, Frazer's discussion groups, while acknowledging the researcher's powerful role, still allow for the interaction of girls who differ in important ways from one another. These groups also diffuse the power of the researcher, providing opportunities for girls to speak up together and to resist a particular conversational direction. Although some differences will always be repressed (for example, Frazer comments on the different taboos and silences surrounding social class for working-class and middle-class girls in her discussion groups), they are less likely to be differences that reflect asymmetries of power between researcher and participant.[47] By rearranging relations of power, discussion groups offer a different perspective on the same issues. While they may not be a suitable forum for soliciting confidences, they are one powerful research tool for negotiating complex and power-laden identities:

> A closed schedule questionnaire, or even an in-depth interview, is more likely to elicit from respondents a unitary and articulated opinion, attitude

or belief. The discussion group elicited, instead, an uncertain negotiation of alternative positions which were frequently unresolved.[48]

My second suggestion is that Gilligan include more interaction between her research conclusions and the girls' interpretations of their own words. As she says,

> The interview process also demonstrated one of the most important benefits of speaking with and listening to girls in this way: it can help girls to develop, to hold on to, or to recover knowledge about themselves, their feelings, and their desires. Taking girls seriously encourages them to take their own thoughts, feelings, and experience seriously, to maintain this knowledge, and even to uncover knowledge that has become lost to them [BVS: 128].

Gilligan herself mentions using feedback techniques in *Meeting at the Crossroads*, in which she describes giving interview extracts back to the girls, explaining her analysis, and inviting their responses.[49] Indeed, "checking back" and offering participants an opportunity to respond to the researcher's interpretations of their lives is a familiar method in progressive ethnography.[50] Frazer, for example, takes account of participants' own descriptions of their experiences. In explaining the girls' narratives, she checked back to ensure that her explanations meshed with the "concepts, categories, and understandings" they used themselves. This approach is akin to a Winchian critique of social science, which in turn is based on Wittgenstein's notion of "forms of life," and his criticisms of insensitive ethnocentric investigations.[51] While checking back is a method with its own pitfalls, Gilligan and her colleagues would do well to develop activities that bring their explanations of girls' disconnection and relational impasse at adolescence more directly back to the girls themselves, for two reasons.

First, Gilligan's tendency to think that a "truth of the matter" in girls' initial responses to interview questions co-exists uneasily alongside her recognition that they may change their minds about those answers, respond skeptically when her analyses are relayed to them, or give different responses depending on the social location of their interviewer. Second, Gilligan urges educators and youth workers to include girls' voices in processes of policy formation, yet she does not fully incorporate this insight into her own work [BVS: 191–92]. Engaging the girls more directly in dialogue in the research process itself is likely not only to produce more complex and difference-sensitive stories about girls' lives, but also to achieve feminist goals of empowerment.[52] More explicit acknowledgment both of the power relations embedded in difference, and of the ways different research methods create specific conditions of possibility for the negotiation of such differences, far from hindering Gilligan's political goals, would serve to make them more attainable.

Just as Gilligan needs to move a collective exploration of power and difference to the center of her feminist method, so our revisions of the political work of allegedly essentialist feminists need to avoid a critique that persistently fragments categories without exploring their empirical adequacy or political importance. Gilligan, far from being "an essentialist," has moved toward a politically informed anti-essentialist method. Laying out salient differences in advance of inquiry, as she does in *Between Voice and Silence*, is a necessary jumping-off point for the construction of anti-essentialist generalizations about girls; feminists have been rightly skeptical of researchers who paid no heed to the significance and interaction of gender, race, or class in formulating research problems. This chapter has suggested, however, that an anti-essentialist research method needs to be even more open to the introduction of new axes of difference and to the asymmetries of power that may obscure those axes, particularly asymmetries between researchers or theorists and the different others they seek to bring into their narratives. These relations of power set the terms for the "scripts" on which much qualitative research is based.

The reconstruction of those feminist projects we have tended to dismiss as naively essentialist has only just begun. As feminists become increasingly exasperated with the superfluity of critique and the paucity of political strategies and solutions the essentialism debates offer, we need to bring our critical skills to bear in excavating and restoring those projects that have been buried underneath the disapprobative rubble of theoretical anti-essentialism. One major area in which the insights of anti-essentialist feminisms have been only tentatively applied is social research programs; yet anti-essentialism constitutes a set of claims precisely about the adequacy conditions of feminist method. By focusing on how power frames difference in the context of Gilligan's research, this chapter has tried to show how the method employed in one feminist project can be refined and nuanced in ways that advance its goals rather than reveal its limitations.

Finally, Carol Gilligan is remarkably perceptive about how women dissociate from relationships. One thing I may well have learned from her and her collaborators is that some recent feminist philosophy exemplifies another form of dissociation: from actual political problems that often seem too overwhelming to address. It is easier by far, but far less fruitful, to analyze the mistakes of allegedly essentialist feminists than to make concrete proposals while fully incorporating a commitment to anti-essentialist method. Here I have shown how this commitment might play out in the context of feminist research; in the next chapter I ask similar questions of feminist organizing against sexual violence.

# Chapter 5

## Between Theory and Practice: MacKinnon and Feminist Activism

As I have been arguing throughout this book, one of the central questions raised by a form of anti-essentialism that urges us to "look and see" is how to give difference its due when it isn't unproblematically there to be discovered. The processes of making generalizations and highlighting differences are necessarily pragmatic tasks but not straightforwardly "empirical" ones. As we saw in my analysis of Gilligan, research methods both discover and construct similarity and difference. The most useful question to pose of these different methods, I have argued, is not whether they are more or less accurate in their descriptions of difference, but rather how they interpret those relations of power that produce similarities and differences. Principled anti-essentialism fails to offer an adequate research methodology: we cannot use general categories without making decisions about inclusion in and exclusion from those categories; moreover, we cannot act politically without these categories. The necessity of categories of some kind invites us to think practically and ethically about issues of process—as Chapter 3 argued, we need to be mindful of the categories we use, since both the tacit status quo and any conscious recategorization creates a reality as well as describing one. So Chapter 4 asked: why did Gilligan pick differences of race and class to broaden her analysis? That choice (and it is a choice) speaks to the politics of the researchers, criticisms of existing work, and to social systems that structure oppression in ways that construct the reality of those differences.

How do we think about these concerns when the differences with which we are confronted arise in real situations of political conflict? When they are embedded in social structures of power, institutionalized, and disciplined in ways that we want effectively to resist? Feminist research always remains, however much the method may be constructed to avoid this dynamic, under the control of the researcher. She often has the leisure to adapt her method in ways that address perceived methodological inadequacies and control the research agenda, as we saw Gilligan and her colleagues do with the girls. By contrast, political practice takes place within the exigencies of situations in which activists are more directly confronted with limited resources, questions of strategy, or conflicts, advancing or responding to emotive demands for inclusion or exclusion within a particular group. Sometimes groups not only have to respond to extant demands, but have to envision which "absent voices" need to be included and how this might be accomplished without condescension. Activists who adopt anti-essentialist positions in theory may have to deal with desires for authenticity ("this is who we really are"), with the identities that are created through practices of resistance, or with oppositional strategies that require the invocation of a group identity, however contingent. Any effort collectively to effect political change must negotiate the processes of identity formation inherent in oppositional intervention into existing systems of meaning. These struggles are not the limitations of an imperfect world in which the dichotomy of essentialism and "difference" fails to guide us; they are the rough ground on which feminist debates about essentialism should be conducted.

In advocating a return to this "rough ground," it initially seemed as if privileging feminist practice and retreating from theory would solve the problem of essentialism. I argued in Chapter 2 that Okin's attempt to ground her generalizations about women in "empirical" realities, however, fails to recognize the complexity of this claim. Similarly, arguments that we can avoid methodological essentialism by privileging practice instead of theory fail to recognize that many of the same forms of essentialism I have identified in feminist theory are also embedded in feminist practice. Merely claiming the primacy of practice, or arguing that a particular theory is grounded in practice, provides no actual information about the shape of that practice or the process by which it generates or justifies a particular theory. Thus, first, this interpretation of the injunction "look and see" fails to tell feminists much about how different forms of practice come to justify different theoretical accounts.

Not only does practice fail always to guide theory, however; theory also fails to guide practice. Feminist theoretical engagement with essentialism, even when it purports to be closely related to practice, often underdetermines the shape of the feminist activism it might endorse. For example, anti-essentialist arguments in political theory often conclude by recommending "coalition building" as a way of breaking down identity group boundaries, thus resisting essentialism while retaining political effectiveness. This theoretical move, however, tells feminists little about the actual shape of anti-essentialist organizing. Do we build coalitions with any group with similar ideology, identity, political goals, or strategic aims? What counts as similar? What criteria do we use in making those decisions? Anti-pornography feminists forming a coalition with religious conservatives to ban "sexually explicit" signs face one set of concerns. Lesbian feminists trying to decide whether to join forces with a gay men's group to campaign for human rights protection face another. Later in this chapter I discuss Catharine MacKinnon's work, and it is worth noting that her legal initiatives have sometimes attracted the support of right-wing political groups. Thus an element of MacKinnon's rhetorical appeal may stem from the convenient fit of her political goals (and even certain aspects of her political theory) with conservative agendas.[1] Is this kind of coalition—and its attendant political problems—a price worth paying for certain gains, or does it compromise feminist political objectives? Merely advocating the loosening of group boundaries or the formation of coalitions does not address these specific, strategic questions. Most theoretical arguments end where many of my concerns begin; anti-essentialist feminist theories often require more content if they are to be genuinely useful in practice.

Widening this gap between theory and practice in the essentialism debates is the lack of connection between the feminist theoretical literature on gender and political identity, and more concrete accounts of how identity has been negotiated within feminist political activism. At a time when much feminist discourse explores the theoretical ramifications of "anti-essentialism" and the limits of generalizing about women, the study of feminist practice has been remarkably uninflected by these concerns. And, as I argued in Chapter 2, philosophers concerned with essentialism and anti-essentialism now uniformly gesture to the need for empirical investigations and practical emphasis without themselves undertaking this research. There is a pressing need for research on the political use of generalizations about women that is both philosophically sophisticated and informed by practice. Without this work, feminist theorists will continue to be stalemated by their own false dichotomies, and practitioners will continue to lack the conceptual tools to investigate empirical contexts.

In this final chapter I turn to concrete forms of feminist practice. I ask how the lessons of the preceding chapters about the construction and negotiation of generalizations about women might inform certain kinds of feminist activism, and how experiences of organizing in turn might shape feminist theorizing about essentialism. "Look and see" is most importantly an injunction to pragmatism—a call to remove oneself from the armchair consideration of "difference" (from where it is all too easy to underestimate the power of "strategic essentialism") and to enter the messier fray of feminist politics. Whatever form our feminist activism takes—and I construe "activism" broadly in this chapter to include any political intervention that has the goal of ameliorating women's oppressions—it ought to be constitutive of how feminists think about essentialism and anti-essentialism.

Feminist theory and practice cannot be nor should be firmly separated— we cannot go to work in the morning thinking practical thoughts and leave off theorizing until we are safely home that evening (nor vice versa). The most challenging and productive forms of feminist engagement, in my experience, require a constant dialectic between ideas gleaned from philosophy books and classroom debate, and the lessons learned in feminist organizations and feminist relationships. There are good intellectual and political reasons for avoiding the privileging of any particular forum for the development of feminist knowledge. Nonetheless, barriers between feminist activism and feminist theory are structurally maintained in familiar ways: the intense competitiveness and individualism of academic careers (especially in light of the current oversupply of new Ph.D.'s) strongly motivate even "progressive" academics to direct their time and energy to research and teaching commitments that are seldom explicitly connected to tangible social change projects, for example. Feminists outside universities, on the other hand, whatever their own educational background and however they stand in relation to the women with whom they work, generally have even fewer material resources and face different imperatives. The kind of tail-chasing I pointed out in Chapter 2 is made possible by keeping the debates within academic feminist theoretical contexts where claims about sameness and difference are not interactive. In fact, they are the kinds of debates that motivated Wittgenstein's famous description of philosophy: "It leaves everything as it is" [PI 124].

In writing this chapter I ran into unanticipated cognitive dissonances: surprised by the lack of case studies of feminist interventions that are theoretically inflected, I found myself trying to mediate two literatures—the sociological and the philosophical—that have relatively little in common. Many feminist theorists claim to want to connect "theory and practice," yet I found few accounts that did so explicitly. Instead I found philosophical work that gestured toward examples from practice without fully integrating them into its terms of argument. The exigencies of feminist activism, however, do not require a more theoretically sophisticated account of why some axes of identity are (in)adequate philosophical grounds for exclusion, but a recognition of the realities of identity and how they play into activist participation. Feeling somewhat adrift, I started to write about my own experience to keep my work grounded in issues in which I had a personal stake. Frustrated by the spiraling theoretical abstractions of some feminist philosophy, I wanted to keep in touch with what I knew about popular paradigms of gender difference, and with the realities of violence against women in particular. But I also often felt that my own experience of feminist activism was somehow lacking: too practical, too unsophisticated, too crude. Throughout its development, this chapter's constructive arguments have been particularly vulnerable to deconstructive criticism. As soon as my claims assumed a more radical shape for which I took political responsibility, an interlocutor (real or imagined) stepped in to point to their philosophical naiveté. Clearly, I want this work to be both philosophically convincing and politically honest. Yet the rhetorical spaces different feminist activities inhabit entail different demands: writing "good" philosophy (good for whom?) requires an elaborate complexity; constructing feminist practice requires oppositional efficacy. Reconciling these two goals has been especially difficult here, my training as a philosopher to qualify every claim conflicting with my political experience, where different kinds of qualifications have been required.

I argue in this chapter that to claim—as Catharine MacKinnon does—that essentialism can be side-stepped as a theoretical problem merely by appealing to feminist practice, begs the question of how essentialism is embedded in practice itself. Feminist theoretical encounters with essentialism, furthermore, often provide insufficient information to make concrete recommendations about the actual shape of anti-essentialist feminist practice. In negotiating that part of the rough ground on which debates about feminist organizing against sexual violence take place, I draw on two of my Wittgensteinian arguments. First, family resemblances enable generalizations about women that are different in kind, not only in their scope. This distinction motivates my critique of MacKinnon as well as my own suggestions for a different kind of anti-essentialist practice. Second, MacKinnon follows the Wittgensteinian injunction to "look and see" by invoking "women's experience" to challenge critics who say her work is methodologically essentialist. But she underestimates the complexity of this injunction and how processes of looking and seeing can never aspire to reflect a transparent reality, whether that reality is reflected in "material conditions," "women's experience," or any other foundational category. Changes to organizations and practices in response to charges that they are essentialist are more than decorative additions to women's already acknowledged commonality. They represent fundamentally different ways of understanding women's identities, particularly in acknowledging the relations of power between women that construct such categories as "women's experience." In casting all women as essentially the same in their relation to a sexuality of dominance and subordination, MacKinnon erases these relations of power as well as the substance of the feminist political organizing against sexual violence that tries to incorporate them into practice. Recognizing this weakness, however, need not lead to giving up on gender as a central category of analysis in this area. Both MacKinnon and I recognize the reality of gender differences and offer feminist justifications for woman-identified activism, but we articulate different notions of inclusion in the category "women."

I then articulate some of the implications I think my own analysis might have for feminist activism against sexual violence. How can we move beyond vague gesturing toward the need for "diversity" or "multiplicity" to an anti-essentialism that provides concrete guidelines for practice? This exposition in turn raises questions of inclusion and exclusion. Does embracing anti-essentialism in this context imply a loss of political efficacy, or even a loss of the ability to justify our use of the category "women"? I take an extreme version of the problem—the issue of including pro-feminist men in feminist anti-sexual violence organizing—and show how feminist anti-essentialism need not give up the kinds of generalizations about women and men that sustain feminist politics. Finally, I ask how we can actually reshape feminist organizations to reflect what we know about essentialism. What organizational structures and forms of representation best facilitate anti-essentialist practice? Particularly with regard to this latter question, I am acutely aware of the limitations entailed in writing about feminist organizing without a more extensive and ongoing dialogue with a community of women preoccupied with similar issues. Writing a philosophical text is in many ways a solitary and univocal process, and thus this chapter is as much a proposal for further investigation under better conditions as a conclusive statement.

## Sexual Violence and Legal Theory

The debate surrounding essentialism and feminist political practice has been most fully developed with regard to feminist anti-sexual violence discourse. In particular, Catharine MacKinnon's theory of sexuality and sexual violence against women and her legal practice (contributing to the emergence of the concept of sexual harassment, as well as the Minneapolis Ordinance which would have made pornography actionable under civil law) have been contested by feminists who argue that her construction of "women" is essentialist.[2] MacKinnon argues that sexuality is the primary locus of women's oppression and that sexual violence is the quintessential expression of male domination in a patriarchal society. Sex is the eroticization of dominance and submission. And sex and violence are inextricably connected through the construction of masculinity as dominance and femininity as subordination. MacKinnon is thus a radical feminist: women's oppression is the result of male dominance, enacted through sexuality, itself disciplined through a plethora of interrelated forms of sexual violence, including sexual harassment, incest, rape, woman beating, sexual slavery, pornography, objectification, and compulsory heterosexuality.[3] Claiming that authoritative liberal understandings of social justice focus on "difference" rather than "dominance," MacKinnon takes a Marxian approach to argue for a legal practice that addresses the totalizing construction of identities through social relations of power.

As with Gilligan's work, much of the power of MacKinnon's theory stems from its strong construction of the category "women" and the explicit relation of this construction to feminist practice. Her theory exhibits a neat congruence with popular political idioms: MacKinnon presents her theory in unequivocal terms, and again, it is the lack of ambiguity in her account that has provoked charges that it is "essentialist." These charges have often been made simply by pointing to possible exclusions in MacKinnon's theory rather than offering alternative accounts of the phenomena she describes; earlier I argued that Gilligan's work has received similarly disappointing critical treatment. Rather like Gilligan, MacKinnon responds that her account successfully avoids methodological essentialism by claiming the privilege of women's experiences and the feminist practice they generate. Her theory is sound, she claims, because it is grounded in the empirical reality of women's lives, and accurately reflects the similarity of women's experiences and of the construction of those experiences under patriarchy. MacKinnon thus invokes an appeal to "empirical reality" and to the grounding of her theory in feminist practice of the kind I have been interrogating. What is the problem of essentialism, then, in this context?

The substance and merits of MacKinnon's view have been extensively debated elsewhere; here I focus particularly on charges that her theory is "essentialist," and specifically on MacKinnon's response that she avoids essentialism by grounding her theory in feminist practice. The charge of essentialism has been made against MacKinnon on several grounds: critics claim that she offers a reductive theory that locates the essence of women's oppression in sexuality, rather than more broadly in a nexus of overlapping social phenomena (such as the sexual division of labor, economic stratification, racism, and so on). Any instance of a sexual desire, act, or identity that might be read as a counter-example to her theory is reconstructed as another confirmation of it.[4] Furthermore, the rhetorical quality of her theory requires reductionism with regard to a number of other key terms: MacKinnon is a feminist "unmodified," while those who reject her analysis of pornography are labeled "liberals" or anti-feminists.[5] Any kind of sexually explicit representation that does not obviously meet her definition of pornography as the eroticization of dominance and submission is either stretched until it does or dismissed as not pornographic.[6] And finally, MacKinnon's claim that women's experiences form the basis of her theory is in fact premised on the experience of a particular group of women and a particular understanding of power.

In positing heterosexuality as foundational to women's oppression, MacKinnon needs to account for sexual acts and identities that inhabit the margins of her theory. By insisting that there is a unitary experience of sexuality in this culture, that sexuality is reducible to relations of domination and subordination where masculinity maps to the former and femininity to the latter, and that there can be no sexuality, let alone sexual pleasure, outside the terms of this dichotomy, MacKinnon is required to explain how queer desires, acts, and identities can be theoretically intelligible. Her account ignores, for example, lesbian sexualities and identities that have radical, disruptive possibilities, instead absorbing lesbian experience to relations of dominance and submission defined within a heterosexual nexus. Thus rather than being *explained*, lesbians are *assimilated* to MacKinnon's theory and in particular to her construction of female sexual identity.

Specifically, MacKinnon argues that "homosexuality" [sic] should be read through the same social relations of power that construct (hetero)sexuality: "Nor is homosexuality without stake in this gendered sexual system. Putting to one side the obviously gendered content of expressly adopted roles, clothing, and sexual mimicry, to the extent the gender of a sexual object is crucial to arousal, the structure of social power which stands behind and defines gender is hardly irrelevant, even if it is rearranged." And MacKinnon argues against lesbian feminist attempts to construct lesbian identities as spaces of resistance:

> Some have argued that lesbian sexuality—meaning here simply women having sex with women, not with men—solves the problem of gender by eliminating men from women's voluntary sexual encounters. Yet women's sexuality remains constructed under conditions of male supremacy; women remain socially defined as women in relation to men; the definition of women as men's inferiors remains sexual even if not heterosexual, whether men are present at the time or not. To the extent gay men choose men because they are men, the meaning of masculinity is affirmed as well as undermined. It may also be that sexuality is so gender marked that it carries dominance and submission with it, whatever the gender of its participants.[7]

There are a number of telling elisions here: first, lesbian sexuality is rarely understood by feminist theorists to consist simply of "women having sex with women" (however "sex" is construed in this phrase).[8] Within lesbian communities, lesbian sexuality is variously understood as a "lifestyle," a complex set of sexual and emotional desires, an aesthetic, a culture, a political identity, and so on.

Second, there is considerable slippage in MacKinnon's writing between an understanding of "women" as a biologically marked category and as a socially constituted collective—at times she seems to suggest that gendered power acts only upon (biological) women and at other times, that anyone (including a biological male) can be "made" a woman through sexual subordination. Either route leads to troubling consequences for MacKinnon's account of resistance: if "women" is a biologically marked category that exists prior to the operation of power, MacKinnon seems to suggest it is overdetermined: once a woman, always a woman. Then the meaning of "women" can perhaps only be resisted at the point of true revolution (although how feminists will get there is unclear), and MacKinnon certainly denies the efficacy of many examples of lesser resistance. If, on the other hand, "women" is a group constituted *through* the exercise of power, MacKinnon implies it may be *larger* than the biological category (however understood), but is still sufficiently overdetermined that it cannot be *smaller*—i.e., all biological females must be women. The over-determination of "women" on either of these interpretations poses a number of difficulties: it entirely erases transgendered experience, especially the subject-position of females passing as men. These individuals fit the phenomenology of neither masculinity nor femininity outlined by MacKinnon, even though she claims these categories are exhaustive. Furthermore, Monique Wittig posits that "women" comprise a group constituted through the exercise of power and defined by material and ideological conditions. Initially echoing MacKinnon's line of argument, Wittig presses the conclusion that while women *are* socially defined as women in relation to men, if they are *not* in relation with men (if they are separatists of various kinds, for example) then they are not women, but lesbians: "lesbians are not women," but rather contingently achieve an identity outside conventional meanings.[9]

Thus, third, while it may be that sexuality is problematically gender-marked even in queer contexts, to reduce all sexuality to equivalent relations of dominance and submission is to beg the question of whether resistance against these relations is possible. A significant body of lesbian feminist theory articulates various ways in which lesbian identities (including, but not reducible to, lesbian sex) are understood to challenge and resist aspects of compulsory heterosexuality as an institution.[10] Rather than responding to the content of these arguments, MacKinnon again merely assimilates them to the terms of her own position.[11] She herself clearly does advocate forms of feminist resistance—anti-pornography ordinances, for example. But it is unclear why MacKinnon believes these legal strategies can stand any hope of overcoming the determinative effects of power she identifies in her theory, and why she believes the effects of queer organizing on contemporary understandings of sexuality so thoroughly fail to do so.[12] MacKinnon attributes an implausibly seamless (and arguably nonfeminist) character to gendered power. If power is this perfectly coherent, then it is not clear how it can be made visible, to open the conceptual window to feminist resistance.

MacKinnon's theory thus narrows the space available to political activism in the course of erasing queer identities and theorizing. This presents troubling inconsistencies not only on the meta-level of her account of power as dominance. Intent on developing her position against a male liberal vanguard, she does not pay much attention—in any of her writing—to debates internal to feminist theory. Her theory, however, while appealing in its clarity and forthrightness, also has negative consequences for any adequate account of feminist consciousness: MacKinnon claims to start from women's experiences to identify the contours of gender dominance. Her conclusions, however, yield the implicit claim that women's experiences that do not conform to her theory are irrelevant to it. Unless MacKinnon invokes a suspiciously strong notion of false consciousness to account for these experiences (and her emphasis on consciousness raising would seem to preclude this), she needs to explain why lesbian feminists who think their sexuality is importantly resistive are wrong. By reducing sexuality to dominance and submission, and re-jecting attempts to resist, subvert, and change this construction, MacKinnon concomitantly erases women's agency, making us into hapless re-enactors of the patriarchal imperative to be subordinate. Power as dominance over-determines in a way that makes empowerment and resistance virtually im-possible. Thus MacKinnon does not need—on her own terms—to look at counter-examples from women's experience.

Because MacKinnon prioritizes sexuality throughout her theoretical proj-ect, the exclusion of queer experience is more readily visible than conceptu-ally similar racial exclusion. My critique emphasizes an account of power that makes possible the assimilation of queer—especially lesbian—experience to the terms of the theory. Critical race theorists have argued that the experi-ences of women of color are likewise assimilated to MacKinnon's theory, which is based in white women's experiences of sexual violence. It is in this latter context that MacKinnon has given her most theoretically complex ri-poste. Angela Harris and Marlee Kline both object to her account on the grounds that it excludes the identities and experiences of oppression of women of color. Kline identifies various manifestations of methodological essentialism in white feminist legal theory. The mistake she attributes to MacKinnon is that of oversimplifying the sites of women's oppression:

> Not only is her construction of the feminist project limited in its capacity
> to capture the complex impact of racism in the lives of women of color . . .
> but her analysis is problematic in two additional, related ways: neither the
> differences in interest and priority that exist between white women and
> women of color nor the unequal power relationship between the groups
> are confronted or dealt with in her work.[13]

Kline posits that MacKinnon's emphasis on sexuality as the primary locus of women's oppression both is reductive and derives from white women's con-struction of feminist practice.

Harris argues in more depth that MacKinnon's work relies on

> gender essentialism—the notion that a unitary, "essential" women's ex-
> perience can be isolated and described independently of race, class, sexual
> orientation, and other realities of experience. The result of the tendency
> toward gender essentialism, I argue, is not only that some voices are si-
> lenced in order to privilege others (for this is an inevitable result of cate-
> gorization, which is necessary both for human communication and polit-
> ical movement), but that the voices that are silenced turn out to be the

same voices silenced by the mainstream legal voice of "We the People"—among them, the voices of black women.[14]

Black women, Harris claims, appear in MacKinnon's work as "white women, only more so."[15] In particular, MacKinnon's feminist legal theory of rape, she argues, fails to take into account the historically and racially specific vulnerability of African-American women to sexual violence. The experience and legacy of slavery and the sexual abuse and exploitation of Black women by white men (especially slave-owners or, after emancipation, male heads of households), the fact that rape of a Black woman during slavery was not a crime, the lynching and continuing disproportionate criminal punishment of Black men for alleged sex crimes against white women, and the complicity of white women in these injustices—all these bring into question any feminist theory or practice that understands rape as simply a "gender issue." This critique is an attack on methodological essentialism in MacKinnon's work. Central to it is the recognition not merely of "differences" between women but of differences of power, or "relations of dominance," in MacKinnon's language. The critique is thus a particularly telling challenge to a theory that purports to place an analysis of power at its core. To address it, MacKinnon needs to justify her selective attention to certain relations of power—such as those between women and men—but not others—those between white women and Black women, for example.

What is MacKinnon's response to her methodological critics? MacKinnon claims to offer a direct reply to these charges, although, like Gilligan, she tends merely to make reference to their existence before once again elaborating the framework that her critics dispute. She argues, first, (in a tu quoque move) that anti-essentialist critiques imply that there is no such thing as the practice of "sex inequality" and second, that there are empirical bases for widely applicable generalizations about women's oppression:

> I want to take up the notion of experience "as a woman" and argue that it is the practice of which the concept of discrimination "based on sex" is the legal theory. That is, I want to investigate how the realities of women's experience of sex inequality in the world have shaped some contours of sex discrimination in the law.[16]

MacKinnon's justification for her theoretical use of sex "unmodified" is that it is based on an "empirical statement about reality" [PT: 47]: "to speak of social treatment 'as a woman' is thus not to invoke any abstract essence or homogeneous generic or ideal type, not to posit anything, far less a universal anything, but to refer to this diverse and pervasive concrete material reality of social meanings and practices" [PT: 48]. She argues that methodological anti-essentialism both trivializes "straight white economically privileged" women's oppression and undercuts the possibility of understanding and remedying the practice of sex inequality. She also makes a point that resonates with Bordo's, albeit in more aggressive terms:

> I also sense . . . that many women, not only women of color and not only academics, do not want to be "just women," not only because something important is left out, but also because that means being in a category with "her," the useless white woman whose first reaction when the going gets rough is to cry. I sense here that people feel more dignity in being part of a group that includes men than in being part of a group that includes that ultimate reduction of the notion of oppression, that instigator of lynch mobs, that ludicrous whiner, that equality coat-tails rider, the white woman [PT: 53].

MacKinnon accepts the point that the otherwise unoppressed white woman is not definitive of women's oppression merely by virtue of this status, but she nonetheless claims that the oppression of the most privileged women is an indicator of the force of sex oppression generally.

Thus on first reading, MacKinnon's response to her anti-essentialist critics might seem to be an "anti anti-essentialist" rejoinder fully in keeping with a Wittgensteinian feminist method. She too wants to "look and see," to permit empirically based and politically effective generalizations about women. She wants her theory to be grounded in feminist practice, to avoid a kind of theory that "proceeds as if you can deconstruct power relations by shifting their markers around in your head" [PT: 45]. And she bases these generalizations on the commonality of women's experiences of sex and sexual violence (or, in her terms, sex *as* sexual violence, sexual violence *as* sex). Patriarchy constructs women uniformly, through defining and controlling discourses and practices, but MacKinnon's feminist oppositional practice, by contrast, is allegedly grounded in women's diverse experiences:

> If we build a theory out of women's practice, comprised of the diversity of all women's experiences, we do not have the problem that some feminist theory has been rightly criticized for. When we have it is when we make theory out of abstractions and accept the images forced on us by male dominance. I said all that so that I could say this: the assumption that all women are the same is part of that bedrock of sexism that the Women's Move-

ment is predicated on challenging. That some academics find it difficult to theorize without reproducing it simply means that they continue to do to women what theory, predicated on the practice of male dominance, has always done to women. It is their notion of what theory is, and its relation to its world, that needs to change [PT: 54].

While I broadly agree with this set of assertions, the kind of theory (and practice) MacKinnon's analysis produces nonetheless both confuses and ignores the responses of her anti-essentialist critics. MacKinnon's rhetorically powerful rejoinders—like Gilligan's—tend to conceal a failure to interrogate the power relations that have generated her own theory and that shape her own story about what constitutes feminist practice. Casting women as a unified group by virtue of their experience of sexuality not only erases differences in that construction but also oversimplifies the exigencies of feminist practice. MacKinnon's appeal to the "empirical" as evidence that her theory is not essentialist allows her successfully to evade the charge that she is making a priori generalizations about women, but, as I argued in Chapter 4, it is not a claim that has any determinate consequences or that constitutes an adequate response to charges of methodological essentialism.

Like Gilligan, MacKinnon agrees that some "theory" as understood outside (radical) feminism may have been essentialist in assuming a biological basis for women's oppression, but easily side-steps any suggestion that her work is essentialist in this sense. In assuming that she is being accused of biological essentialism, however, she fails to grasp the methodological usage of the epithet "essentialist." Thus MacKinnon's first response is to reject the charge of methodological essentialism by sleight of hand—this kind of mistake, she claims, is not *really* essentialism (although this semantic move does not obviate the need to address the problem) [PT: 48; notes 9 and 11]. She nonetheless acknowledges (even if she does not call it "essentialism") the difficulties inherent in constructing a very general account of women's oppression while avoiding methodological pitfalls.

MacKinnon argues, however, that anti-essentialism must imply that there is no such thing as the practice of "sex inequality." But anti-essentialism is not the claim that gender is a useless or even insignificant category in and of itself, merely that arguments about women's oppression should not take the identities of a particular group of women as the epitome of gender oppression. I am sympathetic to MacKinnon's claim, echoing Bordo, that the invocation of class and race differences is used to undercut feminist theories of gender while the reverse is less often true [PT: 50]. But this is a contingent phenomenon that does not necessarily follow from anti-essentialist critique:

in fact, anti-essentialism of the kind for which I have been arguing would insist also that theses in race theory, for example, be inflected by gender difference just as much as the reverse. Anti-essentialists agree that sexual violence, in the forms MacKinnon stresses, contributes to the oppression of all women. It seems clear, as MacKinnon herself comments, that when a woman of any race is raped, for example, she is raped, in some sense, *as a woman*. But, as I argued in Chapter 2, anti-essentialism need not consist solely in the claim that women cannot have shared experiences, but rather consists in a distinctively different way of conceptualizing the similarities and differences between those experiences, and in forms of theory construction that recognize the contextual nature of gender oppression. I suggest that to understand all women's experiences of rape as encapsulated by a unique description of that experience is to ignore the differences of power between women that have led to the privileging of one particular account. MacKinnon ostensibly disagrees with her anti-essentialist critics, but only by accusing them of rejecting all generalizations about women, not by addressing their charge that her theory fails to tell a story about differences of power among them.

MacKinnon does not clarify her position with regard to this stronger anti-essentialist criticism, although she seems hostile to it, and doesn't elaborate on her telling assertion that "how the white woman is imagined and constructed and treated becomes a particularly sensitive indicator of the degree to which women, as such, are despised" [PT: 54]. Thus she simply does not respond to Harris' charge that the context of racialized sexual violence creates both a different experience of that violence for women of color, and a different kind of feminist theory. When Harris argues that the different relations of dominance within which African-American women are situated make rape into a specific kind of feminist issue for them, she is also making an "empirical" argument. Presumably, unless only what white women do counts as feminist practice, Harris can argue that the divergent feminist practice of African-American women against rape emerges from that distinctive experience. Of course, it is sometimes—empirically—the case that women with different experiences and different understandings of feminist issues have successfully worked together by focusing on their common goals. But the point of anti-essentialist critique is to demonstrate that, at least sometimes, feminist practice itself has been constructed to privilege the experiences of a particular group of women.

For example, one of MacKinnon's avowed motivations is to ensure that the previously "sex-blind" law develops provision for sex discrimination understood in radical rather than liberal terms. Without necessarily opposing this goal, however, Kimberlé Crenshaw argues that methodological essentialism in feminist-inspired anti-discrimination law blocks legal recourse for Black women. She presents three specific cases as exemplary of discursive strategies that prevent Black women's experience of oppression from being captured by existing legal conceptualizations. The first is legal resistance to making "Black women" a protected category under anti-discrimination legislation: "The court's refusal in DeGraffenreid [v. General Motors] to acknowledge Black women encounter combined race and sex discrimination implies that the boundaries of sex and race discrimination doctrine are defined respectively by white women's and Black men's experiences." In another type of case, courts have rejected Black women as class representatives in sex discrimination cases: "The court rejected [the plaintiff's] bid to represent all females apparently because her attempt to specify her race was seen as being at odds with the standard allegation that the employer simply discriminated 'against females.'" And finally, this limiting of the representativeness of Black women can also be applied to race: "courts . . . have held that Black women cannot represent an entire class of Blacks due to presumed class conflicts in cases where sex additionally disadvantaged Black women."[17]

Thus even some progressively inspired legal practice contributes to the erasure of the experience of oppression of those with so-called "intersectional identities." MacKinnon doesn't say *how* her account avoids this problem, except to wave toward a practice that is based on the multiplicity of women's experiences. In Chapter 2 I argued that Okin mistakenly accuses Spelman of gender relativism and makes appeal to the "empirical," to preclude essentialism. MacKinnon makes the same move, making the latter claim more nuanced by arguing that her "empirical" argument is grounded in feminist practice. Notice, ironically, how different the respective feminist projects of Okin and MacKinnon are: the former seeks to restore feminism to its rightful place in the liberal pantheon, harshly criticizing the theoretical inflections of postmodern influence in feminist theory. The latter starts from Marxism to reach a starkly radical feminist position. Yet each believes that a plea to the indisputable "empirical" grounds her position. This contradiction, if nothing else, reveals the lack of theoretical support for this reference: MacKinnon's strategy permits her to jettison the criticisms of her anti-essentialist commentators through an important, but ultimately unsatisfactory, rhetorical appeal to practice.

MacKinnon claims to be building a theory from the empirical reality of women's common oppression as identified through feminist practice. This goal, however, is shared by many feminists of different stripes, and I have been arguing that feminists need to develop methods that investigate and elaborate such claims. MacKinnon argues that her opponents adopt an overly abstract theoretical position from which to develop their practice, whereas she grounds her theory in the feminist practice of consciousness-raising. The distinction between theory and practice in MacKinnon's work, however, is never as clear as she would like it to be: doesn't MacKinnon fall into the trap of seeing what she is looking for? Of re-inscribing relations of power within the group "women" even as she purports to describe a universal female reality? Her critics show how she neglects the political salience of racialized constructions of sexuality. But how exactly does this neglect matter for feminist practice? The appeal to feminist "practice" as a route to avoid methodological essentialism provides no more information than the claim that feminist theorists should "look and see." Essentialism can be perpetuated by practices as much as by theory. The challenge facing feminists is to articulate the precise shape of anti-essentialist practice as it is mutually informed by anti-essentialist theory.

### Learning from Practice?

If MacKinnon's account does not adequately describe a feminist practice that is not essentialist, how is essentialism inscribed in feminist activism, and what might anti-essentialist practice look like? There are many sites in which answers to these questions are played out; some of the most interesting are those where feminists have organized against the phenomena she describes as central to women's oppression. The history of feminist activism in this area in fact motivates many of MacKinnon's central claims: much anti-sexual violence organizing in particular is rooted in radical feminist analyses that stress the strength of the connection between gender and violence. Claims, for example, that male violence is concordant with norms of masculinity rather than a feature of a few individual pathologized men, that sex and violence are intimately linked, that acts of sexual violence are prevalent and under-reported, or that petty acts of sexism are contiguous with harassment, rape and murder, are all based in analyses similar to MacKinnon's. Furthermore, sexualized violence really does cross race and class lines; it affects all women. Almost all acts of sexual violence are committed by men. And when this gendered dichotomy of aggressor and victim breaks down, there are plausible reasons to argue, as MacKinnon does, that "exceptional" acts of violence in fact re-inscribe a gender divide. For example, gay men may be queer-bashed because their sexual identity is equated with effeminacy, which in turn is equated with women, which in turn makes them into legitimate targets of violence in the minds of queer-hating misogynists; women who are labeled "aggressors" may in fact acting in self-defense in response to prolonged male violence they have themselves survived. Influential feminist analyses such as MacKinnon's suggest that gender is not only disciplined but actually defined through the nexus of images, attitudes, and social structures that permit and perpetuate sexualized violence.

MacKinnon is right to claim, furthermore, that feminist theories of sexual violence are rooted in feminist practice, and these analytical claims are both generated by and inform, however partially, feminist organizing against sexual violence. They appear in diluted form in the "breaking down myths" training that volunteers typically receive, in pro-survivor feminist counseling strategies, and in the kinds of political goals organizations choose. My experience suggests that many women who are drawn to this kind of feminist work understand themselves as acting in solidarity with women as a group. Women volunteers are encouraged to identify "as women." At all the sexual assault centers and battered women's shelters I know, only women staff phone lines and provide other front-line services. Where men are directly involved in this work it is usually, I think appropriately, as educators or counselors working with other men to challenge male attitudes. And activists working to improve sexual assault legislation often speak of the way it erases "women's experiences" or how the criminal justice system silences "the woman's voice." Thus feminist practice aimed at mitigating sexual violence is, as MacKinnon argues, one of the areas where a universalizing account of women's oppression is indeed both widely accepted and empirically grounded. If generalizations about women are safe in any context, surely it is this one?

Much of the power of MacKinnon's analysis comes from her recognition of the pervasiveness of sexual violence and her anti-liberal insistence that it is made possible by relations of dominance enacted through social groups. But the two opposites of "difference" and "dominance" are not the only choices for feminists; it is possible to retain politically important notions of social group membership without understanding all members of those groups as uniform, and while incorporating recognition of cross-cutting relations of power. The example of feminist organizing against sexual violence is instructive because here, as elsewhere, recognizing the legitimacy and usefulness of certain generalizations about women neither makes relations of dominance between women irrelevant to political practice, nor determines its precise contours.

Just as Okin's claim that women in both "poor" and "Western industrialized" countries are oppressed within the family leaves many questions unanswered, so MacKinnon's claim that sexual violence is the empirical reality of all women elides differences in that reality and under-determines the shape of the practice it generates. At the same time as feminists act on the recognition that women qua women share common concerns, they also face the challenge that many "women's issues" are not straightforwardly universal. Anti-essentialism warns dominant group feminists to be wary of practice that merely "adds on" race or class or sexual identity to an existing approach without attempting a more profound methodological rethinking. Adding "different" women to a pre-existing construction of a feminist problem forces those women to work through constructions that may not reflect their experiences. MacKinnon's critics accuse her of this kind of practice.

There is a risk that women of color, for example, would be "invited in" to organizations that were originally established for and by white women. In grappling with guilt, anger, defensiveness, and the potent mixture of invisible racism and professed anti-racism, white feminists may express a desperate desire to "include." Motivated by abstract political goals, image building, guilt, and good intentions, we have often acted as if the mere fact of intra-organizational diversity were more important than either the political reasons for it or its success and usefulness to women of color. Thus anti-essentialist practice requires more than a simple add-on—an affirmative action slogan on a recruitment poster, a member nominated to act as the "women of color" representative, or the claim that generalizations about gender oppression apply to Other women, only more so. It requires a thorough interrogation of the relations of power that construct feminist "issues" and of the public and hidden transcripts at work when feminists communicate with each other.

The inequalities of power that construct feminist identities through essentialist practice are not always acknowledged. For example, Allison Tom investigated class differences between managerial and trainee women in a self-described feminist bank. She argues that the managerial women, instead of interpreting interpersonal and organizational conflict as indicative of a re-inscription of class relations—as an indication of essentialist practice—understood it as revealing inadequacies on the part of their trainees.[18] I argued in Chapter 4 that entering a feminist zone with a clear sense of the kinds of inequalities and differences generally obscured or made visible by one's position of power or powerlessness generates better research outcomes. Analogously, in feminist practice, stepping back to reflect on the issues emphasized in this book may change our perspective on aspects of our practice previously taken for granted.

Given the value of MacKinnon's analysis and its grounding in certain historically specific kinds of organizing, and given the anti-essentialist critique I have been sketching, what should feminists do differently? Just as the reality of male violence against women is being even more fully documented and revealed as a widespread and cross-cutting social problem, so feminist initiatives are re-evaluating the relevance of their political work to different constituencies of women, to men, and to those who do not fit either of these categories. Feminists working within organizations composed of and representing diverse constituencies of women have raised challenges to the constructions of feminist issues and identities.

For example, many feminists are challenging racism and working toward feminist anti-racist and culturally sensitive therapies.[19] All women *are* oppressed by a sexist legal system, but how this oppression is played out varies widely according to race and class, in ways that have been both quantatively and qualitatively documented by feminists undertaking legal advocacy. Any description of women's oppression under the law which fails to incorporate this observation necessarily presents some women's experiences of oppression as ideal-typical and interprets the legal system's understanding of that oppression as representative of the legal imagination more generally. A wealthy white woman raped by a Black stranger does not only have a very different experience than a poor First Nations woman raped by her white employer; her experience would be constructed differently within the oppressive frameworks of law. The feminist legal practice that may address the oppression of one does not, pace MacKinnon, necessarily remedy the oppression of the other without more specific and sophisticated commitment to addressing oppression from the "bottom up."[20] As part of anti-heterosexist practice, furthermore, feminists can no longer assume that domestic violence only occurs in heterosexual relationships and that lesbian relationships are immune. But nor can we assume that lesbian experiences merely mimic heterosexual violence, copying relations of power and roles found in straight communities.

Effective feminist anti-sexual violence organizing adapts itself to local conditions, matching practice to the particular histories and needs of a community. For example, Nancy Matthews's analysis of racial diversity in a local anti-rape movement documents how historical trends worked against racial integration in feminist campaigning on sexual assault, arguing inter alia that the predominance of white women in the establishment of grass-roots rape crisis centers and their cultural and social links to the second wave of feminism discouraged the involvement of women of color in the anti-rape movement in Los Angeles.[21] She focuses on two feminist organizations: the Rosa Parks Sexual Assault Crisis Center (founded 1984) and the Compton YWCA Sexual Assault Crisis Program, both organized by Black women for local Black communities. Both had bureaucratic (albeit "progressive") parent organizations, and both operated within a framework of community action and social service rather than the dominant feminist political frameworks. They identified quite different priorities for women of color with regard to sexual assault than did their white counterparts. They had to overcome language barriers, a distrust of educators and media, and a different cultural ethic about seeking help from strangers (compounded by tense understandings of who was inside and who was outside the boundaries of the community). They required considerable financial support due to the extra hours of work required for developing culturally appropriate outreach and crisis intervention programs and for working through the multiple problems of their clients. This translated into different practical needs, including incest and alcoholism support groups, gang negotiations, and, in the absence of supporting services, attention to all aspects of clients' well-being. As Matthews quotes the director of the Compton program:

> A woman may come in or call in for various reasons. She has no place to go, she has no job, she has no support, she has no money, she has no food, she's been beaten, and after you finish meeting those needs, or try to meet all those needs, then she may say, by the way, during all this, I was being raped. So the immediate needs have to be met. So that makes our community different from other communities.[22]

In the context of a multiplicity of cultural issues and of the peer counseling roots of crisis intervention work, women of color worked here to deliver services to other women of color. Matthews contrasts this approach with the dominant subculture of the local anti-rape movement, which she describes as "(white) feminism strongly influenced by a lesbian perspective."[23] Black women, she argues, did not have the same political origins and were more likely in this case to identify with a social service orientation and to be less suspicious of government funding. Thus the two communities had different reference systems and political vocabularies, compounded by concerns about racism or homophobia from the other group. While they were in dialogue, each met their objectives through separate and community-appropriate organizing.

Similarly, there is a notion prevalent among white/Anglo feminists that for a woman to move from an abusive male partner to the putatively woman-identified community of a shelter—while it may have negative economic or practical consequences—nonetheless constitutes an improvement in available psychological and political support systems. This understanding is challenged by the recognition that for a woman to leave her home for what is often the only alternative, may also be to leave her linguistic, cultural, racial, ethnic, or religious community behind for a racist, ethnocentric, or otherwise exclusionary milieu. Again, this observation has important consequences for activism.

Feminist anti-essentialist insights also helped my colleagues and me to address problems of exclusion in recruiting and training help-line volunteers. For example, we became more conscious of the implicit mental image most new recruits had of their prospective callers—namely, that they would be young, single or casually dating, heterosexual, Euro-Canadian, and childless. In other words, that the callers would be just like (most of) them. We addressed this familiar problem in two ways: first, as my examples above suggest, by trying to diversify our volunteer body, and second, by actively undermining this "essentialized" image of callers by including training workshops on racism and sexual violence, cultural difference in phone dynamics, challenging heteronormativity, and so on. Such anti-essentialist strategies within feminist organizations are by now quite widespread. For many sexual assault (formerly "rape crisis") centers, the requirement of shared political values now includes that potential members be anti-racist, anti-heterosexist, and responsive to the needs of working-class women and women with disabilities. For example, *Vancouver Women Against Violence Against Women* has included the following sessions in their volunteer training program: "deaf women, deaf culture and sexual violence," "anti-racism," "classism," "Jewish women and anti-Semitism," and "lesbian life," some of which are facilitated by the appropriate caucus. Thus the organization has recognized that a phenomenon (sexual violence) that affects all women affects different women differently due to their social locations, and thus "purely" anti-sexist work disproportionately benefits white, straight, middle-class, able-bodied women. Many feminist organizations are increasingly trying to confront these issues explicitly in their training and development programs.

I also make sense of feminist anti-essentialism in practice by *refraining* from making claims about the sameness of different women's experiences of sexual violence. Just as many of us have been offended by the homophobic man, who, when "propositioned" by another man, says "now I know *exactly* what women mean when they talk about sexual harassment!," so I do not say "I know what you mean—the *exact same* thing happened to me last week." The assimilation (and trivialization) of experience into the language of a dominant Other is a common essentializing moment in feminist practice, as is the appropriation of suffering to meet the needs of its witness.[24] This is the kind of moment that Harris' anti-essentialist critique highlights but that analyses like MacKinnon's tend to ignore. Instead, in identifying patterns in my work I conceptualized the relationships between different women's experiences as "family resemblances" rather than as identity relations. This conceptualization also enabled me to see respect and recognition in the claim that the experiences of ostensibly different women can be similar to my own, notwithstanding important differences. For example, as someone who fortunately did not experience childhood sexual abuse, at the same time as I recognize "that's so terrible, I simply can't relate," I also acknowledge connections between my own experiences of growing up female in a sexist society and the experience of sexual abuse. Refusing to dissociate from survivors, refusing to make "them" into a group distinct from "us," those who did not suffer this experience, is as much a part of effective anti-essentialist practice as is respecting difference. This constant self-reflexive balancing of the dangers of assimilation and dissociation, which happens on the most personal and the most institutionalized levels, is how anti-essentialism should be played out in practice.

These examples represent challenges to a prevalent *feminist* understanding of sexual violence as a set of crimes perpetrated exclusively by men exclusively against their female partners, where these categories are understood as uniform. This strikes me as the kind of commitment dominant group feminists should derive from anti-essentialist feminism, a commitment supported by interrogating attitudes and structures with an eye to power and differences among women. MacKinnon's analysis simply does not give us any tools for understanding and revising these forms of practice. Her theory usefully guides feminist interpretations of sexual violence contra popular liberal descriptions, but for those already converted to a dominance model it provides no theoretical insights or practical guidelines for negotiating oppressive relations of power within oppositional feminist contexts.

However, is there a danger that in challenging MacKinnon's theory of sexual violence, feminists might undermine their own political aims? What are the risks of admitting contextual variation and exceptions within any feminist model, when feminist interpretations in general are already aggressively contested? It would indeed be politically suicidal if the gender skepticism that Bordo identifies as damaging to feminist theory were to spill over into feminist practice. A principled anti-essentialism that merely valorizes difference and makes no serious attempt to understand the history, context, or implications of specific forms of oppression could function as an antifeminist alibi, seeming to de-legitimate any generalization made in the name of politics. This kind of anti-essentialism would thus provide an easy weapon for discourses that seek to deny the salience of social group memberships. This move, however, is not typical of anti-essentialist critiques, although MacKinnon depicts it as such. We should not allow a justified feminist suspicion of principled anti-essentialism to motivate a negative response to the suggestion that we need an anti-essentialist feminist practice; instead, we need to ask how relations of power among women in feminist contexts might change our practice, not to abandon the category "women," but to rethink it so that our practice can become more just and more effective.

### The Challenge of Essentialism, the Risk of Anti-Essentialism

What is most important about anti-essentialist feminist critiques of the kind I have been advocating is their analysis of the ingenuity of oppression within supposedly emancipatory and resistive contexts. For example, Lugones's work has proved extraordinarily valuable to me in pinpointing exactly how my own thinking has tended to re-inscribe privilege by divorcing my experiential knowledge about ethnocentric racism within feminist activism and pedagogy from my philosophical writing, which has tended toward rather abstract analyses of "difference."[25]

Generalizing about gender, however, is an indispensable activity within sites of feminist practice. This crucial observation in part motivates both Gilligan and MacKinnon to make relatively grand claims for the importance and uniformity of gender. The reshaping of feminist practice suggested by anti-essentialism problematizes MacKinnon's argument that generalizing accounts of gender can be based simply on existing practice generated from (some) women's experience. Anti-essentialist practice of the kind I have sketched nevertheless permits politically powerful generalizations about women, and my examples have in fact focused on organizing that continues to place gender, albeit "multiply inflected," at the center of its practice. These examples differ from an essentialist practice: they include analyses of cross-cutting relations of power among women and concomitant shifts in practice as well as recognition of the importance of building alliances with political groups not explicitly focused on gender. They thus echo the claim, often heard in articulations of "postmodern" politics, that coalition building undercuts essentialism. But how far can we take this analysis? How, ultimately, can anti-essentialists justify drawing a boundary around the category "women"? What role might anti-essentialist feminist practices create for pro-feminist men, for example? All political identity claims require some such line drawing; I argued in Chapter 3 that this process should be self-reflexive. But these arguments do not provide much to go on, and their continued invocation as the end of the story again exhibits a "contemptuous attitude toward the particular case."[26]

It is not obvious how some of the theoretical arguments of the preceding chapters might be implemented. Nor is it always obvious how the practice of those, like MacKinnon, who disagree with anti-essentialist claims in feminist philosophy should differ from that of anti-essentialist advocates. These debates came alive for me in the context of my own experience: during the first three years of this book's evolution, I was active in a local feminist anti-sexual violence movement and developed a particular interest in anti-sexual violence organizing on Canadian university campuses. The center in which I worked is based on a university campus and offers services to a clientele composed largely of young English-speaking adults, especially high school and university students. It is a feminist organization and works with both female and male survivors of sexual assault (where the latter are overwhelmingly victims of childhood sexual abuse). How could we avoid methodological essentialism in our practice? I have thought most about this issue in the context of exclusion: how might identity claims exclude, and what criteria can we use in evaluating these exclusions? In the example that follows, I compare a set of responses to claims to exclusion and inclusion in a sexual assault center. Some are power-conscious, others tokenistic, still others power-blind. The question in this context becomes: how can we (as feminist activists with some, however minimal, discursive control over the formation of feminist identities) distinguish productive and just exclusions from pernicious ones?

In pondering the role of the contemporary feminist intellectual, Kathy Miriam writes:

> Most academics probably recognize the distance traveled from earlier dreams for feminist theory—and for feminist theorists as having some important relationship to political praxis. The *reality* of today's intellectual is more aptly depicted in the words of a male professor when, introducing theoretician Judith Butler to the podium at a 1995 conference, he praised her for doing more than anyone else to make feminist theory autonomous from the feminist movement. Whether Butler would wish for such "credit" or not, the male professor's gaffe reveals a general attitude today toward the feminist academic. Perhaps this attitude lurks behind our failure to even pose the question of our role—and dare I say responsibility?—as public intellectuals.[27]

I think often about the responses of members of my intellectual milieu to different genres of feminist theory. I would argue that many times the work most politically and psychologically threatening to those hostile to or ambivalent about feminism exemplifies real women and men as they experience, and are experienced by others through, relations of oppression. Abstract theories that decline to give specific examples of oppressive actions or to generalize about gendered identities feel safe to many readers, especially male readers; they do not see themselves unflatteringly represented.[28] Instead they see only ideas that enable them to keep political discussion at a level of abstraction that often seems more like dissociation, and, of course, to continue to indulge their privilege without challenge.

I remember a moment of crisis in a classroom: teaching introductory feminist theory, I had walked a group of students through a number of difficult concepts that they had initially aggressively resisted. I heard students who had claimed at the beginning of the course that men and women were perfectly equal, talking knowledgeably about oppression and patriarchy. But when I challenged them to work through a series of hypothetical political decisions about representation and exclusion in a feminist organization (for example, "should men be allowed to join?" "will you have a lesbian caucus?") they fell back onto a clichéd liberal language of sameness, inclusion, "special interests" versus equality, individualism, and the symmetry of sexism and separatism ("we can't exclude men, because then we will be repeating exactly what they have done to us"). Eventually, frustrated by their political backtracking, I said in exasperation, "You can't have it both ways. You can't talk about oppression and patriarchy in one breath, then when you're asked to make real decisions and defend a position, turn around and deny that those terms have any basis in reality." Some students saw the importance of this challenge, but many were taken aback: they wanted to feel comfortable in a political language that did not require them to challenge—even to exercise—power, only to accede to its terms. They also wanted to remain in a critical posture, pointing to sexism in their lives and even to the limitations of the feminist theories we were reading, but not defending controversial political positions.

But these observations also highlight what it really means to live a feminist life, to take risks in defending one's politics. When I argue for the reality of gender in the context of sexual violence, I feel as if I am putting myself in the position I required of my students. Separatism and essentialism are presumed by many feminist theorists to go hand-in-hand, yet the insistence on powerfully naming the dichotomous operation of constructions of gender in the context of sexual violence is a form of feminist separation that need not be uncritical about its own line drawing.[29] The categories "women" and "men" can be bounded in ways that capture important realities without implying that all members of each of the two groups are identically situated.

Separatism also need not make line drawing its exclusive focus. Hostile criticisms of feminist separation that direct attention to the illegitimacy of exclusion tend to emphasize what lies outside the line—men, for example. But women-only space is transformational precisely because it directs women's attention toward other women, toward what lies inside the line. Instead of arguing about the possible nature and scope of men's commitments to feminism (an often uncomfortable activity that nonetheless creates space for men, whether literal or metaphorical), the empowering aspect of women-only space for me is the opportunity to place men outside the political picture, to focus on developing a politics that places women at its core.

Having elaborated the philosophical bases of a number of anti-essentialist criticisms, I wanted to accompany this work with an analysis of the political challenges they raise in a particular activist context. Part of my motivation is to offer a language to respond to the browbeating of activists by those who appropriate essentialism talk for anti-feminist purposes. Too often the theoretical moves I have been discussing are divorced from the contexts of power that give them political weight by those who object to generalizations in which they are negatively represented. Likewise the experiences of those who have been illegitimately excluded from political vision can be appropriated to endorse the dominance of different others. This comes through in poorly argued claims that transgender identities, for example, illustrate that gender is "not real," or that generalizations about women and men are a priori illegitimate. In my experience of organizing against sexual violence, it is also revealed in the not uncommon appropriation of the experiences of men who have survived sexual abuse by those who have not. The latter may use the reality of the sexual abuse of boys to deny the systemic nature of girls' and women's sexual victimization by men. Similarly, white men too often invoke the fact of false accusations of rape with racist motivations as evidence that women's testimony of sexual violence should not be believed. Men who make these claims frequently exhibit no substantive political commitment to supporting male survivors or to organizing against racism; their appropriation of these exceptions to feminist generalizations is intended only to buttress their own claims to freeedom from political implication. Thus part of my project is to pick through specific cases of generalizing political claims in the hope of offering some explanations by example, articulating the appropriate use of anti-essentialist criticism.

Consider the following two claims, made by prospective volunteers:

Claim 1: "As a feminist organization, you purport to include the experiences and interests of all women who have survived sexual assault at this university. Yet your volunteer body is not racially, ethnically or culturally diverse, and your training program does not address the needs of women of color or immigrant women who may be dealing with, for example, the threat of deportation when a woman who is not yet a Canadian permanent resident tries to leave her violent husband, or the needs of women of color who face racialized sexual harassment at university."

Claim 2: "Your insistence that only women can work for your help-line and in almost all positions on your co-ordinating committee is exclusionary. Even though men are a minority of survivors of sexual assault, there are male survivors who should be able to speak with men about their experiences and your organization should address this need. Furthermore, many men are very sensitive to these issues and have better feminist politics than many women. And who's to say that a woman of color calling your line wouldn't rather to speak to a man of color about her experience than to a white woman? On what basis have you made gender your fundamental organizing axis?"

Both of these real examples point to forms of exclusion within a feminist organization. In both cases, the identities of the speakers raise additional political questions: the former set of claims was made by women of color and some white women with anti-racist politics. The latter was made by white men who did not themselves identify as survivors of sexual violence, arguing (inconsistently) against their own exclusion, not the exclusion of specific men of color or of specific survivors. Critical comments about the exclusion of men have been made far more often and more volubly by both men and women, and such comments have been given much more attention within the organization than those about exclusion on the grounds of race or sexuality. This reality flags (without over-determining) the different sites of power on which each claim is located. Implicit in both examples are anti-essentialist claims of different kinds. Anti-essentialist feminist activists, while giving careful consideration to both these claims, should take the first much more seriously than the second.

I distinguish the interpretations of these claims offered by power-sensitive and by principled anti-essentialist accounts of gender. The anti-essentialist feminist arguments I have offered might inform, in some contexts, the way we think about the role of men in feminist organizing. In this context, however, the men who invoked "anti-essentialism" to legitimate their own inclusion in feminist projects, or simply to minimize their participation in gender oppression, divorced anti-essentialism from the relations of power that create its feminist political significance. This observation accords with my general argument that merely to recommend "diversity" or "difference" as a political goal is in fact unhelpfully to prescind from judgment on their form and limits in practice. Principled anti-essentialism can operate in political situations not just as a brake on productive feminist inquiry but also in conjunction with anti-feminism. While we remain sensitive to the contingency of generalizations about gender, feminist analyses of power must remain central to our decision making as we evaluate the relative strength of different claims about exclusion.

Critiques of essentialism are compelling because they have carefully shown how textual strategies (such as writing about "difference" not "racism," or "women" not "white women") and political strategies (such as insisting that lesbians keep "their" issues out of feminist organizations) actually reinforce many of the mechanisms of oppression that feminists have criticized in male-dominant societies, where definitions and images of "humanity" (and access to the rights, respect, and so on, that ideally accompany human status) are controlled by powerful men. Feminist anti-essentialism has thus mainly been addressed to analyzing and remedying oppression among different groups of women. It is, however, also relevant to debates surrounding the role of men in feminist discourse and practice. Some feminists have argued that politically salient differences among "women" and among "men" create cross-cutting cleavages, conflicts, and alliances that are not reducible to a formulaic "men" versus "women" in motivating and justifying feminist political action. The essentialist identification of feminist politics with white, straight, middle-class women (in North American contexts) has not only served the factional political interests of those women, it has also delegitimated valued and historically significant political alliances between poor women and poor men, between Black women and Black men, and so on. This extension of anti-essentialism is valuable in deconstructing the race and class biases in certain kinds of radical feminism (which is, not incidentally, the politics that motivated the mainstream feminist rape crisis movement in North America), challenging a conception of gender as a totalizing and fundamental axis of oppression; this anti-essentialism is rightly constructed within a critique of power.

Much anti-sexual violence organizing *has* been inflected by the unsubtle assumption that gender is the only salient axis of oppression, and has thus constructed essentialist practice not only with regard to different groups of women, as I showed above, but also with regard to the category "men." Men are sometimes themselves survivors of sexual violence, and the needs and role of male survivors of childhood sexual abuse in anti-sexual violence organizing confound our gender categories. Especially when these men have *not* gone on to perpetrate sexual abuse, and especially when their abusers included women, they challenge feminists honestly to address the ways "exceptions" might inflect our theory and our practice. The social phenomenon of male sexual violence against other men, whether lovers, acquaintances, or strangers, however common or uncommon, also requires feminist attention.

While this kind of aggression is explicable in feminist terms, it nonetheless challenges a simplistically gendered account of sexually motivated violence, and can nuance feminist analyses in important ways. Some men *are*, furthermore, sometimes falsely accused of acts of sexual violence against women. This is an unpopular claim within feminist circles, and I want to stress that I know that men who deny their implication in acts of sexual violence are very often lying or, at best, self-deceived. Nonetheless, the historical legacy and continued pattern of sex crimes being falsely attributed to Black and poor men, for example, gives feminists good reason not to make a priori assumptions about the truth of all accusations.[30]

Thus anti-essentialism changes how we think about "men" as well as "women" in this context. But isn't this an example of what we were most afraid of—that such caveats would undermine the possibility of feminist politics? I argued in Chapter 2 that the principled anti-essentialism that lies at one end of the spectrum merely pulls the rug out from under feminist feet. If we were to insist that only difference counts, we would be left with no guidelines for sustaining political interventions that rely on counter-hegemonic categories. In particular, discourses of anti-essentialism provide an obvious legitimation strategy to men who wish, for better or worse reasons, to be included in feminist theory or activism, and also to those men who, consciously or not, wish to minimize their own participation in structures of oppression. To argue that power is at work, however, is a claim that needs support: how is power made manifest here? How do we assess whether men who label female feminists "essentialist" for crudely categorizing men in their theories or their practice are making legitimate claims about exclusion from coalition building, are pointing to exceptions that are valid but have minimal implications for practice, or are using "anti-essentialism" as an alibi to disassociate themselves from their implication in sexist oppression? Answering this question not only has important implications for how we as feminist activists justify strategies of resistance in a postmodern world, but it also offers insights into my more global question: How can we effectively combine anti-essentialism and feminist politics?

There are good reasons why men should be excluded from working in feminist organizations of diverse kinds. But how, as a feminist anti-essentialist, can I defend drawing a line around the category "women," with its contested boundaries? And where would I choose to draw that line when the feminisms in which many political theorists of my generation are immersed insist that the re-inscription of duality reifies the very oppressive structures we seek to undermine? How do I justify the implicit claim that gender is the fundamental axis of oppression in this context? I do not believe that all men, however defined, should always be excluded from all forms of feminist politics, however construed. I am evaluating arguments about power that apply within the context of anti-sexual violence organizing in a particular university. We may be able to derive from these arguments a set of critical questions that will prove useful in evaluating claims about inclusion and exclusion in other contexts, but the conclusions we reach in other cases may well differ. A Wittgensteinian attention to the particular case here entails examining the microrelations of power operative in the context in question as well as alluding to generalities that highlight larger group memberships but may fail to capture the local character of those identities.

There are many important ways in which men can be and are involved in anti-sexual violence activism. Valuable political work here includes the efforts of men who form independent or coalitional groups that offer services to (other) male survivors: I have worked with male survivors who want to establish healing solidarity with others in the context of support groups or other services or who want to join together with other anti-sexual violence activists to campaign on specific political issues. In other cases, pro-feminist men argue that they are motivated by their desire to work with other men against violence against women. The educational role of men in this area has been one of the most important contributions of men to feminist political goals and is central to men taking responsibility not just for their own actions, or those of their fellow men, but for changing the construction of masculinity itself. (Of course, much of this work is reformist; in MacKinnon's terms it does not challenge important parts of the larger social structures that perpetuate a sexuality of dominance and submission. But much feminist work in this area also consists of "picking up the pieces," and while this should not be the sole focus of social change efforts, this kind of activism remains valuable, not least to those who use services such as help-lines.) Given these worthy feminist goals, what role can and should men play in organizations with a history of understanding sexual violence through radical feminist analyses?

My argument for feminist separation in this kind of organizing stems from my experience of the reality of gender inequality in dominant regimes of meaning and in women's experiences of sexuality. But this experience is always allied with a sense of the instability and internal diversity of the categories it apprehends. While not a priori opposed to any political alliance of radicals—whether across racial, class, or gender lines—I am opposed to political initiatives that exacerbate women's disempowerment and reinforce a diminished liberal politic that fails to capture the realities of oppression. Certain kinds of alliances between women and men in organizing against sexual violence contingently have these effects because of the self-positioning of the participants and the dominant constructions of sexuality that we are work-ing against. Women's experiences here are diverse yet intelligibly bounded by strong family resemblances. This similarity is clearly not coincidental: it stems from the terms of women's sexual oppression under patriarchy. Mac-Kinnon's mistake is to think that these conditions over-determine a singular experience and erase the possibility of resistance. When I argued against her view, however, I was not arguing against the reality of gender oppression but only against the overdetermined description that she presents as the only truth about women's and men's sexual identities. How does this set of con-cerns play out in the mundane world of volunteer recruitment?

First, as a feminist activist I was confronted with the obviously illegitimate reasons men actually gave for wanting to be involved in anti-sexual violence work and in their objecting to their exclusion from certain spheres (such as answering the help-line). They are worth repeating here, not because they nuance my anti-essentialism—in fact, they are by and large reasons that re-veal little grasp of feminism at all—but because they reveal the dangers of an uncritical embrace of anti-essentialism and the potential loss of separate space and political cohesiveness it entails. They were an object lesson that, in San-dra Harding's words,

> Men love appropriating, directing, judging, and managing everything they can get their hands on—especially the white, Western, heterosexual, and economically overprivileged men with whom most feminist scholars and researchers most often find themselves interacting in various workplace and social institutions. Some have arrogantly tried to do so in the name of feminism, to claim a kind of feminist authority that as men they cannot have, thereby inadvertently revealing that they have not grasped even the most basic feminist principles.[31]

The reasoning of prospective male volunteers amply justifies this skepti-cism: they want to "meet women," they want to "teach" women callers that not all men are bad, or they want to "help" women "become more assertive and stop being victims." They want to learn skills through the organization's training, they want to build their résumés, acquire recommendations, or gain access to particular careers or jobs where involvement of this kind would be a useful bonus, and so on. In a few cases, I have suspected or discovered that men had other implicit and more sinister reasons for their interest in this work: they wanted kudos for being "sensitive," they were titillated by sexual violence, they thought it was a "sexy" and "glamorous" area of feminist ac-tivism, or they wanted to decry bad men and separate themselves off from that category. Most disturbing of all, in some cases they themselves had committed acts of sexual violence and were using the organization either as an ad hoc conscience-salve ("see—it wasn't really rape: how could it be? I work in a sexual assault center!") or simply as a means of further sexual gratification. Sometimes these reasons are on the table, sometimes they are uncomfortably played out in the course of organizing. A disturbing aspect of this latter dynamic is the existence of men who can "talk the talk" on many feminist issues but who resist women's challenges to their problematic assumed authority or behaviors.[32] Such men often anticipate and exploit the fact that a woman is less likely to confront an avowedly "feminist" man about sexist actions, not least because in a feminist context he is likely to have the support of other women.

Thus some motivations and arguments can be straightforwardly discounted as illegitimate from even the most cautious feminist position. There are also consequential reasons why male volunteers should be excluded in this context: women survivors calling us expect and want to speak to women, and most male survivors indicate that they also do. Various cultural norms and taboos about discussing sexual issues with men come into play, as do constraints on speech based on a (multi)cultural perception of men as potential aggressors. Men rarely, if ever, have a sufficiently similar experiential basis for empathy with female survivors. Many sympathetic men can grasp this fear intellectually, but almost never emotionally, and as a result tend to be less empathetic and more authoritarian in their interactions with survivors, both male and female. More controversially, my experience with men in positions of power within the organization has been that men are likely to repeat behaviors learned under patriarchy, which cause them to look for control and dominance. Women also replay gendered patterns such as fear of authority and authoritarian reprisal, conflict avoidance, and so on, but these more often serve to downplay their individual presence within the group rather than to magnify it. Women situate themselves quite differently, tending to be more closely identified with sexual violence as painful and oppressive rather than titillating. Thus in working with men in this particular context, I can point to patterns of behavior and relations of power that, while they are not universally applicable, make the integration of men into the organization problematic.

Of course, not all men exhibit these behaviors consistently. To my mind it is conceptually possible that particular men might become politically involved in this area of activism and successfully avoid all these dynamics. Among the many reasons for feminist anxiety about the exclusion of men, however, one in particular is noteworthy in this context. An implicit reason behind feminist reluctance to insist on women-only space seems to me to be the allure of a "phantom man"—the perfect exception to every generalization about men and masculinity in this culture. Entirely well-versed in feminism, thoroughly cognizant of and resistant to his own privilege, and politically astute (and sexy to boot!), this man represents for many feminists—especially heterosexually identified women—the fantasy worth holding out for, worth compromising our theories and actions to accommodate. The theoretical possibility (and occasional reality) of men who do not conform to feminist predictions is important—just as women need not be overdetermined by oppression, so, I believe, men need not be mere puppets of privilege (indeed, to understand oneself in this way is another instantiation of privilege). But this conceptual opening is, unfortunately, far removed from the reality of men's enactment of masculinities. As many of us remain hopeful that more real men—no matter what their birth sex—will come to create and occupy pro-feminist subject-positions, we need to acknowledge the negative implications of orienting our practice as feminist women toward the accommodation of a phantom. Anti-essentialism has unfortunately often been co-opted as a convenient lexicon not only for keeping open the conceptual space inhabited by Phantom Man (a move I endorse) but also for making the leap to understanding this conceptual space as determinative of women's political action. Sometimes aspirations do provide a ground for political organizing, but in this case the fantasy has negative repercussions: feminists who hold open a space for a hero are likely to have to work with a lot of fakes.[33]

Although dominant and nondominant group men are differently located with regard to other axes of oppression—such as race—the latter are not exempt from the aspects of masculinity noted earlier. Just as different women live (and challenge) their placement in dominant regimes of meaning in different ways, so do different men. But the family resemblances between men's experiences here complement my justification of feminist separation. Men of color in this context negotiated their masculinity differently than white men: they were sometimes less complacent about the prospect of successful social change, sometimes less defensive in the face of an Other's oppression, but sometimes just as (or more) conservative and wedded to dominance. I think of the kinds of things men say about their own desire for inclusion in feminism, and the ways they behave when they are included, and see race, for example, as inflecting but not undercutting that reality.

This is the result of looking and seeing with self-consciousness about the construction of identity. Should we persist, despite these caveats, in trying to break down dichotomous categories, both as a general feminist strategy, and in order to accommodate exceptions to those categories? While we can and do inflect the categories "men" and "women," if we cease to put them at the center of our analysis, and to follow through on this in our practice, we will diminish any feminist political understanding of sexual violence. This would occur in numerous ways, many of which should by now be clear, so let me provide just two further examples.

First, gendered norms of victim blaming are sufficiently strong in contemporary North American culture that to fail to make them visible within our organization would be to lose any empowering or healing way to talk about sexual violence. Put simply, I want a volunteer to say to a female caller who has been raped, "it wasn't your fault," and to mean it; the volunteer therefore requires a framework for understanding how it is that women are blamed for rape and why this is unjust. In other words, she needs a feminist framework that describes and explains dominant cultural ascriptions of femininity. By taking seriously feminist anti-essentialism we do not have to assume that all women experience these ascriptions in the same way. As I argued in Chapter 3, drawing a boundary around the concept "women" need not erase plurality, reify patriarchal constructions of "woman," or be insensitive to "border cases." Rather, we can speak of drawing a line for a particular political purpose while recognizing its contingency. In this case, I highlight the category "women" because I have identified gendered patterns to sexual violence, not because I am making universal claims about all women's experience or all men's complicity.

Second (and this is my worry about much anti-essentialism that is not adequately inflected by an analysis of power), ceasing to invoke gender as a central organizing concept would fit neatly with the conservative discourse of our main political opponents. Their central discursive goals are to avoid the construction of sexual assault on campus as an equity or a human rights issue (both of which require, in Canada, that one find discrimination against a designated social group), and they continually stress the individualistic nature of sexual violence, whereby incidents of date rape and sexual harassment are best understood as misunderstandings or failures of communication between random individuals, who may be men or women. Feminist analyses of sexual assault require a kind of pattern recognition made possible by the use of gendered categories. On the other hand, principled anti-essentialism, by insisting on the fragmentation of those categories, has considerable difficulty making sense of feminist claims, and thus explaining either how or why we should act on them. If our goals become the breakdown of categories, the incorporation of exceptional cases, and the recognition of cross-cutting alliances without regard to the context of power relations within which these concerns are more or less salient, then we fail to understand the feminist content of such claims. Feminist anti-essentialism is a political method for avoid-

ing the re-inscription of relations of oppression, not a justification for ignoring them.

Many of these observations are in keeping with MacKinnon's account of
gendered patterns of power within this context. The difference between us,
however, is that her claims are more ambitious in the breadth of their exclusion and more restrictive in the terms of their inclusion. Her construction
of the relations of domination and subordination that characterize male and
female sexuality under patriarchy cannot make sense of the exceptions to its
own generalizations—the woman who sexually abuses her son, the gay man
who is a victim of sexual assault—without an ad hoc revision of categories to
make these individuals into men and women in its own terms; nor can it grasp
that in the contexts where these generalizations are most applicable—understanding sexual violence, for example—they are nevertheless inflected by differences in women's experiences and relations of power among women. These
differences preclude a uniform understanding of the category "women," and
shape feminist practice in ways that are more than superficial. Negotiating
the rough ground here is a matter of setting up signposts on local roads, not
of drawing a global map. In practice, feminist anti-essentialism is a sensitivity
to the particular case and to the specifics of feminist practice. It includes attention to the particular negative effects of discarding appeals to social group
membership, an awareness of how coalitions may remain possible notwithstanding generalizations, a sensitivity to the construction of feminist issues
within relations of power among women, and a commitment to respect for
the local conditions that shape particular political interventions.

In the humdrum reality of photocopying and phone calls, most of this
analysis passed unnoticed. When we embodied these analyses in practice, we
were always acting within concrete conditions, especially conditions of scar-
city. Like most feminist organizations, we lacked money, space, time, energy,
and political or institutionalized power. Our practice will always be, in many
ways, cruder than our theoretical analyses. Constructing anti-essentialist
feminist theory as has thus far been done brings with it a rather different set
of imperatives than does working through anti-essentialist feminist practice.
The only coherent form of the latter requires that we go on using crude generalizations and revise them as we become aware of specific patterns of oppression and domination that have been re-inscribed by those in positions of
power. Thus there are important ways in which anti-essentialist concerns, in
general, can and should be accommodated within feminist practice. This accommodation only makes sense, however, within a critique of the power relations that motivate feminist anti-essentialism, relations that are frequently
weakened or even erased within anti-essentialist discourses inattentive to

power. In my own context, such a critique entails examining the professed and implicit motives of men wishing to enter the organization, taking into account the negative political consequences of fragmenting or discarding the categories "men" and "women" in our practice, and resisting the pull of organizing around a phantom man who even in his absence draws feminist attention away from other women. Making decisions about who or what to include and exclude is always a strategic process, constrained by practical demands and woefully under-determined by the current state of the essentialism debates in feminist theory.

### Anti-Essentialism and Feminist Organizations

The literature on feminist organizations contains remarkably little about the ways identity and diversity are negotiated within feminist settings. While there is no doubt that feminist activists of the last twenty years have struggled to come to terms with some aspects of methodological essentialism in their political practice, much of the available literature on the internal workings of feminist organizations is in a sociological vein. It offers extended descriptions of feminist organizations with relatively little attention to cross-cutting oppressions crucial to feminist theories of identity, and to the emerging practice of many feminist groups.[34] While rich in case studies, this literature predominantly addresses the relation of feminist organizing to nonfeminist paradigms in organizational social science. Struggles within feminist groups to come to terms with differences among women and with the dangers of essentialism are brought into relief by a second literature that presents the experiences of women marginalized within particular feminist organizations and the politicization of these exclusions.[35] The consequences of anti-essentialism have received perhaps the most attention in the field of queer organizing, and it is here that theoretical models of identity formation have been most closely linked to political practice.[36] This work has yet to be fully integrated with recent feminist analyses of political identity, however, in ways that might suggest revised organizational structures or strategies. There is remarkably little investigation of how feminist groups can adequately address the problems of alliance and coalition formation around issues of common concern to women of all classes, races, ages, and so on—in other words, how to generalize from the successes and failures of particular feminist groups in order to develop methods for understanding and addressing organizational implications of differences among women.

I used the example of men's role in anti-sexual violence organizing to show that feminist anti-essentialists may decide to exclude at the same time as we highlight cross-cutting group memberships and recommend coalition building. Critical discussion of how these decisions should best be made is a project that embeds feminist theory in feminist practice. In the example above I discussed the criteria for exclusion, showing how they are best generated in a particular context by an activist community as a collective project. Making decisions about exclusion and inclusion on the basis of identity, however, not only requires discussion of the substantive claims that justify these decisions. It also requires attention to the group processes within feminist organizations more or less likely to avoid essentialism. How can feminist groups create formal organizational structures that are sensitive to the contingency and complexity of generalizations about women and that are likely to foster anti-essentialist feminist practice? As Carmen Sirianni says, "If alliances among diverse groups of women with multiple interests and identities are central to postmodern feminist politics, . . . then we must pay increasing attention to those organizational features that facilitate and sustain coalitions."[37]

All feminist organizations, whether collectively or hierarchically organized, large or small, have to ask whether the interests of all constituents are justly represented and how intra-organizational processes contribute to essentialist practice. In larger feminist groups with an over-arching structure, questions arise about who represents whom (in a delegation or as elected representative, for example), and how decisions are made so as to take account of the needs of different members of the group. These are very old problems for democratic theory, but they have not yet been adequately connected to anti-essentialist concerns within feminist practice. To avoid essentialism is to address the relations of power among women that permit certain subgroups to define feminist issues and to impose their own identity on a more diverse collectivity.

One of the organizations perhaps most widely studied and politically challenging in this context is the National Women's Studies Association (NWSA). The organization is structurally complex, diverse, and beset with political controversy. Robin Leidner argues in a sympathetic 1991 study that: "The NWSA has worked to develop a system that is efficient but participatory; that protects the rights of individuals and also those of subgroups with special concerns, interests, or viewpoints; and that takes into account an underlying commonality of purpose yet provides means for dealing with conflicting interests and opinions."[38] Leidner points out that existing political frameworks and organizational structures are not suited to this task. The tensions between commonality and difference that I have been discussing in more theoretical contexts raise important questions in organizational practice: how can feminist groups ensure substantive rather than merely formal equality, moving away from structures that simply represent numerical interests to structures that acknowledge inequalities of power? How should feminists juggle sometimes conflicting group or community needs and individual rights? How can organizations ensure that all identities, experiences, or interests are represented, at the same time as they maintain a perspective cognizant of commonality of purpose? How do potentially anti-essentialist structures of representation interact with anarcha-feminist arguments for minimizing hierarchy?

The NWSA's attempts to find workable answers to these questions are instructive for feminists trying to put anti-essentialist theory into practice. The organization has a system of caucuses, each of which can send delegates to the Delegate Assembly and the Co-ordinating Council. This system is an effort to equalize power where constituents' interests may conflict. Caucus members argued that they faced greater costs to participation, including poor incentives to join NWSA, the expense of attending meetings, reduced strength because of smaller numbers, the prejudices of other members, discrimination through self-identification (lesbians), fewer organizational skills or knowledge (working-class women), or the failure of other constituencies to recognize the moral legitimacy of their needs. Similar concerns induced the NWSA to try to offset travel expenses and establish geographical equality. This system, however, raises several questions about the criteria used to decide which differences matter, and how power is understood as constructing these differences. As in the case of excluding or including men from an organization or activity, merely to advocate institutionalizing "difference" or "diversity" does not necessarily constitute an adequate justification for particular organizational structures. Conflict within the NWSA arose in part because the caucus system was conceived by some as a corporatist solution to diverse interests (as the existence of caucuses for relatively "privileged" women such as program administrators implies), and by others as a means of giving additional representational weight to oppressed groups. Is a caucus system legitimated merely as a way of representing "different" interests, or is it intended to provide separate space and additional voice to members of groups that are relatively less powerful as a result of systemic oppression? How can the organization mediate these different strategies of justification, especially when they appear antithetical? Does prioritizing caucuses for women of color, lesbian, and working-class women, for example, also commit white, straight, middle-class feminists to always ceding to requests for asymmetrical representation within an organization? How does the reality of overlapping memberships in these groups change the imperatives of representation?

A more radical difficulty emerges from the demand that the organization change its political priorities and perhaps even its very objectives to accommodate different actual and potential members. In the case of the NWSA, Leidner claims, there was conflict over whether the organization should target the needs of academic women or should prioritize "activist" women and continue to expand its membership base (to, for example, nurses). These dilemmas are particularly acute given the funding crises most feminist organizations periodically experience, which often motivate controversies over the allocation of resources. One response could be to argue that feminist organizations are, by definition, established by a specific group of women to support particular projects and that no single group can hope to be a universally representative entity. In the case of the NWSA, one could argue that it has a legitimate and politically effective position as a feminist organization targeting academic women's projects. Women with political priorities that are not accommodated within existing organizational structures should therefore form independent organizations to further their different projects. As a blanket solution, this response fails to take into account the relative power of established feminist organizations (such that membership is a good in itself), the reality of the (increasingly) diverse constituencies that most feminist organizations draw from or serve, or the problems of women who are generally in a minority within a geographical community and would like to work with a national umbrella organization rather than in their "own" smaller groups. Nor does it accommodate moral demands that more privileged women actively oppose oppressive relations of power, or reconstruct what counts as a relevant project in light of challenges from women who do not see their concerns reflected in existing constructions.

Thus my presentation of Leidner's assessment does not fully capture the texture of ethnocentric racism in the life of an organization. As early as 1981 Chela Sandoval wrote of the hegemonic structure of the NWSA conference and the ghettoization of women of color. She elaborates how anxious appeals to the survival and flourishing of the NWSA itself were repeatedly made by white women in positions of authority to pre-empt internal political critique that might displace their agendas. "Such messages oversaw and guided the imagination of the meanings of racism into permitable arenas."[39] In the case of the NWSA these concerns were brought to a crisis point in 1990, when many of the organization's women of color walked out of the business meeting of the annual conference. Alleging institutional racism following the firing of an African-American woman from the NWSA national office, they left, planning to form a separate organization. This event was the culmination of debates about whom the NWSA represented, with white academic women critically viewed by some as its implicit constituency. Some (white) women in the organization, on the other hand, have perceived the caucus system and the organization's preoccupation with representation and identity as divisive and excessively splintered. The case of the NWSA represents a challenge to feminist understandings of solidarity and difference that is far from theoretical.

Anti-essentialist feminist theory speaks to these issues in feminist organizing, suggesting that we need to bring together experience and study of the actual shape of successfully anti-essentialist feminist practice with anti-essentialist theorizing in ways I can only touch on here. We need to explore not only the "personal" differences that members of an organization bring into any group but also the implications of group differences for our analyses of power, identity politics, and representation. This requires further research into how feminist organizations negotiate diversity: first, at the level of political structures (the efficacy of caucus systems, and the restructuring of organizational objectives, for example), as well as on an interpersonal level (how are feminist organizations structuring their training, group work, and decision making to incorporate political differences among women? How are they dealing with interpersonal conflict and emotional stress caused by internal divisions? What are the characteristics of a "successful" pluralist feminist organization?).[40]

Casting the essentialism debates in this light also refocuses feminist attention on the importance of feminist analyses of power and feminist organizational theory. Social anarchist and anarcha-feminist analyses, for example, have been central in generating radical critiques of conventional organizations, suggesting new organizational structures, and articulating critical feminist accounts of power. But these perspectives are seldom given the prominence in curricula or writing that they merit given recent turns in feminist theory.[41] Too often an interest in collectivist organizing is seen as dated, a throwback to the heady Second Wave, when idealistic radical feminists eschewed structure but slipped into the "tyranny of structurelessness."[42] Concerns about oppression within the feminist movement should focus more closely on feminist organizations, since they are a key locus of political conflict and action on these issues. It is important to know whether feminist organizations are successfully developing anti-essentialist practice sensitive to multiple oppressions and how they are struggling with fragmentation and conflict.

My articulation of anti-essentialism as a set of constructive feminist methods shows why feminist practice needs to inform the construction of theory. We cannot understand the operations of particular relations of power without experiencing them, without making them visible, or without having them made visible to us. MacKinnon is right to assert that this process does not happen from a philosopher's desk; it most often happens when feminists challenge structures of power in ways threatening to patriarchy. But our understanding of dominance and subordination does not simply hatch from the egg of women's experience nor even of feminist practice. It is created through feminist methods, including methods of organizing and decision-making, through the construction of feminist issues and feminist identities. When we become or make others aware of relations of power that permit feminist practice to be partisan, exclusive, or essentialist, we need to have intertwined theoretical and practical tools and skills to address the problem.

Achieving equitable representation in organizations struggling to avoid the re-inscription of oppression and negotiating multiple interests is a problem seemingly far removed from the philosophical discussion of essentialism that began this book. Anti-essentialist feminist practice, however, can be inflected by my Wittgensteinian method, and in many ways it faces the same challenges as feminist research. Merely to assert the primacy of practice—construed by MacKinnon as the struggle to end sexist oppression as it emerges from "women's experience"—as a strategy for avoiding methodological essentialism, begs the question of how that practice has itself been constructed. MacKinnon's attempt to justify her essentialism by appeal to the empirical reality of women's experience and to the exigencies of practice does not speak to questions about the shape of anti-essentialist feminist activism. Even as we move "back to the rough ground" to make sense of these questions, we need constantly to interrogate our own foundations, those presuppositions that seem to require no justification. In failing to do this, MacKinnon's rebuttal of her anti-essentialist critics is ultimately disappointing; she mischaracterizes their concerns and persists with an analysis unwilling to explore the relevance of power-laden differences to feminist organizing.

Understanding how generalizations are constructed through relations of power in the multiple contexts of feminist organizing provides indicators of the future shape of anti-essentialist practice. Organizing against sexual violence—the quintessentially essentialist feminist issue—must be, and has been, rethought in the light of anti-essentialist critique. I offered a specific example of two claims to exclusion, asking how the feminist anti-essentialism I have developed provides criteria for assessing their legitimacy. While anti-essentialism shapes feminist practice, anti-anti-essentialism also informs feminist decision-making about when to include and when to exclude from identity categories and coalition formation. Balancing these two sets of demands requires deeper understandings of systemic oppression than the appeal merely to "difference" can yield. One of the ways they will be brought into equilibrium is through emerging research on their implications for different sites of feminist practice. Here I have only sketched some of the possibilities for this project. Much of this work lies ahead: it is the task of a feminist anti-essentialism that effectively brings together theory and practice.

# Conclusion: "Back to the Rough Ground!"

The central aim of this book is to take the feminist philosophical preoccupation with essentialism more explicitly into the realm of feminist practice. I hoped to demonstrate that the essentialism debates in feminism should not be understood as merely of philosophical interest, narrowly construed, but rather as touching on feminists' most practical concerns as we investigate and seek to change our lives. The anti-essentialist position I have sketched pins down the amorphous problem of essentialism at the same time as it recommends methods that avoid it. This position endeavors to mediate some of the central questions of diverse feminist theoretical camps and brings a new sense of interdisciplinarity to feminist philosophy.

In Chapters 1 and 2, I distinguished different meanings of the epithet "essentialist," arguing that essentialisms (of the metaphysical and biological varieties) prior to social constructionism are not what is at stake in contemporary feminist debates. The "problems" of essentialism do include concerns with materiality (of bodies, for example) and social ontology, but again these concerns are located within social constructionist discourses rather than prior to them. The kind of methodological essentialism that allows the experiences and identities of certain more powerful groups of women to stand in for larger feminist claims, however, deserves to be challenged. More than this, we need to find ways of avoiding methodological essentialism while continuing to justify politically enabling feminist claims. We can evade the fruitless tail-chasing of the debates between anti-essentialists and "anti-anti-essentialists," I argued in Chapter 3, by developing an alternative Wittgensteinian feminism that conceptualizes the connections between women as family resemblances, while still allowing for purposive line drawing. How we justify the placement of these boundaries around categories is a central political question for feminists, and the simple injunction to "look and see," leaves this political question unanswered, even unposed. Therefore in the last two chapters I turned to instances of feminist practice to ask how anti-essentialism might inform feminist research methods and feminist organizing while I investigated the work of Carol Gilligan and Catharine MacKinnon, the two contemporary feminists most often accused of methodological essentialism.

It is both the great strength and the difficulty of Wittgensteinian method in philosophy that it eschews large conclusions. My analyses here have tended to be local, contextual, and carefully bordered with caveats about the wider implications of my claims. It is tempting to conclude with a grand summing up, but this would risk disloyalty to my method. Nevertheless, I am not so deeply ensnared by Wittgenstein's own picture as to believe that no broader conclusions derive from my arguments. The concept in political philosophy that has come up again and again in this book is *power*. It is the power of the researcher, I argued in my analysis of Gilligan's method, that enables her to construct the identities of her participants to be like her own. And her theory construction risks essentialism by imposing on girls' narratives a preconceived, if vague, account of their psychology that is not sensitive to its own contingency—precisely because it does not recognize how it is power-laden.

Similarly, MacKinnon's appeal to "feminist practice" as the basis of strong claims about sexual violence neglects the ways political practice is itself constructed in contexts where some women, however well-intentioned or politically astute, have discursive power over the construction of "women's experience" or "empirical reality." I am certainly not suggesting that power is always a negative force or that we eradicate or even minimize power, only that power is always inevitably at work in any feminist context. Those feminist methods that are the least likely to make the mistakes that I have labeled as essentialism have the most fully developed understanding of the workings of power. They recognize that their own oppositional theories cannot take place outside relations of power, and they incorporate self-reflexive mechanisms and political dialogue into their processes of theory building. Most specifically, they are methods that understand how power constructs identity and that develop strategies for undercutting the hegemony of dominant group feminists in the construction of political meaning.

This version of anti-essentialist feminism suggests a new approach to generalizations in feminist discourse. A principled anti-essentialism that fragments all generalizing claims may be naively indifferent to the salience of social group membership, and many have pointed out how deconstructive approaches to feminist theory run the risk of losing an importantly radical shape and degenerating into methodological individualism or a shallow form of liberalism.[1] Power-sensitive anti-essentialism does not reject generalizations per se but evaluates them in the ways I have been suggesting in this book; it requires broad analyses of the mechanisms by which some social groups come to be more powerful in the first place. Many of the claims I have made in the course of my argument are premised on feminist, anti-racist, anti-heteronormative, and class analyses. To be politically convincing, any anti-essentialist feminism requires a larger account of the axes along which power operates to create structures of oppression based on social group membership. Thus a radical theoretical framework that understands social groups as central to conceptualizing oppression is a prerequisite of politically effective feminist anti-essentialism rather than antithetical to it.

If an analysis of power is at the heart of politically compelling anti-essentialism, then what account of power follows?[2] Radical interpretations of Foucault in particular have generated renewed contemporary interest in feminist conceptions of power within political theory.[3] These accounts provide rich and valuable theoretical insights into power as a "capillary" social phenomenon, for example. If understanding power is at the heart of the essentialism debates, however, feminists need more theoretically developed accounts and more evidence of how power is exercised and circulates among women and within diverse feminist groups. The account of power I have been working with operates at the larger social structural and interpersonal levels. Many philosophers working in a tradition from Hegel and Marx, Nietzsche, and Foucault through to feminists such as Butler and Wittig, have argued that subjects are constituted through power, and that the process of becoming a subject—*assujettissement* in Foucault's language—is also a process of subjection.[4] My Wittgensteinian approach dovetails with this account in its familiar insistence that "women" is not a category prior to the exercise of power, but rather is constituted through it. Despite the corollary that power constrains the possibilities open to individual agents, I would argue that it need not over-determine their actions or how those actions should be interpreted. The already-constructed nature of even biological understandings of femaleness reveals the extent to which relations of power are constitutive of feminist investigation. Any feminist theory of power, furthermore, must see power equally at work in feminist contexts. Spaces of feminist resistance that are self-conscious about the effects of patriarchal power must also be self-conscious about their own implication in power relations, including the inheritance of tactics of power from patriarchy. Much of this book consists of examples and case studies to support this claim. In the course of articulating them, I hope also to have pointed to some desiderata for a future feminist account of power.

Several anti-anti-essentialist feminists mention their disquiet when the fragmentation of gender is not accompanied by calls to inflect other identity categories. The epithet "essentialist" is used disproportionately to undermine feminist claims, they argue, whereas the very concepts used to effect this venture—ostensibly presented as symmetrical with gender—remain themselves unchallenged. In other words, critics claim that anti-essentialists say that gender must be inflected with race but not that race must be inflected with gender, for example. I have often been struck by the unabashed ignorance of feminist work (especially writing on race by feminists of color) evinced by many men working in critical race theory. While many white feminists have also ignored and appropriated the work of feminists of color, there seems to be an asymmetry. I suspect that power is at work here, too: the ghettoization and low status of feminist philosophy are partly effects of its population by women. Women scholars are lauded for their interest in men: working on race can at least be read as an interest in men of color (and their scholarship). But men (including both white men and men of color working in critical race theory) are less willing to be demeaned by an intellectual association with feminism, and are most often able to circulate successfully in prestigious intellectual communities where this knowledge is not demanded of them. And we as feminist philosophers may be more willing to criticize our white feminist women colleagues for their inattention to race than to take on men who talk blithely about race without understanding that their racialized subjects are also gendered.

All of these facets of academic politics contribute to the familiar erasure of (scholarship by) women of color. It is an important observation that feminists are required to inflect their categories while critical race theorists less often are. But this imposed construction highlights yet another iteration of essentialism: women of color writing about gender and race oppression are often construed as "feminists" *rather than* "critical race theorists," reiterating the problematic ontology that forces them to partition their identities. The allegation of asymmetry between race and gender does point to a disturbing trend in certain political theoretical approaches, but analysis of this trend should not obscure the abundance of writing that takes on the project of theorizing from critical race–feminist perspectives.[5] Throughout this book, I have focused on feminist discourses that place gender in the foreground, and have asked how feminism might re-articulate its methods of analyzing gender in the light of anti-racist or anti-heteronormative critique. Another way of thinking about these debates is to place identity categories other than gender center stage, to ask how oppositional discourses that are inflected by feminism but do not prioritize gender might apply my Wittgensteinian method.

Methodological essentialism is of enormous significance, for example, in political theories of race. In particular, many theorists are grappling with the same dilemma I faced at the beginning of the book: how can we formulate a coherent concept of race (using labels like "people of color" or "Black") that highlights the socially constructed, sometimes ad hoc, and complex nature of racial categories, at the same time as it acknowledges that use of the concept of race is currently central both to racism and to anti-racism?[6] This question generates four sets of questions for critical race theory. First, how can we understand the concept of "race" itself? Answers to this question range from deconstructive accounts to revisions of Afrocentricity.[7] Second, just as there are women of every possible racial identity, so any given racial group is divided into genders, sexualities, ages, classes, and so on. Can any theory of race and racism adequately capture the varying experiences of oppression of a young African-American working-class man in Alabama and a middle-aged Black Caribbean female university professor in small-town New England? Should this be its goal? To pose this question is to approach my own questions about gender from the other side, asking how a theory that foregrounds race for a particular purpose might conceptualize itself as analyzing oppression along other axes. Third, this interrogation of racial identities has meshed with attempts to theorize so-called "intrasectional" identities—such as mixed race—and the challenges they raise for understanding identity categories as bounded and homogeneous.[8] I would suggest that understanding the relations between members of different racial groups as family resemblances answers certain questions and raises others for philosophers of race and racism, questions that are in many ways analogous to those faced by feminist philosophers. Finally, anti-essentialism in critical race theory, as in feminism, aims to understand the power relations that persistently problematize some racial identities and render others neutral or invisible. Thus it recommends the critical study of dominant identities (such as "whiteness") in order to reveal their particular social construction and implications in structures of oppression.[9]

Similarly, examples from queer theory have featured throughout my discussion. Methodological essentialism is an important issue as we construct explanatory models of sexuality, in political theory building, and in grounding political activism; again, Wittgensteinian anti-essentialist critique could be fruitfully developed. In Chapter 1 I asked how we might define "lesbians" given feminist concerns about the historical continuity of the term's referents. And in Chapter 3 I asked how purposive line drawing might lead us to include "men" in the category "lesbians" and suggested some reasons why this might not be a useful course of action. Wittig's suggestion that "lesbians are not women" reverses this strategy, arguing that "women" takes its meaning from heterosexual systems of thought and heterosexual economic systems and that lesbians should thus be excluded from the category. Taking the family resemblance approach to the question "who is a lesbian?" highlights even more starkly issues of power: on the one hand, heteronormativity and lesbophobia manufacture lesbianism as a marginalized and stigmatized subject position; on the other, lesbian feminists have struggled to seize discursive control over the construction of a counter-hegemonic political identity. Anti-essentialism, then, has to intervene in these debates to point out politically significant exclusions, without undercutting the possibility of radical politics.[10]

To emphasize any axis of power in a political analysis is to draw a line in a particular place in order to show something. That this line draws attention only to one aspect of any political reality does not invalidate it, but does suggest caution in recognizing limits and exclusions. This book has developed answers to two objections I identified at the outset. I now have a reply to the objection that "anti-essentialism" necessarily implies that invocation of any social group is suspect. Family resemblance generalizations should be made with self-consciousness of their own partiality and contingency in the context of relations of power; they nonetheless select important social realities and can still be ontologically and politically justified. The fact that rape is a crime overwhelmingly committed by men against women, for example, is constructed in different ways in different theoretical accounts, but its existence as a social reality lends meaning to generalizations using gender. However, I also have a response to the objection that anti-essentialist critique necessitates an endless proliferation of categories. In any particular case, certain axes of difference will construct the problem under investigation. Having an adequate analysis of relations of power may help to make visible which axes these are, and social and political theorists are under orders, I believe, to familiarize themselves with literatures outside their usual ambit in order to understand where their own accounts are located. Here is also a reason to support the familiar injunction that the reality of overlapping oppressions implies that the field of feminist theory cannot (and should not) be artificially separated from critical race theory, queer theory, and so on. This approach to method certainly raises tough intellectual and political challenges, but the difficulty of theorizing in the midst of complexity and contingency cannot justify ignoring anti-essentialist critique.

Looking at these methodological questions with gender, race, class, and sexuality in mind—to take some, but by no means all politically relevant categories—shows how difficult it is to remain true to Wittgensteinian anti-essentialism, to stay mindful of complexity. Whenever we conceptualize political problems, we emphasize particular aspects of political identity and sideline others. The inevitability and necessity of this process should not distract us from its limits: we need political theories that explain oppression in terms of social group membership, but we also need the context and interconnectedness of those theories to be spelled out. Throughout this book I have been acutely aware of the ineluctable "et cetera" that characterizes much self-defined pluralist feminist theory. Often the very arguments that aim to stress the importance of context are content to fall back on a mantra of "gender, race, and class," or to gesture toward the countless "differences" that are to figure in their analyses, without considering which matter more, or why. While this ineluctable et cetera crucially highlights the way any categorization erases difference, it is not an et cetera that can be uncritically appended to ward off claims of exclusion. Merely to say "and so on" is not enough to do justice to the excluded, particularly the excluded who most often appear in the unnamed categories following the tag.

For example, class is often given as an item on the list of differences worthy of feminist attention, even as many analyses side-step the structural critiques that have enabled leftists to make sense of class oppression. In other words, it is fashionable for feminists in North America to treat class as one of a string of differences among women, but it is less fashionable to claim allegiance to socialist or other analyses of the structural determinants of class. The very thin notions of social class membership that are evinced by much radical North American political theory allow "gender, race, and class" to remain an empty gesture. It cannot be enough to point to the mere fact that class differences among women are important for feminist theory and practice. We need thicker ways of understanding class membership as an economic and cultural phenomenon in North America. Therefore the very listing of differences that aims to avoid essentialism sometimes manages paradoxically to re-inscribe it by failing to offer adequate analyses of specific relations of power.

All of these contexts represent attempts to articulate better understandings of the links between identity in political theory and in political practice. And that, I believe, is all to the good: I have increasingly come to believe that feminist theory should be, as has been said in another context of politics simpliciter, "the art of the possible." Our contributions to even the "highest" forms of theory should be motivated by the need better to understand and change women's lives. This claim is more controversial than it might first appear: our ways of investigating and changing feminist realities are complex and contested, and the kind of feminist philosophy recommended by a practically oriented anti-essentialism is not uncontroversial. It is interdisciplinary, assertively political, and strongly connected to feminist activism and hence to feminist communities outside the academy. All these qualities are threatening to conventional contemporary understandings of the institutionalized discipline of philosophy itself, even though they find support in the work of many canonical philosophers—Wittgenstein among them—often neglected by feminists as well as our detractors. Both feminists and those hostile to feminism have charged that the study of research methods or of political organizations are simply not subjects appropriate to philosophy. But a consequence of my arguments is that our philosophical lives should not be technical and private affairs, lived among other specialists. If feminist philosophy has a vocation, it is constantly to return to the question of why philosophizing matters, and how, if it all, it might make the world a better place for women. In arguing for a feminist anti-essentialism that is intimately intertwined with political practice, I hope to go some way toward answering that question.

# Notes

## Introduction: Philosophy and Purity

1. María Lugones, "Purity, Impurity, and Separation," *Signs* 19 (1994), 463.
2. Lugones, "Purity, Impurity, and Separation," 467.
3. Terry Eagleton, "Ludwig Wittgenstein: The Terry Eagleton Script," in *Wittgenstein: The Terry Eagleton Script/The Derek Jarman Film* (London: British Film Institute, 1993), 55. See also Naomi Scheman's treatment of the same narrative, in "Forms of Life: Mapping the Rough Ground," in *The Cambridge Companion to Wittgenstein*, edited by Hans Sluga and David G. Stern (Cambridge: Cambridge University Press, 1996), 383.
4. Lugones, "Purity, Impurity, and Separation," 476. "Transparency" for Lugones is specifically "group relative:" "Individuals are transparent with respect to their group if they perceive their needs, interests, ways, as those of the group and if this perception becomes dominant or hegemonical in the group . . . So, as transparent, one becomes unaware of one's own difference from other members of the group," 474.
5. Eagleton, "Ludwig Wittgenstein," 55.
6. Lugones, "Purity, Impurity, and Separation," 464.
7. Marilyn Frye, "The Necessity of Differences: Constructing a Positive Category of Women," *Signs* 21 (1996): 1006–7.
8. Wendy Brown, *States of Injury: Power and Freedom in Late Modernity* (Princeton: Princeton University Press, 1995), 79.
9. Brown, *States of Injury*, 78–9.
10. Lugones actually says, "White women theorists seem to have worried more passionately about the harm the claim [that some feminist generalizations are exclusionary] does to theorizing than about the harm the theorizing did to women of color." María Lugones, "On the Logic of Pluralist Feminism," in *Feminist Ethics*, ed. Claudia Card (Lawrence: University Press of Kansas, 1991), 41.
11. See Allison Weir, *Sacrificial Logics: Feminist Theory and the Critique of Identity* (New York: Routledge, 1996).
12. Examples of this genre include: Jane Roland Martin, "Methodological Essentialism, False Difference, and Other Dangerous Traps," *Signs* 19 (1994): 630–57; Teresa de Lauretis, "Upping the Anti (sic) in Feminist Theory," in *Conflicts in Feminism*, eds. Marianna Hirsch and Evelyn Fox Keller (New York: Routledge 1991); Elizabeth Grosz, "Sexual Difference and the Problem of Essentialism," in *The Essential Difference*, eds. Naomi Schor and Elizabeth Weed (Bloomington: Indiana University Press, 1994).
13. See Linda Alcoff, "Cultural Feminism Versus Poststructuralism: The Identity Crisis in Feminist Theory," and Sandra Harding, "The Instability of the Categories of Feminist Theory," both in *Feminist Theory in Practice and Process*, edited by Micheline Malson, Jean F. O'Barr, Sarah Westphal, and Mary Wyer (Chicago: University of Chicago Press,

1989), and Iris Marion Young, "Gender As Seriality: Thinking About Women as a Social Collective," in *Intersecting Voices: Dilemmas of Gender, Political Philosophy, and Policy* (Princeton: Princeton University Press, 1997).

14. I discuss Susan Moller Okin's attempt to develop the former strategy in Chapter 2. The latter approach is apparent in both Frye, "The Necessity of Differences," and Weir, *Sacrificial Logics.*

### Chapter 1: Essentialism and Anti-Essentialism in Feminist Theory

1. Nancy Fraser, "The Uses and Abuses of French Discourse Theories for Feminist Politics," in *Critical Theory Now*, ed. Philip Wexler (London: Falmer Press, 1991), 99.

2. Joan Scott, "Deconstructing Equality-Versus-Difference: Or, The Uses of Poststructuralist Theory for Feminism," *Feminist Studies* 14 (1988): 47.

3. bell hooks, *Yearning: Race, Gender and Cultural Politics* (Toronto: Between the Lines, 1990), 28.

4. Nancy Fraser and Linda Nicholson "Social Criticism Without Philosophy: An Encounter Between Feminism and Postmodernism," in *Feminism/Postmodernism*, ed. Linda Nicholson (New York: Routledge, 1990), 32.

5. Elizabeth Grosz, *Volatile Bodies: Toward a Corporeal Feminism* (Bloomington: Indiana University Press, 1994), esp. 16–24.

6. Ibid., 18.

7. Chantal Mouffe, "The Legacy of m/f," in *The Woman in Question*, eds. Parveen Adams and Elizabeth Cowie (Cambridge: MIT Press, 1990), 4.

8. See Martin "Methodological Essentialism;" Jane Gallop, Marianne Hirsch, Nancy Miller, "Criticizing Feminist Criticism," in *Conflicts in Feminism*, eds. Hirsch and Fox Keller; Teresa de Lauretis, "The Essence of the Triangle or, Taking the Risk of Essentialism Seriously: Feminist Theory in Italy, the US, and Britain," *differences* 1:2 (1989): 3–37; "In a Word," interview by Ellen Rooney with Gayatri Spivak, in *The Essential Difference*, eds. Schor and Weed; Natalie Stoljar, "Essence, Identity and the Concept of Woman," *Philosophical Topics* 23 (Fall 1995): 261–93; Charlotte Witt, "Anti-Essentialism in Feminist Theory," *Philosophical Topics* 23 (Fall 1995): 321–44.

9. Betty Friedan, *The Feminine Mystique* (New York: Norton, 1963); bell hooks, "Black Women: Shaping Feminist Theory," in *Feminist Theory: From Margin to Center* (Boston: South End Press, 1984).

10. Elizabeth V. Spelman, *Inessential Woman: Problems of Exclusion in Feminist Thought* (Boston: Beacon Press, 1988).

11. See David DeGrood, *Philosophies of Essence* (Amsterdam: B. R. Gruner, 1976); Baruch Brody, *Identity and Essence* (Princeton: Princeton University Press, 1980). For an analysis of Wittgenstein's critique of essentialism in his own context, see Garth Hallett, *Essentialism: A Wittgensteinian Critique* (Albany: SUNY Press, 1991).

12. John Locke, *An Essay Concerning Human Understanding*, ed. John W. Yolton (London: Dent, 1961 [1690]), 3:3:15.

13. See Margaret Atherton, "The Inessentiality of Lockean Essences," *Canadian Journal of Philosophy* 14 (1984): 277–93.

14. Plato, *Euthyphro*, esp. 5C–16A.

15. Nancy Tuana, *The Less Noble Sex: Scientific, Religious, and Philosophical Conceptions of Woman's Nature* (Bloomington: Indiana University Press, 1993), esp. 3–17, 53–66, 79–87.

16. See Mary Briody Mahowald, ed., *Philosophy of Woman: An Anthology of Classic to Current Concepts* (Indianapolis: Hackett, 3rd edition, 1994 [1978]).

17. Lauretis, "The Essence of the Triangle," 5–6.

18. See Mary Daly, *Gyn/Ecology: The Metaethics of Radical Feminism* (Boston: Beacon Press, 1978), esp. 315–320, 385–424.

19. Audre Lorde, "An Open Letter to Mary Daly," in *Sister/Outsider* (Freedom: The Crossing Press, 1984), 67.

20. Andrea Dworkin, *Intercourse* (New York: Free Press, 1987), 137, 124, 127–8.

21. Mary Wollstonecraft, *A Vindication of the Rights of Woman* (London: Penguin, 1992 [1792]), 142.

22. Martha Nussbaum, "Human Functioning and Social Justice: In Defense of Aristotelian Essentialism," *Political Theory* 20 (1992): 206.

23. Ibid., 205.

24. Seyla Benhabib, "Feminism and Postmodernism: An Uneasy Alliance," in Seyla Benhabib, Judith Butler, Drucilla Cornell, and Nancy Fraser (with introduction by Linda Nicholson), *Feminist Contentions: A Philosophical Exchange* (New York: Routledge, 1995).

25. Benhabib, "Feminism and Postmodernism," in *Feminist Contentions*, Benhabib et al., 19.

26. See Vicky Kirby, "Corporeal Habits: Addressing Essentialism Differently," *Hypatia* 6:3 (1991): 4–24.

27. Grosz, "Sexual Difference," 84.

28. Tuana, *The Less Noble Sex*, 44–6.

29. See Anne Fausto-Sterling, *Myths of Gender: Biological Theories About Women and Men* (New York: Basic Books, 2nd edition, 1992).

30. John D'Emilio, "Capitalism and Gay Identity," in *The Material Queer: A LesBiGay Cultural Studies Reader*, ed. Donald Morton (Boulder: Westview, 1996); Jeffrey Escoffier, "Sexual Revolution and the Politics of Gay Identity," *Socialist Review* 15:4 (1985): 119–53; Michel Foucault, *The History of Sexuality*, Volume 1 (New York: Vintage, 1980).

31. For example, Hester Eisenstein, *Contemporary Feminist Thought* (Boston: G. K. Hall, 1983).

32. Sara Ruddick, *Maternal Thinking: Toward a Politics of Peace* (New York: Ballantine, 1989).

33. Ibid., 28–57.

34. The history of this debate is discussed in *The Woman in Question*, eds. Adams and Cowie; Linda Nicholson, "Interpreting Gender," *Signs* 20 (1994): 79–105; Grosz, *Volatile Bodies*.

35. Judith Butler, *Bodies that Matter: On the Discursive Limits of "Sex"* (New York: Routledge, 1993), 5.

36. Herculine Barbin, *Herculine Barbin: Being the Recently Discovered Memoirs of a Nineteenth Century French Hermaphrodite*, with introduction by Michel Foucault (New York: Pantheon, 1980); Susan Bordo, *Unbearable Weight: Feminism, Western Culture and the Body* (Berkeley: University of California Press, 1993); Kate Bornstein, *Gender Outlaw: On Men, Women and the Rest of Us* (New York: Vintage Books, 1995); Anne Fausto-Sterling, "The Five Sexes: Why Male and Female Are Not Enough," *The Sciences* 33 (March/April 1993):

20–25; Suzanne J. Kessler, "The Medical Construction of Gender: Case Management of Intersexed Infants," *Signs* 16 (1990): 3–26; Henry Rubin, "Transformations: Emerging Female to Male Transsexual Identities," Ph.D. diss., Department of Sociology, Brandeis University, 1996.

37. Diana Fuss, *Essentially Speaking: Feminism, Nature and Difference* (New York: Routledge, 1989), 2–3.

38. Steven Epstein, "Gay Politics, Ethnic Identity: The Limits of Social Constructionism," *Socialist Review* 17:3 (1987): 11.

39. Fuss, *Essentially Speaking*, 3.

40. Ibid., 19–20.

41. Ibid., 20.

42. See Hallett, *Essentialism*.

43. It is worth noting here that although I discuss this position with regard to feminist theory, the enterprise of establishing definitions that are based on necessary and sufficient conditions has been largely discredited among philosophers of language.

44. Judith Butler, "Contingent Foundations: Feminism and the Question of 'Postmodernism,'" in *Feminist Contentions*, Benhabib et al.

45. Judith Butler, *Gender Trouble: Feminism and the Subversion of Identity* (New York: Routledge, 1990), 34.

46. See for example Nussbaum, "Human Functioning and Social Justice;" Seyla Benhabib, "Subjectivity, Historiography and Feminist Politics," in *Feminist Contentions*, Benhabib et al.

47. Ludwig Wittgenstein, *The Blue Book* (Oxford: Blackwell, 1958), 18.

48. Monique Wittig, *The Straight Mind and Other Essays* (Boston: Beacon Press, 1992), esp. 21–32.

49. Wittig, "The Category of Sex," in *The Straight Mind*, 2.

50. Fuss, *Essentially Speaking*, 43.

51. Fuss's response to this charge, elsewhere in the text, seems to be that essentialism should be "deployed" rather than avoided. This claim is under-explored, however, and is also in tension with her use of the reductio as a decisive argument against Wittig. See Eleanor Kuykendall's review essay "Subverting Essentialisms," *Hypatia* 6:3 (1991): 208–17.

52. See for example Valerie Lehr, "The Difficulty of Leaving 'Home': Gay and Lesbian Organizing to Confront AIDS," in *Mobilizing the Community*, eds. Robert Fisher and Joseph Kling (Newbury Park: Sage, 1993), and David Halperin, "The Queer Politics of Michel Foucault," in *Saint Foucault: Towards a Gay Hagiography* (Oxford: Oxford University Press, 1995) for accounts of political actions that attempt to use this framework.

53. Henry Rubin, "Transformations," 40–98.

54. Martin, "Methodological Essentialism," 640.

55. See for example Lillian Faderman, *Surpassing the Love of Men: Romantic Friendship and Love Between Women from the Renaissance to the Present* (New York: Morrow, 1981); Judith Halberstam, *Female Masculinity* (Durham, N.C.: Duke University Press, 1998).

56. Denise Riley, *Am I That Name? Feminism and the Category of "Woman" in History* (Basingstoke: Macmillan, 1988).

57. Benhabib, "Feminism and Postmodernism," in *Feminist Contentions*, Benhabib et al., 22.

58. Fraser and Nicholson, "Social Criticism Without Philosophy," 33.

59. Benhabib, "Subjectivity, Historiography, and Politics," in *Feminist Contentions*, Benhabib et al., 113.

60. Benhabib, "Feminism and Postmodernism," in *Feminist Contentions*, Benhabib et al., 28.

61. See Joan Scott, "Experience," in *Feminists Theorize the Political* eds. Judith Butler and Joan Scott (Routledge: New York, 1992).

62. Fuss, *Essentially Speaking*, 114.

63. bell hooks, "Essentialism and Experience," in *Teaching To Transgress: Education as the Practice of Freedom* (New York: Routledge, 1994), 90

## Chapter 2: Feminist Method and Generalizing about Women

1. Spelman, *Inessential Woman*, 187.

2. Julia Kristeva, "Woman Can Never Be Defined," in *New French Feminisms: An Anthology*, ed. Elaine Marks and Isabelle de Courtivron (Amherst: University of Massachusetts Press, 1980), 137.

3. Spelman, *Inessential Woman*, 3–4.

4. Ibid., 138.

5. Here I follow Becky Thompson's usage of "eating problems" rather than "eating disorders" on the grounds that the latter tends to medicalize and individualize social problems that have obvious cultural roots (see following note).

6. For responses from feminist critics who argue that dominant *feminist* constructions of eating problems are prone to criticism for falsely generalizing, see Dawn Atkins, ed., *Looking Queer: Body Image and Identity in Lesbian, Bisexual, Gay, and Transgendered Communities* (Binghamton, N.Y.: Harrington Park, 1998); hooks's critiques of Naomi Wolf in *Outlaw Culture: Resisting Representations* (New York: Routledge, 1994), 94–102; Becky Thompson, *A Hunger So Wide and So Deep: A Multiracial View of Women's Eating Problems* (Minneapolis: University of Minnesota Press, 1994).

7. Combahee River Collective, "A Black Feminist Statement," in *All the Women Are White, All The Blacks Are Men, But Some of Us Are Brave*, eds. Gloria T. Hull, Patricia Bell Scott, and Barbara Smith (New York: The Feminist Press, 1982), 16.

8. Ibid., 16.

9. bell hooks, "Men: Comrades in Struggle," in *Feminist Theory*, 67–81. For an implicit response to the Combahee River Collective and hooks that challenges the assumption that feminist separatism necessarily weakens racial solidarity, see Jackie Anderson, "Separatism, Feminism, and the Betrayal of Reform," *Signs* 19 (1994): 437–48.

10. Shane Phelan, *Identity Politics: Lesbian Feminism and the Limits of Community* (Philadelphia: Temple University Press, 1989), 166.

11. Rubin, "Transformations," 40–98. Contrast this account with Judith Halberstam's work: see especially "F2M: The Making of Female Masculinity," in *The Lesbian Postmodern*, ed. Laura Doan (New York: Columbia University Press, 1994); "Transgender Butch: Butch/FTM Border Wars and the Masculine Continuum," in Judith Halberstam, *Female Masculinity*.

12. This problem is particularly acute in the history of trans-people: consider, for example, the contrast between Rubin's Foucauldian position and that of Leslie Feinberg,

who tacitly argues that transgendered people constitute a stable and continuous historical category. Leslie Feinberg, *Transgender Warriors: Making History from Joan of Arc to Dennis Rodman* (Boston: Beacon Press, 1996).

13. Fraser and Nicholson, "Social Criticism Without Philosophy," 35.

14. See Gayatri Chakravorty Spivak, "Criticism, Feminism, and the Institution," in *The Post-Colonial Critic: Interviews, Strategies, Dialogues*, ed. Sarah Harasym (New York: Routledge, 1990).

15. Spelman, *Inessential Woman*, ix.

16. Ibid., 125.

17. Lugones, "On the Logic of Pluralist Feminism," 41.

18. Stoljar, "Essence, Identity and the Concept of Woman," 280.

19. Ibid., 282.

20. Spelman, *Inessential Woman*, especially 137–59.

21. Ibid., 176.

22. Susan Moller Okin, "Gender Inequality and Cultural Differences," *Political Theory* 22 (1994): 5.

23. Ibid., 7.

24. Ibid., 13.

25. Ibid., 20.

26. For an excellent analysis of the essentializing construction of the "third world woman" in western feminist texts that speaks precisely to Okin's mistakes, see Chandra Mohanty, "Under Western Eyes: Feminist Scholarship and Colonial Discourses," in *Third World Women and the Politics of Feminism*, eds. Chandra Talpade Mohanty, Ann Russo, and Lourdes Torres (Bloomington, Ind.: Indiana University Press, 1991).

27. Clifford Geertz, "Anti Anti-Relativism," *American Anthropologist* 86 (1984): 263–78.

28. Martin, "Methodological Essentialism," 631.

29. Susan Bordo, "Feminism, Postmodernism, and Gender Skepticism," in *Unbearable Weight*, 217.

30. Ibid., 230.

31. Ibid., 225 (italics in original).

32. Ibid., 233.

33. Spelman, *Inessential Woman*, 12.

34. María Lugones, "Playfulness, 'World'-Travelling, and Loving Perception," in *Lesbian Philosophies and Cultures*, ed. Jeffner Allen (Albany: SUNY Press, 1990), 164, 165.

35. Barbara Christian, "The Race for Theory," in *Making Face, Making Soul/Haciendo Caras: Creative and Critical Perspectives by Feminists of Color*, ed. Gloria Anzaldúa (San Francisco: Aunt Lute, 1990), 338–39.

36. bell hooks, *Sisters of the Yam: Black Women and Self-Recovery* (Toronto: Between the Lines, 1993), 14–15.

37. Spivak, "In a Word," in *The Essential Difference*, eds. Schor and Weed, 175.

### Chapter 3: Philosophical Investigations (in a Feminist Voice)

1. Ludwig Wittgenstein, *Philosophical Investigations*, 2nd ed., translated by G. E. M. Anscombe (Oxford: Blackwell, 1997 [1953]), § 67. All further references to this text will be indicated by the abbreviation PI followed by paragraph or page numbers.

2. See for example Seyla Benhabib, "Epistemologies of Postmodernism," in *Feminism / Postmodernism*, ed. Nicholson; Elizabeth Potter, "Gender and Epistemic Negotiation," in *Feminist Epistemologies*, eds. Linda Alcoff and Elizabeth Potter (New York: Routledge, 1993); Lorraine Code, "Taking Subjectivity into Account," in *Feminist Epistemologies*, eds. Alcoff and Potter.

3. An increasing number of feminists are appropriating Wittgenstein's philosophy. See Judith Mary Green and Blanche Radford Curry, "Recognizing Each Other Amidst Diversity: Beyond Essentialism in Collaborative Multi-Cultural Feminist Theory," *Sage* 8:1 (1991): 39–49; Chantal Mouffe, "Feminism, Citizenship and Radical Democratic Politics," in *Feminists Theorize the Political*, eds. Butler and Scott; Linda Nicholson, "Interpreting Gender"; Stoljar, "Essence, Identity and the Concept of Woman"; Linda Zerilli, "Doing Without Knowing: Feminism's Politics of the Ordinary," *Political Theory* 26 (1998): 79–105; Susan Hekman, "Backgrounds and Riverbeds: Feminist Reflections, *Feminist Studies* 25 (1999): 427–48; Wendy Lee-Lampshire, "The Sound of Little Hummingbird Wings: A Wittgensteinian Investigation of Forms of Life as Forms of Power," *Feminist Studies* 25 (1999): 409–26; Wendy Lee-Lampshire, "Spilling all Over the 'Wide Fields of Our Passions': Frye, Butler, Wittgenstein and the Context(s) of Attention, Intention and Identity (Or: From Arm Wrestling Duck to Abject Being to Lesbian Feminist)," *Hypatia* 14:3 (1999): 1–16; Naomi Scheman, ed., *Feminist Interpretations of Ludwig Wittgenstein* (University Park, Pa.: Penn State Press, in press).

4. There is every reason (including some direct biographical evidence) to believe that Wittgenstein was hostile to feminism and to women in general, despite his close contact with successful philosophers such as Alice Ambrose and Elizabeth Anscombe. See Ray Monk, *Wittgenstein: The Duty of Genius* (London: Vintage, 1990), 72–3, 498 for Wittgenstein's asides on women, feminism, and philosophy.

5. Peta Bowden, *Caring: Gender-Sensitive Ethics* (New York: Routledge, 1997); Theodore Schatzki, *Social Practices: A Wittgensteinian Approach to Human Activity and the Social* (Cambridge: Cambridge University Press, 1996); James Tully, *Strange Multiplicity: Constitutionalism in an Age of Diversity* (Cambridge: Cambridge University Press, 1995).

6. Ludwig Wittgenstein, *Tractatus Logicus-Philosophicus* (London: Routledge and Kegan Paul, 1981).

7. Jacob Hale offers an articulation of the concept "women" that relies on thirteen criteria, no single one of which is either necessary or sufficient. See "Are Lesbians Women?" *Hypatia* 11:2 (1996): 94–121. Hale "clusters" these criteria, and in a similar vein it has been suggested to me (by Allen Carlson) that my position might be nuanced as follows: "women" is defined by reference to a finite number of disjunctive sets of sufficient conditions (i.e. x is a woman if and only if x exhibits characteristics {a and b and c} or {d and e and f} or {a and c and f}, and so on finitely). The characteristics invoked can be, as they are for Hale, either biological (presence of breasts) or an individual gender presentation (dressing as a woman), or an intersubjective experience of gender (being oppressed as a woman). The list of characteristics and hence sets is finite because "women" in its current uses continues to pick out only some individuals by reference to identifiable criteria, albeit not the narrow set of criteria most people imagine.

8. The fullest articulation of this view appears in Ludwig Wittgenstein, *On Certainty*, eds. G. E. M. Anscombe and G. H. von Wright (New York: Harper Torchbooks, 1969).

9. G. P. Baker and P. M. S. Hacker, *An Analytical Commentary on the Philosophical Investigations* (Oxford: Blackwell, 1980), 544.

10. G. E. Moore, "Wittgenstein's Lectures in 1930–33," in *Philosophical Papers* (London: Allen and Unwin, 1959), 322–3.

11. Baker and Hacker, *An Analytical Commentary*, 685.

12. Wittgenstein, *Blue Book*, 18.

13. Lugones, "On The Logic of Pluralist Feminism," 41 (italics in original).

14. See, for example, Susan Bordo, *Unbearable Weight*; Elizabeth Grosz, *Volatile Bodies*; Iris Marion Young, "The Scaling of Bodies and the Politics of Identity," in *Justice and the Politics of Difference* (Princeton: Princeton University Press, 1990), and "Throwing Like a Girl: A Phenomenology of Feminine Body Comportment, Motility, and Spatiality," in *Throwing Like a Girl and Other Essays in Feminist Philosophy and Social Theory* (Bloomington Ind.: Indiana University Press, 1990).

15. Wittgenstein, *On Certainty*, § 152.

16. See Suzanne Kessler and Wendy McKenna, *Gender: An Ethnomethodological Approach* (New York: John Wiley and Sons, 1978), and Holly Devor, *Gender Blending: Confronting the Limits of Duality* (Bloomington, Ind.: Indiana University Press, 1989).

17. Kessler, "The Medical Construction of Gender."

18. The terms "transsexuality," "transgender," and other trans- labels are obviously contested both inside and outside trans- communities. One common distinction is to use "transgendered" to describe those whose gender presentation does not conform to their sex assignment, but who have made no (or limited) body modifications, while "transsexed" describes those who aspire to or have undergone "sex reassignment" surgery. I follow that distinction here, using the deliberately imprecise adjective "trans-" to capture a wider range of identities than either "transgendered" or "transsexed" can describe. For a discussion of the diversity of trans- communities, see Leslie Feinberg, *Trans Liberation: Beyond Pink or Blue* (Boston: Beacon Press, 1998), 43–62.

19. See, for example, Alice Domurat Dreger, *Hermaphrodites and the Medical Invention of Sex* (Cambridge, Mass.: Harvard University Press, 1998); Julia Epstein and Kristina Straub, eds., *Body Guards: The Cultural Politics of Gender Ambiguity*, (New York: Routledge, 1991); Michel Foucault's introduction and the main text of *Herculine Barbin*; Suzanne Kessler, *Lessons from the Intersexed* (Baltimore: Rutgers, 1998).

20. Janice G. Raymond, *The Transsexual Empire: The Making of the She-Male*, 2nd edition (New York: Teachers College, 1994 [1979]). See Sandy Stone, "The Empire Strikes Back: A Posttranssexual Manifesto," in *Body Guards*, eds. Epstein and Straub, for the best-known response to Raymond, and Raymond's "Introduction to the 1994 Edition" of *The Transsexual Empire*, xxii–xxiii for a disappointing riposte to Stone; Jan Morris, *Conundrum* (London: Faber, 1974). Morris's conservatism on gender issues emerges in several widely cited passages, for example, "Such are the superficials of my new consciousness and...I must add to them a frank enjoyment, *which I think most honest women will admit to*, of the small courtesies men now pay me, the standing up or the opening of doors, which really do give one a cherished or protected feeling, undeserved perhaps but very welcome," 148 (italics added).

21. Morris, *Conundrum*, 9, 14–15.

22. Donna Eder, Suzanne Staggenborg, and Lori Sudderth, "The National Women's Music Festival, Collective Identity and Diversity in a Lesbian-Feminist Community," *Journal of Contemporary Ethnography* 23 (1995): 485–515; Monica Kendel, Holly Devor, and Nancy Strapko, "Feminist and Lesbian Opinions about Transsexuals," in *Gender Blending*, eds. Vern L. Bullough, Bonnie Bullough, and James Elias (Amherst, N.Y.: Prometheus

Books, 1997); Jay Prosser, *Second Skins: Body Narratives of Transsexuality* (New York: Columbia University Press, 1998), 171–7.

23. Bornstein, *Gender Outlaw*; Leslie Feinberg, *Stone Butch Blues* (Ithaca: Firebrand, 1993); *Transgender Warriors*; Prosser, *Second Skins*; Susan Stryker, "My Words to Victor Frankenstein Above the Village of Chamounix: Performing Transgender Rage," *GLQ: A Journal of Lesbian and Gay Studies*, 1:3 (1994): 237–54.

24. Sandy Stone, "The Empire Strikes Back," 289–93; Jacob Hale, "Tracing A Ghostly Memory in My Throat: Reflections on Ftm Feminist Voice and Agency," in *Men Doing Feminism*, ed. Tom Digby (New York: Routledge, 1998), 103–108.

25. See for example Bornstein, *Gender Outlaw*.

26. For answers to these questions, in addition to works already cited, see C. Jacob Hale, "Leatherdyke Boys and Their Daddies: How to Have Sex Without Women and Men," *Social Text* 15: 3/4 (1997): 223–39; "Suggested Rules for Non-Transsexuals Writing About Transsexuals, Transsexuality, Transsexualism, or Trans—." http://www.actlab.utexas.edu/~sandy/hale.rules.html; Minnie Bruce Pratt, *S/he* (Ithaca: Firebrand, 1995); Henry Rubin, "Reading Like a (Transsexual) Man," in *Men Doing Feminism* ed. Digby; Naomi Scheman, "Queering the Center By Centering the Queer: Reflections on Transsexuals and Secular Jews," in *Feminists Rethink the Self*, ed. Diana Tietjens Meyers (Boulder: Westview, 1997).

27. Rubin, "Transformations," 205–217. In his forthcoming book *Always Already Men* (Chicago: University of Chicago Press), Rubin places greater emphasis on understanding essentialist claims to authenticity through his Foucauldian framework, reading them as emergent "technologies of the self" (Rubin, personal communication, April 14, 1999).

28. Scheman, "Queering the Center by Centering the Queer," in Meyers, ed., *Feminists Rethink the Self*, 141.

29. Jacquelyn Zita, "Male Lesbians and the Postmodernist Body," *Hypatia* 7:4 (1992): 106–27.

30. Ibid., 117.

31. Linda Zerilli, "Doing Without Knowing," 454.

32. Kristeva, "Woman Can Never Be Defined."

33. Judith Butler, "For a Careful Reading," in *Feminist Contentions*, 132.

34. Spelman, *Inessential Woman*, 187.

35. Friedan, *The Feminine Mystique*, 326.

36. Spelman, *Inessential Woman*, 140.

37. Kathy Ferguson, "Interpretation and Genealogy in Feminism," *Signs* 16 (1991) : 337.

38. Martin, "Methodological Essentialism," 637–8.

39. Young, "Gender as Seriality," 23.

40. Ibid., 28.

41. Linda Alcoff and Laura Gray, "Survivor Discourse: Transgression or Recuperation?" *Signs* 18 (1993): 260–90; Nancy Potter, "The Severed Head and Existential Dread: The Classroom as Epistemic Community and Student Survivors of Incest," *Hypatia* 10:2 (1995): 69–92.

42. See Cressida Heyes, ed. *APA Newsletter on Feminism and Philosophy* (Fall 1999) for a discussion of the backlash against feminist philosophy within academia.

**Chapter 4: "Look and See": Gilligan and Feminist Research**

1. Jill McLean Taylor, Carol Gilligan, and Amy M. Sullivan, *Between Voice and Silence: Women and Girls, Race and Relationship* (Cambridge: Harvard University Press, 1996). Hereafter references to this book are given in parentheses in the main text using the abbreviation BVS followed by a page number.

2. See Shulamit Reinharz, *Feminist Methods in Social Research* (New York: Oxford University Press, 1992).

3. For accounts of potential basic tenets of "feminist research" see Sandra Harding, "Introduction: Is There a Feminist Method?" in *Feminism and Methodology*, ed. Sandra Harding (Bloomington, Ind.: Indiana University Press, 1987); Liz Stanley, *Feminist Praxis: Research, Theory and Epistemology in Feminist Sociology* (London: Routledge, 1990), esp. 20–47; Mary Margaret Fonow and Judith Cook, "Back to the Future: A Look at the Second Wave of Feminist Epistemology and Methodology," in *Beyond Methodology: Feminist Scholarship as Lived Research*, eds. Mary Margaret Fonow and Judith Cook (Bloomington, Ind: Indiana University Press, 1991); Maria Mies, "Towards a Methodology for Feminist Research," in *Theories of Women's Studies*, eds. Gloria Bowles and Renate Duelli Klein (Boston: Routledge, 1983).

4. For one of the best known early feminist arguments against this social scientific tradition, see Ann Oakley, "Interviewing Women: A Contradiction in Terms," in *Doing Feminist Research*, ed. Helen Roberts (Boston: Routledge and Kegan Paul, 1981).

5. Mies, "Towards a Methodology for Feminist Research."

6. Diane L. Wolf, "Situating Feminist Dilemmas in Fieldwork," in *Feminist Dilemmas in Fieldwork*, ed. Diane Wolf (Boulder: Westview, 1996), 28.

7. Lynn Cannon, Elizabeth Higginbotham, and Marianne Leung, "Race and Class Bias in Qualitative Research on Women," *Gender and Society* 2 (1988): 459 (italics added).

8. Maxine Baca Zinn, Pierrette Hondagneu-Sotelo, and Michael A. Messner, eds. *Through the Prism of Difference: Readings on Sex and Gender* (Needham Heights, Mass.: Allyn and Bacon, 1997).

9. Catherine Kohler Riessman, "When Gender is Not Enough: Women Interviewing Women," *Gender and Society* 1 (1987): 190.

10. Ibid., 190.

11. Laura Nader, "Up the Anthropologist: Perspectives Gained From Studying Up," in *Anthropology for the Nineties*, ed. Johnetta Cole (New York: Free Press, 1988); Maxine Baca Zinn, "Field Research in Minority Communities: Ethical, Methodological, and Political Observations by an Insider," *Social Problems* 27 (1979): 209–19; Marjorie DeVault, "Ethnicity and Expertise: Racial-Ethnic Knowledge in Sociological Research," *Gender and Society* 9 (1995): 612–31; Patricia Zavella, "Feminist Insider Dilemmas: Constructing Ethnic Identity with Chicana Informants," *Feminist Dilemmas*, ed. Wolf.; Carol B. Stack, "Writing Ethnography: Feminist Critical Practice," *Feminist Dilemmas*, ed. Wolf.

12. Judith Stacey, "Can There Be A Feminist Ethnography?," *Women's Studies International Forum* 11:1 (1988): 21–27.

13. Gilligan's work on this issue forms part of several research projects with other investigators and is reported in numerous books and articles to date. In presenting this body of literature, by and large, as exemplary of "Gilligan's" method, I do not intend to erase the contributions of her co-authors, minimize the collaborative nature of the research, or sug-

gest that there is a unitary authorial voice in these studies. Rather I want to avoid stylistic awkwardness, to stress how the later books rework ideas first presented in *In a Different Voice*, and acknowledge that Gilligan is the only author common to all the studies.

14. See Carol Gilligan, *In a Different Voice: Psychological Theory and Women's Development*, 2$^{nd}$ edition. (Cambridge: Harvard University Press, 1993 with new "Letter to Readers" [1982]); Carol Gilligan, J. Ward, and Jill McLean Taylor, eds., *Mapping the Moral Domain: A Contribution of Women's Thinking to Psychological Theory and Education* (Cambridge: Harvard University Press, 1988); Carol Gilligan, Nona P. Lyons, and Trudy J. Hanmer, eds., *Making Connections: The Relational Worlds of Adolescent Girls at Emma Willard School*, (Cambridge: Harvard University Press, 1990); Carol Gilligan, Annie G. Rogers, and Deborah L. Tolman, eds., *Women, Girls and Psychotherapy: Reframing Resistance* (New York: Harrington Park Press, 1991); Lyn Mikel Brown and Carol Gilligan, *Meeting at the Crossroads: Women's Psychology and Girls' Development* (Cambridge: Harvard University Press, 1992).

15. Gilligan, *In a Different Voice*. For one of the most sophisticated and charitable critical readings of *In a Different Voice*, see Susan J. Hekman, *Moral Voices, Moral Selves: Carol Gilligan and Feminist Moral Theory* (University Park, Penna.: Penn State Press, 1995), esp. 1–33.

16. Bordo, *Unbearable Weight*, 233.

17. Gilligan, *In a Different Voice*, 2.

18. *Making Connections*, eds. Gilligan, Lyons and Hanmer, 9.

19. Linda Kerber, "Some Cautionary Words for Historians," *Signs* 11 (1986): 309.

20. Nancy Chodorow, *The Reproduction of Mothering: Psychoanalysis and the Sociology of Gender* (Berkeley: University of California Press, 1978).

21. See for example Linda Nicholson, "Women, Morality, and History," in *An Ethic of Care: Feminist and Interdisciplinary Perspectives*, ed. Mary Jeanne Larrabee (New York: Routledge, 1993).

22. Fraser and Nicholson, "Social Criticism Without Philosophy," 32–33 (italics in original).

23. See Michele Moody-Adams, "Gender and the Complexity of Moral Voices," in *Feminist Ethics*, ed. Card.

24. See "Part III: Checking the Data," in *An Ethic of Care*, ed. Larrabee.

25. Carol Gilligan, "Joining the Resistance: Psychology, Politics, Girls and Women," *Michigan Quarterly Review* 29 (1990): 501–46.

26. Judith Stacey, "On Resistance, Ambivalence and Feminist Theory: A Response to Carol Gilligan," *Michigan Quarterly Review* 29 (1990): 537–46.

27. Gilligan, "Joining the Resistance," 526.

28. Gilligan, *In a Different Voice*, xii–xiii.

29. See Gilligan, *In a Different Voice*, 2; Carol Gilligan, "Reply," *Signs* 11 (1986): 324–33.

30. Gilligan, *In a Different Voice*, xiii–xv.

31. See Gilligan, "Joining the Resistance."

32. For example, Christine Di Stefano, *Configurations of Masculinity: A Feminist Perspective on Modern Political Theory* (Ithaca: Cornell University Press, 1991).

33. See for example Mary Cooper, "Gilligan's Different Voice: A Perspective for Nursing," *Journal of Professional Nursing* 5 (1989): 10–16; Robin Leidner, "Stretching the Boundaries of Liberalism: Democratic Innovation in a Feminist Organization," *Signs* 16 (1991): 263–89; Nel Noddings, "An Ethic of Caring and Its Implications for Instructional Arrangements," in *The Education Feminism Reader*, ed. Lynda Stone (New York: Routledge,

1994); Fiona Robinson, *Globalizing Care: Ethics, Feminist Theory, and International Relations* (Boulder: Westview, 1999); Suzanna Sherry, "Civic Virtue and the Feminine Voice in Constitutional Adjudication," *Virginia Law Review* 72 (1986): 543–616; Joan Tronto, *Moral Boundaries: A Political Argument for an Ethic of Care* (New York: Routledge, 1993).

34. Gilligan, "Reply."

35. María Lugones, "On the Logic of Pluralist Feminism," 38.

36. Brown and Gilligan, *Meeting at the Crossroads*, 25–31.

37. Ibid., 29. Emphasis in original.

38. See, for example, Taylor, Gilligan, and Sullivan, *Between Voice and Silence*, 14. They state: "In *Meeting at the Crossroads* (1992) Lyn Mikel Brown and Carol Gilligan, observing the effects of different interviewers on girls' responses, noted in particular how an African American girl's interview conversation differs when an African American woman is listening rather than a white interviewer, and also how a playful interviewer can elicit a very different girl from the one who takes a more formal approach." In fact, both issues are treated quite marginally in that text and in the context of larger similarities.

39. Clifford Geertz, *Works and Lives: The Anthropologist as Author* (Stanford: Stanford University Press, 1988), 140.

40. See Sandra Harding, *Whose Science? Whose Knowledge? Thinking From Women's Lives* (Ithaca: Cornell University Press, 1991).

41. Brown and Gilligan, *Meeting at the Crossroads*, 7–17.

42. James C. Scott, *Domination and the Arts of Resistance: Hidden Transcripts* (New Haven: Yale University Press, 1990), 5.

43. Adrienne Rich, "Compulsory Heterosexuality and Lesbian Existence," *Signs* 5 (1980): 631–60.

44. Neither the sexualities of the researchers nor any explicit analysis of heteronormativity is presented in any discussion either of the retreat process, the interpretive community, or the research itself. Members of the research team may have identified as lesbian, bisexual or another queer moniker, but this is not mentioned in the book.

45. María Lugones and Elizabeth V. Spelman, "Have We Got a Theory for You!: Feminist Theory, Cultural Imperialism, and the Demand for the 'The Woman's Voice,'" in *Women and Values: Readings in Recent Feminist Philosophy*, ed. Marilyn Pearsall (Belmont, Calif: Wadsworth, 1986).

46. Elizabeth Frazer, "Teenage Girls Talking about Class," *Sociology* 22 (1988): 343–58; "Feminist Talk and Talking about Feminism: Teenage Girls' Discourses of Gender," *Oxford Review of Education* 15 (1989): 281–90; "Talking about Gender, Race and Class," in *Researching Language: Issues of Power and Method*, Deborah Cameron, Elizabeth Frazer, and Penelope Harvey (London: Routledge, 1992).

47. Frazer, "Teenage Girls Talking about Class."

48. Frazer, "Talking about Gender, Race and Class," 99.

49. Brown and Gilligan, *Meeting at the Crossroads*, 228–32.

50. See Stacey, "On Resistance, Ambivalence and Feminist Theory"; Frazer, "Talking about Gender, Race and Class"; Katherine Borland, "'That's Not What I Said': Interpretive Conflict in Oral Narrative Research," in *Women's Words: The Feminist Practice of Oral History*, eds. Sherna Gluck and Daphne Patai (New York: Routledge, 1991).

51. Peter Winch, *The Idea of a Social Science* (London: Routledge and Kegan Paul, 1958). See also Wittgenstein, *Philosophical Investigations* §§ 19, 23, 241, pp. 174, 226.

52. Frazer, "Talking about Gender, Race and Class," 100.

## Chapter 5: Between Theory and Practice: MacKinnon and Feminist Activism

1. For a critique of MacKinnon's rhetoric, see Brown, "The Mirror of Pornography," in *States of Injury*, 77–95; for an analysis of her alleged conservatism, see Gayle Rubin, "Thinking Sex: Notes for a Radical Theory of the Politics of Sexuality," in *American Feminist Thought at Century's End: A Reader*, ed. Linda S. Kauffman (Oxford: Blackwell, 1993), 35–43.

2. Catharine MacKinnon, *Sexual Harassment of Working Women* (New Haven: Yale University Press, 1979); "Minneapolis Ordinance: Excerpts," in *Women Against Censorship*, ed. Varda Burstyn (Vancouver: Douglas and MacIntyre, 1985).

3. MacKinnon articulates this view most fully in *Toward a Feminist Theory of the State* (Cambridge, Mass.: Harvard University Press, 1989), especially "Sexuality," 126–54, and "Sex Equality: On Difference and Dominance," 215–36.

4. Brown, *States of Injury*, esp. 87–90.

5. Catharine MacKinnon, *Feminism Unmodified: Discourses on Life and Law* (Cambridge, MA: Harvard University Press, 1987), 48–50.

6. MacKinnon, *Feminism Unmodified*, 148–50 and 171–74.

7. MacKinnon, *Toward a Feminist Theory of the State*, 141–42.

8. For a discussion of the "essentializing" of sex, see Marilyn Frye, "Lesbian 'Sex,'" in *Lesbian Philosophies and Cultures*, ed. Allen.

9. Wittig, *The Straight Mind*, 32.

10. Rich, "Compulsory Heterosexuality and Lesbian Existence"; Wittig, *The Straight Mind*; Allen, ed., *Lesbian Philosophies and Cultures*.

11. Legal theorist Carl Stychin has argued in a similar vein that MacKinnon assimilates gay male pornography to straight porn in ways that assume rather than investigate whether the same relations of dominance and submission are enacted: Carl F. Stychin, "Exploring the Limits: Feminism and the Legal Regulation of Gay Male Pornography," *Vermont Law Review* 16 (1992): 857–900.

12. For a lesbian feminist critique, including anecdotal information about MacKinnon's responses to criticism, see Patricia A. Cain, "Feminist Jurisprudence: Grounding the Theories," in *Feminist Legal Theory: Readings in Law and Gender*, eds. Katharine T. Bartlett and Rosanne Kennedy (Boulder: Westview, 1991), esp. 272–75.

13. Marlee Kline, "Race, Racism and Feminist Legal Theory," *Harvard Women's Law Journal* 12 (1989): 140–41.

14. Angela Harris, "Race and Essentialism in Feminist Legal Theory," in *Feminist Legal Theory*, eds. Bartlett and Kennedy, 238.

15. Ibid., 242.

16. Catharine MacKinnon, "From Practice to Theory, or What is a White Woman Anyway?," in *Radically Speaking*, eds. Diane Bell and Renate Klein (Melbourne: Spinifex, 1996), 46. Hereafter references to this article will be given in the main text using the abbreviation PT and a page number in parentheses.

17. Kimberlé Crenshaw, "Demarginalizing the Intersection of Race and Sex: A Black Feminist Critique of Antidiscrimination Doctrine, Feminist Theory and Antiracist Politics," in *Feminist Legal Theory*, eds. Bartlett and Kennedy, 59, 60, 63. See also Kimberlé Crenshaw, "Mapping the Margins: Intersectionality, Identity and Violence Against Women of Color," *Stanford Law Review* 43 (1993): 1241–99; Martha Minow, *Making All The Difference: Inclusion, Exclusion, and American Law* (Ithaca, N.Y.: Cornell University Press, 1990).

18. Allison Tom, "Children of Our Culture? Class, Power and Learning in a Feminist Bank," in *Feminist Organizations: Harvest of the New Women's Movement*, eds. Myra Marx Ferree and Patricia Yancey Martin (Philadelphia: Temple University Press, 1995).

19. See Jeanne Adleman and Gloria Enguidanos, eds., *Racism in the Lives of Women: Testimony, Theory, and Guides to Antiracist Practice* (Binghamton: Harrington Park, 1996); Laura Brown and Maria Root, eds., *Diversity and Complexity in Feminist Therapy* (New York: The Haworth Press, 1990), passim.

20. Crenshaw, "Demarginalizing the Intersection of Race and Sex," 64.

21. Nancy Matthews, "Surmounting a Legacy: The Expansion of Racial Diversity in a Local Anti-Rape Movement," *Gender and Society* 3 (1989): 518–32.

22. Ibid., 527.

23. Ibid., 529.

24. See Elizabeth V. Spelman, *Fruits of Sorrow: Framing Our Attention to Suffering* (Boston: Beacon Press, 1997), 113–32 for an analysis of the appropriation of suffering, especially in the context of racial differences among women.

25. See for example María Lugones, "Hablando cara a cara/Speaking Face to Face: An Exploration of Ethnocentric Racism," in *Making Face, Making Soul/Haciendo Caras: Creative and Critical Perspectives by Feminists of Color*, ed. Gloria Anzaldúa (San Francisco: Aunt Lute, 1990).

26. Wittgenstein, *Blue Book*, 18.

27. Kathy Miriam, "Disciplining Feminism: Reflections on the (Im)possibility of the Feminist Academic as Public Intellectual," Paper presented at the Radical Philosophy Association Conference, San Francisco, November 1998, 1.

28. I am indebted to Mary Gebhart for making this point in this way.

29. I use the term in Marilyn Frye's sense: "Feminist separation is, of course, separation of various sorts or modes from men and from institutions, relationships, roles and activities which are male-defined, male-dominated and operating for the benefit of males and the maintenance of male privilege—this separation being initiated or maintained, at will, *by women.*" Marilyn Frye, "Some Reflections on Separatism and Power," in *The Politics of Reality* (Freedom, Calif.: The Crossing Press, 1983), 96. Emphasis in original.

30. Angela Davis gives the example of a Black woman who, having been acquitted of the murder of the white prison guard who had raped her, lobbied on behalf of a Black man falsely convicted of raping a white woman. Few white women or organized anti-rape groups took up this cause, a reluctance Davis construes as "one of those historical episodes confirming many Black women's suspicions that the anti-rape movement was largely oblivious to their special concerns." Angela Davis, *Women, Race and Class* (New York: Vintage, 1983), 175.

31. Harding, *Whose Science? Whose Knowledge?*, 280.

32. See David Kahane, "Male Feminism as Oxymoron," in *Men Doing Feminism*, ed. Digby.

33. I am indebted to Peter Hovmand for his helpful suggestions and discussion of these points.

34. See for example Myra Ferree and Beth Hess, eds. *Controversy and Coalition: The New Feminist Movement*, 2nd edition (Boston: Twayne, 1994 [1985]); Ferree and Martin, eds. *Feminist Organizations*.

35. See Adleman and Enguidanos, eds. *Racism in the Lives of Women*; Constance Backhouse and David H. Flaherty, eds. *Challenging Times: The Women's Movement in Canada and*

*the United States* (Montreal: McGill-Queens University Press, 1993), esp. 160–81; Eder, Staggenborg, and Sudderth, "The National Women's Music Festival"; Tom, "Children of Our Culture?"; Robin Leidner, "Stretching the Boundaries of Liberalism"; Matthews, "Surmounting a Legacy"; Sandra Morgen, "The Dream of Diversity, the Dilemmas of Difference: Race and Class Contradictions in a Feminist Health Clinic," in *Anthropology for the Nineties*, ed. Sole; Carmen Sirianni, "Learning Pluralism: Democracy and Diversity in Feminist Organizations," in *Nomos XXXV: Democratic Community*, eds. John Chapman and Ian Shapiro (New York: New York University Press, 1993).

36. See Epstein, "Gay Politics, Ethnic Identity"; Diana Fuss, ed. *Inside/Out: Lesbian Theories, Gay Theories* (New York: Routledge, 1991); Lehr, "The Difficulty of Leaving 'Home'"; Shane Phelan, *Identity Politics*, and *Getting Specific: Postmodern Lesbian Politics* (Minneapolis: University of Minnesota Press, 1994).

37. Sirianni, "Learning Pluralism," 299.

38. Leidner, "Stretching the Boundaries of Liberalism," 265.

39. Chela Sandoval, "Feminism and Racism: A Report on the 1981 National Women's Studies Association Conference," in *Making Face, Making Soul*, ed. Anzaldúa, 59.

40. See the Canadian Research Institute for the Advancement of Women report, *Looking for Change: A Documentation of National Women's Organizations Working towards Inclusion and Diversity*, December 1996.

41. Kathleen Iannello's book is a rare contemporary investigation of feminist organizing with an eye to anarcha-feminist frameworks. See Iannello, *Decisions without Hierarchy: Feminist Organization Theory and Practice* (New York: Routledge, 1992).

42. Jo Freeman's classic analysis of the drawbacks of collectivist organizing argued that without formal structures guaranteeing a certain procedural fairness, feminist organizations risked other forms of injustice emerging from the dominance of charismatic personalities, nepotism, and so on. Jo Freeman, "The Tyranny of Structurelessness," *Berkeley Journal of Sociology* 17 : 2 (1972): 151–64. See also Cathy Levine's less well-known riposte, "The Tyranny of Tyranny," mimeograph (Montreal: Black Rose, 1984).


## Conclusion: "Back to the Rough Ground!"


1. See for example Christine Di Stefano, "Dilemmas of Difference" in *Feminism/Postmodernism*, ed. Nicholson.

2. I attempt to answer this question in a paper-in-progress, "What Do Feminists Need a Theory of Power to Explain?," presented at the American Philosophical Association Eastern Division Conference, December 1998.

3. For example, Sandra Lee Bartky, *Femininity and Domination: Studies in the Phenomenology of Oppression* (New York: Routledge, 1990); Nancy Fraser, *Unruly Practices: Power, Discourse, and Gender in Contemporary Social Theory* (Minneapolis: University of Minnesota Press, 1989); Susan Hekman, ed., *Feminist Interpretations of Michel Foucault* (University Park, Penna.: Penn State Press, 1996); Jana Sawicki, *Disciplining Foucault: Feminism, Power and the Body* (New York: Routledge, 1991).

4. Judith Butler, *The Psychic Life of Power* (Stanford: Stanford University Press, 1997).

5. Much Black feminist writing, for example, takes on the essentialist construction of both gender and race in radical political theory, as captured by the title of the classic collection *All the Women Are White, All the Blacks Are Men, But Some of Us Are Brave*. See also

hooks, "Reflections on Race and Sex," in *Yearning;* "Feminist Scholarship: Black Scholars," in *Teaching to Transgress;* Patricia Hill Collins, *Black Feminist Thought: Knowledge, Consciousness, and the Politics of Empowerment* (New York: Routledge, 1990).

6. See for example, David Theo Goldberg, *Racist Culture: Philosophy and the Politics of Meaning* (Oxford: Blackwell, 1993); Lucius Outlaw, *On Race and Philosophy* (New York: Routledge, 1996).

7. For a range of different positions within this spectrum, see for example, Henry Louis Gates, Jr., ed. *"Race," Writing and Difference* (Chicago: University of Chicago Press, 1986); K. Anthony Appiah, *In My Father's House: Africa in the Philosophy of Culture* (New York: Oxford University Press, 1992); Molefi K. Asante, *Afrocentricity* (Trenton, NJ: Africa World Press, 1988).

8. See Naomi Zack, ed., *American Mixed Race: The Culture of Microdiversity* (Lanham, Md.: Rowman and Littlefield, 1995) and Naomi Zack, *Race and Mixed Race* (Philadelphia: Temple University Press, 1993); Ruth Colker, *Hybrids: Bisexuals, Multiracials and Other Misfits Under Law* (New York: New York University Press, 1996).

9. For examples of critical approaches to the study of whiteness within feminism see Ruth Frankenberg, *White Women, Race Matters: The Social Construction of Whiteness* (Minneapolis: University of Minnesota Press, 1993); Chris J. Cuomo and Kim Q. Hall, eds., *Whiteness: Feminist Philosophical Narratives* (Lanham, Md.: Rowman and Littlefield, 1999).

10. Again, an extensive literature addresses these issues. See for example Ann Ferguson, "Is There a Lesbian Culture?" Julia Penelope, "The Lesbian Perspective," and Claudia Card, "Pluralist Lesbian Separatism," in *Lesbian Philosophies and Cultures,* ed. Allen; Ruth Ginzberg, "Audre Lorde's (Nonessentialist) Lesbian Eros," Elisabeth D. Däumer, "Queer Ethics; or, The Challenge of Bisexuality to Lesbian Ethics," and Sarah Lucia Hoagland, "Why *Lesbian* Ethics?" in *Adventures in Lesbian Philosophy,* ed. Claudia Card (Bloomington: Indiana University Press, 1994); Arlene Stein, "Sisters and Queers: The Decentering of Lesbian Feminism," *Socialist Review* 22:1 (1992): 33–55; Vera Whisman, "Identity Crises: Who is a Lesbian Anyway," and Lisa Kahaleole Chang Hall, "Bitches in Solitude: Identity Politics and Lesbian Community," in *Sisters, Sexperts, Queers: Beyond the Lesbian Nation,* ed. Arlene Stein (New York: Plume, 1993); Verta Taylor and Leila Rull, "Women's Culture and Lesbian Feminist Activism: A Reconsideration of Cultural Feminism," *Signs* 19 (1993): 32–61; Verta Taylor and Nancy Whittier, "Collective Identity and Lesbian Feminist Mobilization," in *Frontiers of Social Movement Theory,* eds. Aldon Morris and Carol McClurg Mueller (New Haven: Yale University Press, 1992).

# Bibliography

Adams, Parveen, and Elizabeth Cowie, eds. *The Woman in Question*. Cambridge, Mass.: MIT Press, 1990.

Adleman, Jeanne, and Gloria Enguidanos, eds. *Racism in the Lives of Women: Testimony, Theory, and Guides to Antiracist Practice*. Binghamton, N.Y.: Harrington Park, 1996.

Alcoff, Linda. "Cultural Feminism versus Poststructuralism: The Identity Crisis in Feminist Theory." In *Feminist Theory in Practice and Process*, eds. Micheline Malson, Jean F. O'Barr, Sarah Westphal, and Mary Wyer. Chicago: University of Chicago Press, 1989.

Alcoff, Linda, and Laura Gray. "Survivor Discourse: Transgression or Recuperation?" *Signs* 18 (1993): 260–90.

Allen, Jeffner, ed. *Lesbian Philosophies and Cultures*. Albany: SUNY Press, 1990.

Anderson, Jackie. "Separatism, Feminism, and the Betrayal of Reform." *Signs* 19 (1994): 437–48.

Appiah, K. Anthony. *In My Father's House: Africa in the Philosophy of Culture*. New York: Oxford University Press, 1992.

Asante, Molefi K. *Afrocentricity*. Trenton, N.J.: Africa World Press, 1988.

Atherton, Margaret. "The Inessentiality of Lockean Essences." *Canadian Journal of Philosophy* 14 (1984): 277–93.

Atkins, Dawn. *Looking Queer: Body Image and Identity in Lesbian, Bisexual, Gay, and Transgendered Communities*. Binghamton, N.Y.: Harrington Park, 1998.

Baca Zinn, Maxine. "Field Research in Minority Communities: Ethical, Methodological, and Political Observations by an Insider." *Social Problems* 27 (1979): 209–19.

Baca Zinn, Maxine, Pierrette Hondagneu-Sotelo, and Michael A. Messner, eds. *Through the Prism of Difference: Readings on Sex and Gender*. Boston: Allyn and Bacon, 1997.

Backhouse, Constance, and David Flaherty, eds. *Challenging Times: The Women's Movement in Canada and the United States*. Montreal: McGill-Queens University Press, 1992.

Baker, G. P., and P. M. S. Hacker. *An Analytical Commentary on the Philosophical Investigations*. Oxford: Blackwell, 1980.

Barbin, Herculine. *Herculine Barbin: Being the Recently Discovered Memoirs of a Nineteenth Century French Hermaphrodite* with introduction by Michel Foucault. New York: Pantheon Books, 1980.

Bartky, Sandra Lee. *Femininity and Domination: Studies in the Phenomenology of Oppression*. New York: Routledge, 1990.

Benhabib, Seyla, Judith Butler, Drucilla Cornell, and Nancy Fraser, with introduction by Linda Nicholson. *Feminist Contentions: A Philosophical Exchange*. New York: Routledge, 1995.

Bordo, Susan. *Unbearable Weight: Feminism, Western Culture and the Body*. Berkeley: University of California Press, 1993.

Borland, Katharine. "'That's Not What I Said': Interpretive Conflict in Oral Narrative

Research." In *Women's Words: The Feminist Practice of Oral History*, eds. Sherna Gluck and Daphne Patai. New York: Routledge, 1991.

Bornstein, Kate. *Gender Outlaw: On Men, Women and the Rest of Us*. New York: Vintage Books, 1995.

Bowden, Peta. *Caring: Gender-Sensitive Ethics*. New York: Routledge, 1997.

Brody, Baruch. *Identity and Essence*. Princeton: Princeton University Press, 1980.

Brown, Laura, and Maria Root, eds. *Diversity and Complexity in Feminist Therapy*. New York: Haworth, 1990.

Brown, Lyn Mikel, and Carol Gilligan. *Meeting at the Crossroads: Women's Psychology and Girls' Development*. Cambridge, Mass.: Harvard University Press, 1992.

Brown, Wendy. *States of Injury: Power and Freedom in Late Modernity*. Princeton: Princeton University Press, 1995.

Butler, Judith. *Gender Trouble: Feminism and the Subversion of Identity*. New York: Routledge, 1992.

——. *Bodies That Matter: On the Discursive Limits of "Sex."* New York: Routledge, 1993.

——. *The Psychic Life of Power*. Stanford: Stanford University Press, 1997.

Cain, Patricia A. "Feminist Jurisprudence: Grounding the Theories." In *Feminist Legal Theory: Readings in Law and Gender*, eds. Katharine T. Bartlett and Rosanne Kennedy. Boulder: Westview, 1991.

Canadian Research Institute for the Advancement of Women, *Looking for Change: A Documentation of National Women's Organizations Working Towards Inclusion and Diversity*. Ottawa: CRIAW/ICREF, December 1996.

Cannon, Lynn Weber, Elizabeth Higginbotham, and Marianne Leung. "Race and Class Bias in Qualitative Research on Women." *Gender and Society* 2 (1988): 449–62.

Card, Claudia, ed. *Adventures in Lesbian Philosophy*. Bloomington: Indiana University Press, 1994.

Chodorow, Nancy. *The Reproduction of Mothering: Psychoanalysis and the Sociology of Gender*. Berkeley: University of California Press, 1978.

Christian, Barbara. "The Race For Theory." In *Making Face, Making Soul/Haciendo Caras: Creative and Critical Perspectives by Feminists of Color*, ed. Gloria Anzaldúa. San Francisco: Aunt Lute, 1990.

Code, Lorraine. "Taking Subjectivity Into Account." In *Feminist Epistemologies*, eds. Linda Alcoff and Elizabeth Potter. New York: Routledge, 1993.

Colker, Ruth. *Hybrids: Bisexuals, Multiracials and Other Misfits Under Law*. New York: New York University Press, 1996.

Combahee River Collective. "A Black Feminist Statement." In *All the Women Are White, All the Blacks Are Men, but Some of Us Are Brave*, eds. Gloria T. Hull, Patricia Bell Scott, and Barbara Smith. New York: The Feminist Press, 1982.

Cooper, Nancy. "Gilligan's Different Voice: A Perspective for Nursing." *Journal of Professional Nursing* 5 (1989): 10–16.

Crenshaw, Kimberlé. "Demarginalizing the Intersection of Race and Sex: A Black Feminist Critique of Antidiscrimination Doctrine, Feminist Theory and Antiracist Politics." In *Feminist Legal Theory*, eds. Katharine T. Bartlett and Rosanne Kennedy. Boulder: Westview, 1991.

——. "Mapping the Margins: Intersectionality, Identity and Violence Against Women of Color." *Stanford Law Review* 43 (1993): 1241–99.

Cuomo, Chris J., and Kim Q. Hall, eds. *Whiteness: Feminist Philosophical Narratives*. Lanham, Md.: Rowman and Littlefield, 1999.

Daly, Mary. *Gyn/Ecology*. Boston: Beacon Press, 1978.

Davis, Angela. *Women, Race and Class*. New York: Vintage, 1983.

DeGrood, David. *Philosophies of Essence*. Amsterdam: B. R. Gruner, 1976.

de Lauretis, Teresa. "The Essence of the Triangle or, Taking the Risk of Essentialism Seriously: Feminist Theory in Italy, the US, and Britain." *differences* 1:2 (1989): 3–37.

———. "Upping the Anti (sic) in Feminist Theory." In *Conflicts in Feminism*, eds. Marianne Hirsch and Evelyn Fox Keller. New York: Routledge, 1990.

D'Emilio, John, "Capitalism and Gay Identity," in *The Material Queer: A LesBiGay Cultural Studies Reader*, ed. Donald Morton (Boulder: Westview, 1996).

DeVault, Marjorie. "Ethnicity and Expertise: Racial-Ethnic Knowledge in Sociological Research." *Gender and Society* 9 (1995): 612–31.

Devor, Holly. *Gender-Blending: Confronting the Limits of Duality*. Bloomington: Indiana University Press, 1989.

Di Stefano, Christine. "Dilemmas of Difference: Feminism, Modernity, and Postmodernism." In *Feminism/Postmodernism*, ed. Linda Nicholson. New York: Routledge, 1990.

———. *Configurations of Masculinity: A Feminist Perspective on Modern Political Theory*. Ithaca: Cornell University Press, 1991.

Dreger, Alice Domurat. *Hermaphrodites and the Medical Invention of Sex*. Cambridge, Mass.: Harvard University Press, 1998.

Dworkin, Andrea. *Intercourse*. New York: Free Press, 1987.

Eagleton, Terry and Derek Jarman, *Wittgenstein: The Terry Eagleton Script/The Derek Jarman Film* (London: British Film Institute, 1993).

Eder, Donna, Suzanne Staggenborg, and Lori Sudderth. "The National Women's Music Festival: Collective Identity and Diversity in a Lesbian-Feminist Community." *Journal of Contemporary Ethnography* 23 (1995): 485–515.

Eisenstein, Hester. *Contemporary Feminist Thought*. Boston: G. K. Hall, 1983.

Epstein, Julia, and Kristina Straub, eds. *Body Guards: The Cultural Politics of Gender Ambiguity*. New York: Routledge, 1991.

Epstein, Steven. "Gay Politics, Ethnic Identity: The Limits of Social Constructionism." *Socialist Review* 17:3 (1987): 9–54.

Escoffier, Jeffrey. "Sexual Revolution and the Politics of Gay Identity." *Socialist Review* 15:4 (1985): 119–53.

Faderman, Lillian. *Surpassing the Love of Men: Romantic Friendship and Love Between Women from the Renaissance to the Present*. New York: Morrow, 1981.

Fausto-Sterling, Anne. *Myths of Gender: Biological Theories About Women and Men*, 2nd ed. New York: Basic Books, 1992.

———. "The Five Sexes: Why Male and Female Are Not Enough." *The Sciences* 33 (March/April 1993): 20–25.

Feinberg, Leslie. *Stone Butch Blues*. Ithaca: Firebrand Books, 1993.

———. *Transgender Warriors: Making History from Joan of Arc to Dennis Rodman*. Boston: Beacon, 1996.

———. *Trans Liberation: Beyond Pink and Blue*. Boston: Beacon, 1998.

Ferguson, Kathy. "Interpretation and Genealogy in Feminism." *Signs* 16 (1991): 322–39.

Ferree, Myra, and Beth Hess, eds. *Controversy and Coalition: The New Feminist Movement*, 2nd ed. Boston: Twayne, 1994 [1985].

Ferree, Myra Marx, and Patricia Yancey Martin, eds. *Feminist Organizations: Harvest of the New Women's Movement*. Philadelphia: Temple University Press, 1995.

Fonow, Mary Margaret, and Judith Cook, eds. *Beyond Methodology: Feminist Scholarship as Lived Research*. Bloomington: Indiana University Press 1991.

Foucault, Michel. *The History of Sexuality*. Volume 1. New York: Vintage, 1980.

Frankenberg, Ruth. *White Women, Race Matters: The Social Construction of Whiteness*. Minneapolis: University of Minnesota Press, 1993.

Fraser, Nancy. *Unruly Practices: Power, Discourse, and Gender in Contemporary Social Theory*. Minneapolis: University of Minnesota Press, 1989.

———. "The Uses and Abuses of French Discourse Theories for Feminist Politics." In *Critical Theory Now*, ed. Philip Wexler. London: Falmer Press, 1991.

Fraser, Nancy, and Linda Nicholson. "Social Criticism without Philosophy: An Encounter between Feminism and Postmodernism." In *Feminism/Postmodernism*, ed. Linda Nicholson. New York: Routledge, 1990.

Frazer, Elizabeth. "Teenage Girls Talking about Class." *Sociology* 22 (1988): 343–58.

———. "Feminist Talk and Talking about Feminism: Teenage Girls' Discourses of Gender." *Oxford Review of Education* 15 (1989): 281–90.

———. "Talking about Gender, Race and Class." In *Researching Language: Issues of Power and Method*. eds. Deborah Cameron, Elizabeth Frazer, and Penelope Harvey. London: Routledge, 1992.

Freeman, Jo. "The Tyranny of Structurelessness." *Berkeley Journal of Sociology* 17 (1972): 151–64.

Friedan, Betty. *The Feminine Mystique*. New York: Norton, 1963.

Frye, Marilyn. "Some Reflections on Separatism and Power." In *The Politics of Reality*. Freedom, Calif.: Crossing Press, 1983.

———. "Lesbian 'Sex.'" In *Lesbian Philosophies and Cultures*, ed. Jeffner Allen. Albany: SUNY Press, 1990.

———. "The Necessity of Differences: Constructing a Positive Category of Women." *Signs* 21 (1996): 991–1010.

Fuss, Diana. *Essentially Speaking: Feminism, Nature and Difference*. New York: Routledge, 1989.

Fuss, Diana, ed. *Inside/Out: Lesbian Theories, Gay Theories*. New York: Routledge, 1991.

Gallop, Jane, Marianne Hirsch, and Nancy Miller. "Criticizing Feminist Criticism." In *Conflicts in Feminism*, eds. Marianne Hirsch and Evelyn Fox Keller. New York: Routledge, 1991.

Gates, Henry Louis Jr., ed. *"Race," Writing and Difference*. Chicago: University of Chicago Press, 1986.

Geertz, Clifford. "Anti Anti-Relativism." *American Anthropologist* 86 (1984): 263–78.

———. *Works and Lives: The Anthropologist as Author*. Stanford: Stanford University Press, 1988.

Gilligan, Carol. "Reply by Carol Gilligan." *Signs* 11 (1986): 324–33.

———. "Joining the Resistance: Psychology, Politics, Girls and Women." *Michigan Quarterly Review* 29 (1990): 501–46.

———. *In a Different Voice: Psychological Theory and Women's Development*, 2nd ed. Cambridge, Mass.: Harvard University Press, 1993 [1982].

Gilligan, Carol, J. Ward, and J. Taylor, eds. *Mapping the Moral Domain: A Contribution of Women's Thinking to Psychological Theory and Education.* Cambridge, Mass.: Harvard University Press, 1988.

Gilligan, Carol, Nona P. Lyons, and Trudy J. Hanmer, eds. *Making Connections: The Relational Worlds of Adolescent Girls at Emma Willard School.* Cambridge, Mass.: Harvard University Press, 1990.

Gilligan, Carol, Annie G. Rogers, and Deborah L. Tolman, eds. *Women, Girls and Psychotherapy: Reframing Resistance.* Binghamton, N.Y.: Harrington Park, 1991.

Goldberg, David Theo. *Racist Culture: Philosophy and the Politics of Meaning.* Oxford: Blackwell, 1993.

Green, Judith Mary, and Blanche Radford Curry. "Recognising Each Other Amidst Diversity: Beyond Essentialism in Collaborative Multi-Cultural Feminist Theory." *Sage* 8:1 (1991): 39–49.

Grosz, Elizabeth. "Sexual Difference and the Problem of Essentialism." In *The Essential Difference,* eds. Naomi Schor and Elizabeth Weed. Bloomington: Indiana University Press, 1994.

———. *Volatile Bodies: Toward a Corporeal Feminism.* Bloomington: Indiana University Press, 1994.

Halberstam, Judith. "F2M: The Making of Female Masculinity." In *The Lesbian Postmodern,* ed. Laura Doan. New York: Columbia University Press, 1994.

———. *Female Masculinity.* Durham, N.C.: Duke University Press, 1998.

Hale, C. Jacob. "Suggested Rules for Non-Transsexuals Writing About Transsexuals, Transsexuality, Transsexualism, or Trans—." http://www.actlab.utexas.edu/~sandy/hale.rules.html

———. "Are Lesbians Women?" *Hypatia* 11:2 (1996): 94–121.

———. "Leatherdyke Boys and Their Daddies: How To Have Sex without Women and Men." With response by Eve Kosofsky Sedgwick. *Social Text* 15: 3/4 (1997): 223–39.

———. "Tracing A Ghostly Memory in My Throat: Reflections on Ftm Feminist Voice and Agency." In *Men Doing Feminism,* ed. Tom Digby. New York: Routledge, 1998.

Hallett, Garth. *Essentialism: A Wittgensteinian Critique.* Albany: SUNY Press, 1991.

Halperin, David M. "The Queer Politics of Michel Foucault." In *Saint Foucault: Towards a Gay Hagiography.* New York: Oxford University Press, 1995.

Harding, Sandra. "The Instability of the Analytical Categories of Feminist Theory." In *Feminist Theory in Practice and Process,* eds. Micheline Malson, Jean F. O'Barr, Sarah Westphal, and Mary Wyer. Chicago: University of Chicago Press, 1989.

———. *Whose Science? Whose Knowledge? Thinking From Women's Lives.* Ithaca: Cornell University Press, 1991.

Harding, Sandra, ed. *Feminism and Methodology.* Bloomington: Indiana University Press, 1987.

Harris, Angela. "Race and Essentialism in Feminist Legal Theory." In *Feminist Legal Theory: Readings in Law and Gender,* eds. Katharine T. Bartlett and Rosanne Kennedy. Boulder: Westview, 1991.

Hekman, Susan J., "Backgrounds and Riverbeds: Feminist Reflections," *Feminist Studies* 25 (1999): 427–48.

———. *Moral Voices, Moral Selves: Carol Gilligan and Feminist Moral Theory.* University Park: Penn State Press, 1995.

Hekman, Susan J., ed. *Feminist Interpretations of Michel Foucault*. University Park: Penn State Press, 1996.

Heyes, Cressida J. "Anti-Essentialism in Practice: Carol Gilligan and Feminist Philosophy." *Hypatia* 12:3 (1997): 142–63.

———. "What Do Feminists Need a Theory of Power to Explain?" Paper presented at the Eastern Division meeting of the American Philosophical Association, December 1998.

Heyes, Cressida J., ed. "American Philosophical Association Newsletter on Feminism and Philosophy," Fall 1999.

Hill Collins, Patricia. *Black Feminist Thought: Knowledge, Consciousness and the Politics of Empowerment*. New York: Routledge, 1991.

hooks, bell. *Feminist Theory: From Margin to Center*. Boston: South End Press, 1984.

———. *Yearning: Race, Gender and Cultural Politics*. Toronto: Between the Lines, 1990.

———. *Sisters of the Yam: Black Women and Self-Recovery*. Toronto: Between the Lines, 1993.

———. *Outlaw Culture: Resisting Representations*. New York: Routledge, 1994.

———. *Teaching to Transgress: Education as the Practice of Freedom*. New York: Routledge, 1994.

Iannello, Kathleen. *Decisions without Hierarchy: Feminist Interventions in Organization Theory and Practice*. New York: Routledge, 1992.

Kahane, David J. "Male Feminism as Oxymoron." In *Men Doing Feminism*, ed. Tom Digby. New York: Routledge, 1998.

Kendel, Monica, Holly Devor, and Nancy Strapko. "Feminist and Lesbian Opinions about Transsexuals." In *Gender Blending*, eds. Vern L. Bullough, Bonnie Bullough, and James Elias. Amherst, N.Y.: Prometheus Books, 1997.

Kerber, Linda. "Some Cautionary Words for Historians." *Signs* 11 (1986): 304–10.

Kessler, Suzanne J. "The Medical Construction of Gender: Case Management of Intersexed Infants." *Signs* 16 (1990): 3–26.

———. *Lessons from the Intersexed*. Baltimore: Rutgers, 1998.

Kessler, Suzanne, and Wendy McKenna. *Gender: An Ethnomethodological Approach*. New York: John Wiley and Sons, 1978.

Kirby, Vicky. "Corporeal Habits: Addressing Essentialism Differently." *Hypatia* 6:3 (1991): 4–24.

Kline, Marlee. "Race, Racism, and Feminist Legal Theory." *Harvard Women's Law Journal* 12 (1989): 115–50.

Kristeva, Julia. "Woman Can Never Be Defined." In *New French Feminisms: An Anthology*, eds. Elaine Marks and Isabelle de Courtivron. Amherst: University of Massachusetts Press, 1980.

Kuykendall, Eleanor. "Subverting Essentialisms." *Hypatia* 6:3 (1991): 208–17.

Larrabee, Mary Jeanne, ed. *An Ethic of Care: Feminist and Interdisciplinary Perspectives*. New York: Routledge, 1993.

Lee-Lampshire, Wendy, "The Sound of Little Hummingbird Wings: A Wittgensteinian Investigation of Forms of Life as Forms of Power," *Feminist Studies* 25 (1999): 409–26.

———. "Spilling All Over the 'Wide Fields of Our Passions': Frye, Butler, Wittgenstein and the Context(s) of Attention, Intention and Identity (Or: From Arm Wrestling Duck to Abject Being to Lesbian Feminist)," *Hypatia* 14:3 (1999): 1–16.

Lehr, Valerie. "The Difficulty of Leaving 'Home': Gay and Lesbian Organizing to Confront AIDS." In *Mobilizing the Community*, eds. Robert Fisher and Joseph Kling. Newbury Park: Sage, 1993.

Leidner, Robin. "Stretching the Boundaries of Liberalism: Democratic Innovation in a Feminist Organization." *Signs* 16 (1991): 263–89.

Levine, Cathy. "The Tyranny of Tyranny." Mimeograph. Montreal: Black Rose, 1984.

Locke, John. *An Essay Concerning Human Understanding*, ed. John W. Yolton. London: Dent, 1961 [1690].

Lorde, Audre. "An Open Letter to Mary Daly." In *Sister/Outsider*. Boston: Crossing Press, 1984.

Lugones, María C. "Purity, Impurity, and Separation." *Signs* 19 (1994): 458–79.

———. "Playfulness, 'World'-Travelling, and Loving Perception." In *Lesbian Philosophies and Cultures*, ed. Jeffner Allen. Albany: SUNY Press, 1990.

———. "Hablando Cara á Cara/Speaking Face to Face: An Exploration of Ethnocentric Racism." In *Making Face, Making Soul/Haciendo Caras: Creative and Critical Perspectives by Feminists of Color*, ed. Gloria Anzaldúa. San Francisco: Aunt Lute, 1990.

———. "On the Logic of Pluralist Feminism." In *Feminist Ethics*, ed. Claudia Card. Lawrence: University Press of Kansas, 1991.

Lugones, María C., and Elizabeth V. Spelman. "Have We Got a Theory for You! Feminist Theory, Cultural Imperialism and the Demand for 'The Woman's Voice.'" In *Women and Values: Readings in Recent Feminist Philosophy*, ed. Marilyn Pearsall. Belmont, Calif.: Wadsworth, 1986.

MacKinnon, Catharine. *Sexual Harassment Of Working Women*. New Haven: Yale University Press, 1979.

———. "Minneapolis Ordinance—Excerpts." In *Women Against Censorship*, ed. Varda Burstyn. Vancouver: Douglas and MacIntyre, 1985.

———. *Feminism Unmodified: Discourses on Life and Law*. Cambridge, Mass.: Harvard University Press, 1987.

———. *Toward a Feminist Theory of the State*. Cambridge, Mass.: Harvard University Press, 1989.

———. "From Practice to Theory, or What is a White Woman Anyway?" In *Radically Speaking: Feminism Reclaimed*, eds. Diane Bell and Renate Klein. Melbourne: Spinifex, 1996.

Mahowald, Mary Briody, ed. *Philosophy of Woman: An Anthology of Classic to Current Concepts*, 3rd ed. Indianapolis: Hackett, 1994 [1978].

Martin, Jane Roland. "Methodological Essentialism, False Difference, and Other Dangerous Traps." *Signs* 19 (1994): 630–57.

Matthews, Nancy. "Surmounting a Legacy: The Expansion of Racial Diversity in a Local Anti-Rape Movement." *Gender and Society* 3 (1989): 518–32.

Mies, Maria. "Towards a Methodology for Feminist Research." In *Theories of Women's Studies*, eds. Gloria Bowles and Renate Duelli Klein. Boston: Routledge, 1983.

Minow, Martha. *Making All the Difference: Inclusion, Exclusion and American Law*. Ithaca: Cornell University Press, 1990.

Miriam, Kathy, "Disciplining Feminism: Reflections on the (Im)possibility of the Feminist Academic as Public Intellectual," paper presented at the Radical Philosophy Association Conference, San Francisco, November 1998.

Mohanty, Chandra Talpade. "Under Western Eyes: Feminist Scholarship and Colonial

Discourses." In *Third World Women and the Politics of Feminism*, eds. Chandra Talpade Mohanty, Ann Russo, and Lourdes Torres. Bloomington: Indiana University Press, 1991.

Monk, Ray. *Ludwig Wittgenstein: The Duty of Genius*. London: Vintage, 1990.

Moody-Adams, Michele M. "Gender and the Complexity of Moral Voices." In *Feminist Ethics*, ed. Claudia Card. Lawrence: University Press of Kansas, 1991.

Moore, G. E. "Wittgenstein's Lectures in 1930–33." In *Philosophical Papers*. London: Allen and Unwin, 1959.

Morgen, Sandra. "The Dream of Diversity, the Dilemmas of Difference: Race and Class Contradictions in a Feminist Health Clinic." In *Anthropology for the Nineties*, ed. Johnetta Sole. New York: Free Press, 1988.

Morris, Jan. *Conundrum*. London: Faber, 1974.

Mouffe, Chantal, "The Legacy of m/f." In *The Woman in Question*, eds. Parveen Adams and Elizabeth Cowie. Cambridge, Mass.: MIT Press, 1990.

———. "Feminism, Citizenship, and Radical Democratic Politics." In *Feminists Theorize the Political*, eds. Judith Butler and Joan Scott. New York: Routledge, 1992.

Nader, Laura. "Up the Anthropologist: Perspectives Gained from Studying Up." In *Anthropology for the Nineties*, ed. Johnetta Sole. New York: Free Press, 1988.

Nicholson, Linda. "Interpreting Gender." *Signs* 20 (1994): 79–105.

Noddings, Nel. "An Ethic of Caring and Its Implications for Instructional Arrangements." In *The Education Feminism Reader*, ed. Lynda Stone. New York: Routledge, 1994.

Nussbaum, Martha. "Human Functioning and Social Justice: In Defense of Aristotelian Essentialism." *Political Theory* 20 (1992): 203–46.

Oakley, Ann. "Interviewing Women: A Contradiction in Terms." In *Doing Feminist Research*, ed. Helen Roberts. Boston: Routledge and Kegan Paul, 1981.

Okin, Susan Moller. "Gender Inequality and Cultural Differences." *Political Theory* 22 (1994): 5–24.

Outlaw, Lucius. *On Race and Philosophy*. New York: Routledge, 1996.

Phelan, Shane. *Identity Politics: Lesbian Feminism and the Limits of Community*. Philadelphia: Temple University Press, 1989.

———. *Getting Specific: Postmodern Lesbian Politics*. Minneapolis: University of Minnesota Press, 1994.

Plato. *Euthyphro*.

Potter, Elizabeth. "Gender and Epistemic Negotiation." In *Feminist Epistemologies*, eds. Linda Alcoff and Elizabeth Potter. New York: Routledge, 1993.

Potter, Nancy. "The Severed Head and Existential Dread: The Classroom as Epistemic Community and Student Survivors of Incest." *Hypatia* 10:2 (1995): 69–92.

Pratt, Minnie Bruce. *S/he*. Ithaca: Firebrand Books, 1995.

Prosser, Jay. *Second Skins: The Body Narratives of Transsexuality*. New York: Columbia University Press, 1998.

Raymond, Janice G. *The Transsexual Empire: The Making of the She-Male*, 2nd ed. New York: Teachers College, 1994 [1979].

Reinharz, Shulamit. *Feminist Methods in Social Research*. New York: Oxford University Press, 1992.

Rich, Adrienne. "Compulsory Heterosexuality and Lesbian Existence." *Signs* 5 (1980): 631–60.

Riessman, Catherine Kohler. "When Gender is Not Enough: Women Interviewing Women." *Gender and Society* 1 (1987): 172–207.

Riley, Denise. *Am I That Name? Feminism and the Category of 'Woman' in History*. Basingstoke: Macmillan, 1988.

Robinson, Fiona. *Globalizing Care: Ethics, Feminist Theory, and International Relations*. Boulder: Westview, 1999.

Rubin, Gayle. "Thinking Sex: Notes for a Radical Theory of the Politics of Sexuality." In *American Feminist Thought at Century's End*, ed. Linda Kauffman. Oxford: Blackwell, 1993.

Rubin, Henry Samuel. "Transformations: Emerging Female to Male Transsexual Identities." Ph.D. dissertation, Department of Sociology, Brandeis University, 1996.

———. "Reading Like a (Transsexual) Man." In *Men Doing Feminism*, ed. Tom Digby. New York: Routledge, 1998.

———. *Always Already Men: Female-To-Male Transsexual Subjectivity and Embodiment*. Chicago: University of Chicago Press, forthcoming.

Ruddick, Sara. *Maternal Thinking: Toward a Politics of Peace*. New York: Ballantine, 1989.

Sandoval, Chela. "Feminism and Racism: A Report on the 1981 National Women's Studies Association Conference." In *Making Face, Making Soul/Haciendo Caras: Creative and Critical Perspectives by Feminists of Color*, ed. Gloria Anzaldúa. San Francisco: Aunt Lute, 1990.

Sawicki, Jana. *Disciplining Foucault: Feminism, Power and the Body*. New York: Routledge, 1991.

Schatzki, Theodore. *Social Practices: A Wittgensteinian Approach to Human Activity and the Social*. Cambridge: Cambridge University Press, 1996.

Scheman, Naomi. "Forms of Life: Mapping the Rough Ground." In *The Cambridge Companion to Ludwig Wittgenstein*, eds. Hans Sluga and David G. Stern. Cambridge: Cambridge University Press, 1996.

———. "Queering the Center by Centering the Queer: Reflections on Transsexuals and Secular Jews." In *Feminists Rethink the Self*, ed. Diana Tietjens Meyers. Boulder: Westview, 1997.

Scheman, Naomi, ed. *Feminist Interpretations of Ludwig Wittgenstein*. University Park, Pa.: Penn State Press, forthcoming.

Scott, James. *Domination and The Arts of Resistance: Hidden Transcripts*. New Haven: Yale University Press, 1990.

Scott, Joan. "Deconstructing Equality-Versus-Difference: Or, The Uses of Poststructuralist Theory for Feminism." *Feminist Studies* 14 (1988): 33–51.

———. "Experience." In *Feminists Theorize the Political*, eds. Judith Butler and Joan Scott. New York: Routledge, 1992.

Sherry, Suzanna. "Civic Virtue and the Feminine Voice in Constitutional Adjudication." *Virginia Law Review* 72 (1986): 543–616.

Sirianni, Carmen. "Learning Pluralism: Democracy and Diversity in Feminist Organizations." In *Nomos XXXV: Democratic Community*, eds. John Chapman and Ian Shapiro. New York: New York University Press, 1993.

Spelman, Elizabeth V. *Inessential Woman: Problems of Exclusion in Feminist Thought*. Boston: Beacon Press, 1988.

———. *Fruits of Sorrow: Framing Our Attention to Suffering*. Boston: Beacon Press, 1997.

Spivak, Gayatri Chakravorty. "Criticism, Feminism and the Institution." In *The Post-Colonial Critic: Interviews, Strategies, Dialogues*, ed. Sarah Harasym. New York: Routledge, 1990.

Spivak, Gayatri Chakravorty, with Ellen Rooney. "In a Word: Interview." In *The Essential Difference*, eds. Naomi Schor and Elizabeth Weed. Bloomington: Indiana University Press, 1994.

Stacey, Judith. "Can There Be a Feminist Ethnography?" *Women's Studies International Forum* 11 (1988): 21–27.

———. "On Resistance, Ambivalence and Feminist Theory: A Response to Carol Gilligan." *Michigan Quarterly Review* 29 (1990): 537–46.

Stanley, Liz. *Feminist Praxis: Research, Theory and Epistemology in Feminist Sociology*. London: Routledge, 1990.

Stein, Arlene. "Sisters and Queers: The Decentering of Lesbian Feminism." *Socialist Review* 22:1 (1992): 33–55.

Stein, Arlene, ed. *Sisters, Sexperts, Queers: Beyond the Lesbian Nation*. New York: Plume, 1993.

Stoljar, Natalie. "Essence, Identity and the Concept of Woman." *Philosophical Topics*, 23 (1995): 261–93.

Stone, Sandy. "The Empire Strikes Back: A Posttranssexual Manifesto." In *Body Guards: The Cultural Politics of Gender Ambiguity*, eds. Julia Epstein and Kristina Straub. New York: Routledge, 1991.

Stryker, Susan. "My Words to Victor Frankenstein above the Village of Chamounix: Performing Transgender Rage." *GLQ: A Journal of Lesbian and Gay Studies*, 1 (1994): 237–54.

Stychin, Carl. "Exploring the Limits: Feminism and the Legal Regulation of Gay Male Pornography." *Vermont Law Review* 16 (1992): 857–900.

Taylor, Jill McLean, Carol Gilligan, and Amy M. Sullivan. *Between Voice and Silence: Women and Girls, Race and Relationship*. Cambridge, Mass.: Harvard University Press, 1996.

Taylor, Verta, and Leila Rull. "Women's Culture and Lesbian Feminist Activism: A Reconsideration of Cultural Feminism." *Signs* 19 (1993): 32–61.

Taylor, Verta, and Nancy Whittier. "Collective Identity and Lesbian Feminist Mobilization." In *Frontiers of Social Movement Theory*, eds. Aldon Morris and Carol McClurg Mueller. New Haven: Yale University Press, 1992.

Thompson, Becky. *A Hunger So Wide and So Deep: A Multiracial View of Women's Eating Problems*. Minneapolis: University of Minnesota Press, 1994.

Tom, Allison. "Children of Our Culture? Class, Power and Learning in a Feminist Bank." In *Feminist Organizations: Harvest of the New Women's Movement*, eds. Myra Marx Ferree and Patricia Yancey Martin. Philadelphia: Temple University Press, 1995.

Tronto, Joan, *Moral Boundaries: A Political Argument for an Ethic of Care* (New York: Routledge, 1993).

Tuana, Nancy. *The Less Noble Sex: Scientific, Religious, and Philosophical Conceptions of Woman's Nature*. Bloomington: Indiana University Press, 1993.

Tully, James. *Strange Multiplicity: Constitutionalism in an Age of Diversity*. Cambridge: Cambridge University Press, 1995.

Weir, Allison. *Sacrificial Logics: Feminist Theory and the Critique of Identity*. New York: Routledge, 1996.

Winch, Peter. *The Idea of a Social Science*. London: Routledge and Kegan Paul, 1958.

Witt, Charlotte. "Anti-Essentialism in Feminist Theory." *Philosophical Topics*, 23 (1995): 321–44.

Wittgenstein, Ludwig. *Philosophical Investigations*, 2nd ed. Translated by G. E. M. Anscombe. Oxford: Blackwell, 1997 [1953].

———. *The Blue Book*. Oxford: Blackwell, 1958.

———. *On Certainty*, eds. G. E. M. Anscombe and G. H. von Wright. New York: Harper Torchbooks, 1969.

———. *Culture and Value*. Chicago: University of Chicago Press, 1980.

———. *Tractatus Logicus-Philosophicus*. London: Routledge and Kegan Paul, 1981.

Wittig, Monique. *The Straight Mind and Other Essays*. Boston: Beacon Press, 1992.

Wolf, Diane L., ed. *Feminist Dilemmas in Fieldwork*. Boulder, Colo.: Westview, 1996.

Wollstonecraft, Mary. *A Vindication of the Rights of Woman*. London: Penguin, 1992 [1792].

Young, Iris Marion. "The Scaling of Bodies and the Politics of Identity." In *Justice and the Politics of Difference*. Princeton: Princeton University Press, 1990.

———. "Throwing Like a Girl: A Phenomenology of Feminine Body Comportment, Motility, and Spatiality." In *Throwing Like a Girl and Other Essays in Feminist Philosophy and Social Theory*. Bloomington: Indiana University Press, 1990.

———. "Gender as Seriality: Thinking About Women as a Social Collective." In *Intersecting Voices: Dilemmas of Gender, Political Philosophy, and Policy*. Princeton: Princeton University Press, 1997.

Zack, Naomi. *Race and Mixed Race*. Philadelphia: Temple University Press, 1993.

Zack, Naomi, ed. *American Mixed Race: The Culture of Microdiversity*. Lanham, Md.: Rowman and Littlefield, 1995.

Zerilli, Linda, "Doing Without Knowing: Feminism's Politics of the Ordinary," *Political Theory* 26 (1998): 435–58.

Zita, Jacquelyn N. "The Male Lesbian and the Postmodernist Body." *Hypatia* 7:4 (1992): 106–27.

# Index

sex/gender, 97, 116, 119, 149, 151, 157, 169
Organizations, 8, 42, 143, 156, 170, 175–77. *See also* Feminist, organizing
Outlaw, Lucius, 204 n.6

Patriarchy, 4, 12, 26, 53, 56, 101, 113–14, 116, 126, 144, 148, 150, 184
Penelope, Julia, 204 n.10
"Phantom man," 171, 174
Phelan, Shane, 59, 193 n.10, 203 n.36
*Philosophical Investigations. See* Wittgenstein, Ludwig
Philosophy, 25, 81
   abstraction in, 1–2
   impact on feminism, 61
   as institutionalized profession, 4, 188
   philosophical therapy, 13, 83, 85, 87, 101–2
   skepticism toward, 85
Plato, 190 n.14
Plurality, 85, 97, 187
Political philosophy, 2, 7,10, 25, 50, 82, 88
Political practice, 11, 52, 61, 71, 96, 98, 112, 139, 162
Political strategy, 9, 95, 133, 136
Postmodern, 18, 56, 59, 71, 92, 153, 161
   feminism, 60, 70
Poststructuralism, 36, 38–39, 68
Potter, Elizabeth, 195 n.2
Potter, Nancy, 197 n.41
Power, 147, 182–84
   analysis of, 75, 136, 149
   of dominant feminists, 54, 57, 63, 66, 72, 177, 182–83
   domination and submission, 145–49, 155, 173, 179
   empowerment, 148, 164
   of girls, 110, 112–23, 135–36
   exercise of, 32, 93–94, 119, 146–47, 163
   Foucauldian, 46, 59
   mechanism of, 16, 88
   micro-relations of, 168
   relations of, 55, 69, 100, 128–29, 138, 144, 157, 165, 170, 178, 186
   interrogation of, 151, 156, 161
   in the research process, 104–5, 108, 120, 126–28, 130–33
   among women, 15–16, 51, 67, 107, 143, 148, 152, 154, 160–61, 173
Pratt, Minnie Bruce, 197 n.26
Pro-feminist men, 143, 155, 164, 167–68, 171

Prosser, Jay, 91, 197 nn.22–23
Psychology, 102, 113–14, 126
   feminist, 110
   of gender, 15, 111, 113, 119
Purity, 2–5

Queer, 147, 148
   politics, 59, 89, 174
   theory, 32, 89, 92, 186

Race, 123–4, 127, 184, 185
Racism, 12, 21–22, 55, 59, 62, 70–71, 127, 148, 156–58, 177, 185
Radical feminism, 25, 32, 62, 91, 144, 151, 153–54, 166, 168
Rape. *See* Sexual violence
Raymond, Janice, 90–91, 196 n.20
Reductionism, 19
Reinharz, Shulamit, 198 n.2
Relationship, 114–15, 118, 122–28, 133, 136, 178
Relativism, 22, 28, 64–67
Research methods, 12, 104, 111, 125–26, 132, 134, 138
   anti-essentialist, 136
   feminist, 105–6
   objective, 106
   politics of, 119
   power relations within, 15, 127
   quantitative, 106
Rich, Adrienne, 200 n.43, 201 n.10
Riessman, Catherine, 108–9, 198 n.9–10
Riley, Denise, 192 n.56
Robinson, Fiona, 200 n.33
Rogers, Annie, 199 n.14
Rooney, Ellen, 190 n.8
Root, Maria, 202 n.19
Rough ground, 3–4, 9–10, 13, 63, 75, 79, 97, 100, 102, 139, 142, 173, 179
Rubin, Gayle, 201 n.1
Rubin, Henry, 42, 59, 93, 192 n.36, 53, 193 nn.11–12, 197 nn.26–27
Ruddick, Sarah, 32, 191 nn.32–33
Rull, Leila, 204 n.10

Sandoval, Chela, 177, 203 n.39
Sawicki, Jana, 203 n.3
Schatzki, Theodore, 82, 195 n.5
Scheman, Naomi, 93, 189 n.3, 195 n.3, 197 nn.26, 28
Scientific discourse, 30
Scott, James, 128, 129, 200 n.42
Scott, Joan, 190 n.2, 193 n.61
Separatism, 41, 58–59, 163, 202 n.29

104, 122, 129, 143–45, 147, 150,
159, 170, 182
Women of color, 55, 62–63, 70–71, 108,
117, 123–24, 127–28, 148–49, 152–
53, 156–58, 177, 184
Women's studies, 99
Womyn-born-womyn, 91–92

Young, Iris Marion, 99, 190 n.13, 196 n.14,
197 nn.39–40

Zack, Naomi, 204 n.8
Zavella, Patricia, 198 n.11
Zerilli, Linda, 95, 195 n.3, 197 n.31
Zita, Jacquelyn, 93, 197 nn.29–30

www.ingramcontent.com/pod-product-compliance
Lightning Source LLC
Chambersburg PA
CBHW022310280326
41932CB00010B/1053